Questions – A User's Guide

A. M. Howcroft

Bri,

Hope you and Trevor have fun
asking each other (& Chief!) some
new questions after reading this!

Anthony.

For Gillian & Freya

Contents

1. INTRODUCTION

The art and science of asking questions
is the source of all knowledge.

Adolf Berle

It is better to know some of the questions
than all of the answers.

James Thurber

Why should I care?

Questions govern every aspect of your life. They're the mechanism by which you learn; the tools you use to build relationships. Your questions signal your credibility and knowledge at work, and help in selecting those who'll be your colleagues. The people you encounter will have varying degrees of training in asking questions. Some will know how to extract information from you, whether you wish to surrender that data or not, others will attempt to persuade you to buy goods, join causes, or take actions; all by using questions. You may feel that asking questions is an innate skill; something everybody grasps. You're probably right. As we shall discover, this skill may be one of the most profound characteristics that make you human. That doesn't mean you can't improve though. Most people can swim, but our style, expertise, and technique can vary tremendously. If you want to swim faster, you may have to unlearn some techniques, master new ones, study, train, and even change your diet. Luckily, you don't have to stop eating chocolate or give-up doughnuts to master the art of asking good questions. Fundamentally, we all know questions are critical in all our communications. We use them at work, at home, and even for internal debates with ourselves. Questions are the primary way that we learn about the world, but equally they can be used to attack or defend, and they reveal far more about our inner thought processes than we might imagine.

Research shows that the questions you ask—and those that others ask you—can change your mind. In this book, we're going to take a trip through the world of questions. There'll be some details on techniques and useful tricks you can use; but we'll also have fun by looking at the strangest interview questions; seeing how Hollywood has taken to the art of questions; and discover the only animal to have asked a question of a human. We'll look at the origins, ethics, and history of questioning; learn why the chicken crossed the road; and spend some time considering answers. What is a question, without an answer? We'll even explore why politicians don't seem capable of giving a proper answer.

Increasingly, technology is used as a tool to answer questions for us, and so we'll examine the latest trends and see what might come next. Since different industries employ different questioning methods, we'll take a whistlestop tour through teaching, law, sales, psychiatry, literature, journalism, and more. Finally, we'll summarise our learnings and share tips on how to improve your questioning skills, as well as on how to avoid being manipulated by others—with a few cautionary tales in between. But first, let me tell you why I wrote this book.

How to go faster

A few years ago, I took up running to keep fit and lose a bit of my beer belly. I'd run two or three times a week; and once a month I'd do a 10k run (6.2 miles) as fast as I could. My times were typically between 51 and 53 minutes. I compared my time to the runners at a local 10k race (they published a spreadsheet with all the results), and the data showed I'd be in the 40–50th percentile, finishing in the middle of the pack, had I actually done the race. I also looked at the most recent time from Mo Farah, the multiple world and Olympic gold medallist—who ran his last competitive 10k in 27 minutes, 28 seconds. I was relieved to see that Mo Farah wasn't quite twice as fast as me. I asked myself the following question: *How can I run faster?*

The answer was on the cover of every running magazine: use cross-training, diet, running programs (including tempo, speed work, long slow distance, and hills in your routine), how to avoid and recover better from injury, use psychology, run in groups, and the most popular—buy new equipment, especially shoes (and sports bras for women) to make you faster. It was all a little overwhelming. Each month I tried a technique or bought a new pair of shoes and it might make me 30 seconds faster, but then I'd slip back in the following month. I wasn't making any true progress, and my times had been static for a year. Then one day, while I was discussing this problem with a friend at the gym, he asked me: 'To run faster, do you need to take longer strides or increase your cadence?' For non-runners, cadence is simply the number of steps you take per minute. A higher cadence means more steps.

This was an interesting question that cut through the

noise of options and got to the heart of the matter. I didn't know the answer, so I went home and searched the internet. The answer I discovered was, perhaps predictably, 'both'. The fundamental basics of running faster are to take more steps with a longer stride in a given time period. Not very helpful, but on social media—especially in the blogs by other runners—the advice was to change your cadence first. Apparently, this is easier to achieve, and with a lower chance of injury. The other runners warned that increasing your cadence may feel like you're taking tiny baby-steps, but once your legs were used to the speed, then stride length would naturally revert to its normal distance and you'd be faster.

I decided to give it a go. On the next run, on the same course which had seen me finish in 51 minutes 29 seconds only seven days earlier, I attempted to alter my cadence. It felt weird. I didn't bother looking at my sportswatch because this run was about training my body to move my legs faster, rather than aiming for any specific pace. At the end of the run, my sports watch beeped and I looked down to discover a finish time of 45 minutes 29 seconds. An improvement of 6 minutes. I was blown away. Nothing else in my routine had changed that week, and my initial reaction was that my watch was broken! I tried again a week later and went a little faster. This was amazing. I checked the spreadsheet from the race, to see how my new result compared. Suddenly, I had moved from being a 'middle of the pack' guy, to a runner in the top 10 percent. In my age group, I was actually in the top 5 percent!

The next day, I was at my desk, dialled into a conference call reviewing my team's sales performance with upper management. The usual commentary was flowing around, and the same ideas, which were all trying to answer the basic question: 'How do we sell more?' It suddenly struck me that we were falling into the same trap that I'd experienced with my running. We needed our questions to be more specific, more informed. We should be asking (and testing) questions like: 'To sell more, do we need to lower the price, or increase the marketing budget?' We needed to get better at asking questions. I also knew that I could only directly change the behaviour of one person. If we needed to get better at asking questions, it had to start with me. The next day, I set out to learn more.

For much of my career, I've been selling or building computer systems that specialise in answering questions. I've used sales questions to understand my customers' business and the challenges they faced. Later, these customers would use my products to answer their questions, and I'd see which companies got the most value, and how they approached their biggest issues. After my revelation from knocking 6 minutes off my running time in one week, I began to take a closer look at the techniques and approaches involved—or the theory of questioning, if you want to call it that. This book is a summary of my personal research and experience. I don't promise to have all the answers, but I do have lots of questions.

The right question

To start, we need to agree that there's a difference between a question and a good question—or perhaps it might be better to phrase that as *the right question*. In Michael Crichton's book, *Jurassic Park*, there's a scene where the park owner Hammond and his chief scientist are both insistent that the dinosaurs are not breeding. They have a large electronic map that shows the location of the creatures, and a screen displaying the count for each type: the stegosaurs, tyrannosaurs, hadrosaurs, compys, and pterosaurs through to the velociraptors. Using motion sensors and image recognition from live-video streams, they tally the number of dinosaurs every 15 minutes. The screen shows they have the correct number of dinosaurs: 238. Meanwhile, Malcolm, the mathematician of chaos and complexity theory, believes the dinosaurs *are* breeding, and is determined to prove it.

"Can you have the computer search for a different number of animals?" he asks.

They tell him they can, and setting the number to 300, they let the system start counting. It stops after identifying 292 dinosaurs. The number of predatory velociraptors in the tally leaps from an expected count of 8 up to 37—which, as anyone who's seen the movie knows—is a big problem! Malcolm explains to the shocked Hammond and scientist that the computer was set to look for a certain number of animals because they were worried about losing them. The question framed by the programmer was: 'Have we accounted for all 238 of our dinosaurs?' Hammond and the scientist were viewing the counts as the answer to a completely different question: 'How many dinosaurs do we have in total?' This mismatch between the question they thought they were asking, and the question the system was tackling, highlighted a massive issue that would catapult them into a nightmare scenario.

This scene is such a good example of questioning—both the philosophy (don't accept everything at face value), and the understanding of how certain questions may stand in the way of effective communication—plus the ability to ask a good question for clarification. Most importantly, it shows the huge difference between asking *a question* and asking *the right question*. Sometimes, the underlying goal is the same, but the phrasing can make a big difference. If you need any more convincing, ask yourself which of the following is more likely to get a positive response:

"Should we get a marriage contract and apply for a joint mortgage?"

or

"You're amazing. Will you marry me?"

Unsolved questions

- Can we live forever?
- Do aliens exist?
- Who *really* shot JFK (and why)?
- (When) will Artificial Intelligence make computers smarter than people?
- Why do we dream?
- Why are prime numbers different?
- Who was Jack the Ripper?
- How do we cure cancer?
- Is there a (physics) theory of everything?
- Where is the nuclear bomb lost off Tybee Island, Georgia?*
- What is the Voynich Manuscript about?
- Where is Antony and Cleopatra's tomb?
- What is dark matter?
- Can we time-travel?

* Okay, this may not be the biggest unsolved question in the world, unless you happen to live in Tybee.

Origins

The way in which language first appeared in humans is a tough question. There are multiple theories, but without a time machine, it seems unlikely we will discover the definitive answer—until we see language emerge in another species, or prompt it, perhaps. We should make the distinction here between speech and language. Language can be based on gestures alone, and a written language could exist without speech, although it's hard to imagine how that might occur in practical terms—the examples available are from groups of people that have died out, taking their spoken language with them. Most theories of human language focus on vocalisation as the starting point. Some theories place song before speech, so perhaps it will be a magpie or a nightingale that develops talk next, rather than our fellow primates.

Two of the most respected writers in this field have been Steven Pinker and Noam Chomsky. The basic view of Chomsky is that a chance mutation occurred that allowed language to develop pretty much in one-step, although many of the pre-requisites were already in place, such as our descended larynx. We should point out that several other animals do have a similar larynx, or one that can be lowered to permit large sounds such as roaring or barking, including dogs, deer, cats of all types, goats, and more; so while this may be a requirement, it's not the magic element that produces language. Most experts today though, favour the so-called continuity theories, which believe that language evolved gradually from gestures and vocalisations through to some basic nouns, with syntax developing over a longer period. Steven Pinker is in this camp, with a view that language is largely an innate ability.

Another challenge in exploring the origins of language is that nobody can agree when it first occurred. We can be confident that social interaction of the level required to make certain tools, structures, and artwork probably required co-operation and therefore language; and this certainly took place in the past 200,000 years. However, the homo split from the earlier pan group of apes took place over 2 million years before this, and there is increasing evidence to show a very broad range of species followed, from australopithecus, through homo erectus, neanderthal and homo habilis, up to the modern homo sapiens.

Before we become mired in debate about the timing and process through which language evolved, or was given to us by a benevolent god or alien, we should switch our focus to the origins of *questions*. Other primates have shown they can make tools and communicate using gestures, and many animals use effective vocalisations—think of a meerkat calling out warning sounds about a snake or falcon—and yet we have no evidence of these creatures asking any questions. We'll explore this in more detail in the chapter 'Non-human questions', but for now let's take it as fact. Humans are the only species to ask questions (although there's a case to suggest this may have been true for other extinct hominids). What's more, human children can ask questions before they master language, initially by gestures and/or facial expressions, and then via intonation and simple words.

A baby sees a dog, points at the animal and looks to his mother.

"Dog", says the mother.

The baby laughs and gurgles. This may happen on several separate occasions. Then one day the baby points, and with a rising tone says,

"Dagga?"

"Yes, dog", the mother answers.

It appears that questioning is part of the fundamental core of language, and may be the thing that distinguishes language from other, more basic forms of communication. Certainly, the primary function of questions appears to be one of education, and it is necessary for all children to *learn* their native language. This would be true unless language were an innate, genetic ability which came fully formed. We know this is not so, and it informs jokes such as the ones where English-speaking parents tell their friends they're learning Mandarin Chinese to talk to their adopted Chinese baby. Social interaction is the mechanism by which babies learn language, and there are more than 7,000 languages across the planet with a myriad of styles and approaches, from tonal through to accented. Yet despite the structural and social differences, research has demonstrated that all children of all nationalities use a rising pitch for classic yes/no questions. In fact, for several languages including Portuguese, using a rising tone is the only way to form a question from a declarative statement For example:

"That is a dog" (no rising tone) is a statement.

"That is a *dog*" (rising tone on the word 'dog') is a question.

One point here is that I could imply the two questions above with just the word 'dog' and a rising tone. That's very important because it means you don't need syntax or grammar to ask questions. In other words, questions are a cognitive capability, not just a part of language. We can see that from a questioning gesture or facial expression.

Although the origins of language are obscured, the ability to ask questions is, as mentioned, at the core of language, and may even be the precursor to full language development. We should consider whether questions form the basis from which cognitive abilities develop. If you imagine two hominids, one able to learn by forming and asking questions, and the other without this capability—which one do you think is going to survive and thrive in a hostile environment? Which one will have more children, and how will their cognitive abilities continue to develop? We don't know much about the other hominid groups roaming the planet when homo sapiens began its rise, but it's easy to imagine a group with rapidly growing cognitive abilities having a significant advantage, even if other races were physically stronger. Given that we can ask questions without full language, by pointing for example; we might argue that questions came first and helped expand our cognitive abilities to a threshold where language became possible. We might say that *we're thinking creatures because we can ask questions.*

The very first question

Without any written records, it's hard to track down the first questions ever asked—humanity was speaking long before we were writing. Apart from tallies of food, some of the earliest written materials were religious works. The first question in the Bible is Satan quizzing Eve about God's instructions on which fruit could be eaten. Clearly though, this was not the first question in the chronological sequence of biblical events. At some point prior to this, Satan the fallen angel had questioned God's authority, and was cast out of heaven with his followers as a result.

If we go further back in time, before Christianity, much of the earliest known writing was in the form of marks on clay to record stores of grain and other items. One of the first known pieces of literature is the *Epic of Gilgamesh*, a series of Sumerian poems from before 2000 years BC. The oldest surviving version was created by the Babylonians. The language is sophisticated and contains many questions. The first one comes in the prologue, where the narrator is describing the city of Uruk: 'Climb upon the wall of Uruk; walk along it, I say; regard the foundation terrace and examine the masonry: is it not burnt brick and good?'

Given the complexity of the language, this was not the first place where humans were asking questions, but cave paintings and scraps of bones from around firepits give us little to work with. Given the impossibility of tracking down the true origins of questions, perhaps we should switch to more modern times.

The film industry has grown from jerky, silent sequences of images in the late 1800s to fully featured and immersive

IMAX and 4D experiences, soon to be supplemented by Virtual or Augmented Reality, no doubt. In silent films, there were no verbal questions asked, for obvious reasons. Dialogue, scene breaks, and exposition were provided by the title cards that appeared between sections of film. These were known in the trade as intertitles, and at the first ever Academy Awards in 1929 an Oscar was given to *The Red Mill* for 'Best Title Writing'. This was the only time this prize was awarded, as 'talkie' movies soon made these intertitles redundant. When sound first arrived at the movie theatre though, it wasn't speech, but sound effects, such as the noise that accompanied the film of Charles Lindbergh's take-off during his flight to Paris; and the cheering crowds greeting his homecoming in America. Movies like *Don Juan* and *Sunrise* had soundtracks that consisted of musical scores, and some background sound effects. Although the 1927 movie *The Jazz Singer*, starring Al Johnson, has retained its legendary status as the first talkie in popular culture, it wasn't—previous films had included dialogue. *The Jazz Singer* is remembered largely due to its commercial success, helped significantly by Al Johnson's celebrity status before appearing in the movie, and so the film's reputation is not entirely due to the use of sound. The commercial success of this movie drove other studios to experiment. I spent a few hours hunting down the first questions from these early movies, without much luck. Like our written artefacts, it seems that many of the first pieces of movie history have been lost, damaged, or were never preserved in the first place. Hollywood though, has produced some memorable scenes based on questions—see the sidebar for some of the best-known ones.

We have better records in the computer age. The first ever question asked on Google was supposedly: "When was the internet invented?" While Google is used by a huge swathe of the world's population to search for information and to answer questions on many topics (along with Chinese equivalents such as Alibaba, or Microsoft's equivalent, Bing), the firm actually set up a specific site for questions, called Google Answers. On this site, the first question—a 'test' question—was removed, but the second question, the first 'true' one was: "Why is the sky blue?" asked on 9 April 2002. It seems to be the quintessential kids' question that adults, especially if they are scientific, love to hear, since it has a good answer. It's so stereotypical that it's easy to imagine an engineer deliberately seeding this to start the site. In reality, kids ask much tougher questions:

> "Santa is a stranger so why do we let him into our house?"
> "When will you die?"
> "Why don't we get a *four*-bedroomed house so mum and dad don't have to share a room?"
> "How did you get so wrinkly?"
> "Where do thoughts come from?"

Although we're talking about firsts, we should probably also mention the great science fiction writer Isaac Asimov who famously invented the three laws of robotics, popularising them in his collection of stories *I, Robot*. Asimov's favourite short story by his own hand was apparently, 'The Last Question'. The plot involves successive generations of humans asking a supercomputer: "How can the net amount of entropy of the universe be massively decreased?" This is really asking how to reverse the second law of thermodynamics, or to put it more simply: How do we stop the universe from using up all the energy and dying? Each time it's asked, the computer states that there is insufficient data to answer the question. Eventually, all humanity dies or merges with the computer, which does not function within the standard space-time continuum, but inhabits hyperspace. At some point after this; when the universe has ceased to exist, the computer finally discovers an answer. Since there's nobody alive to tell, the computer decides to demonstrate the results. "Let there be light!" it says, and there was light.

Famous questions from Hollywood movies

Mrs. Robinson, you're trying to seduce me, aren't you?
Dustin Hoffman, *The Graduate*

Aren't you a little short for a stormtrooper?
Carrie Fisher, *Star Wars*

Have you ever danced with the devil in the pale moonlight?
Jack Nicholson, *Batman*

Is it safe?
Laurence Olivier, *Marathon Man*

Who ya gonna call?
Theme song, *Ghostbusters*

You've gotta ask yourself a question: 'Do I feel lucky?' Well, do ya, punk?
Clint Eastwood, *Dirty Harry*

What's your favourite scary movie?
The killer, *Scream*

You want the truth?
Jack Nicholson, *A Few Good Men*

You know how to whistle, don't you Steve?
Lauren Bacall, To Have and Have Not

You talkin' to me?
Robert De Niro, *Taxi Driver*

2. TECHNIQUES

If you ask too many questions, you will find no answers,
only more questions.

Monica Fairview

Categorising questions

There are multiple ways of categorising questions, and it's quite possible for some questions to fit into several categories. We can ask a rhetorical question such as 'Is the Pope Catholic?' without expecting an answer, but the question is also a yes/no type, so counts as a closed, polar, and rhetorical question. We can break questions down by grammar and structure, or by the purpose of the question (a common approach in professional classification systems). We can divide questions into sub-groups based on relevance and importance; e.g. essential questions like 'What does it mean to live a good life?' vs tactical ones such as 'What should I eat for dinner?' Here's a quick rundown of the most common classifications people use:

Open/closed
Open: What did you do this weekend?
(may inspire a long answer)
Closed: Did you see *Jurassic Wars* this weekend?
(typical yes/no response)

Most training teaches that open questions are good and closed questions are bad, but the truth is that both types have value. Closed questions are a useful tool and can help you control a conversation or get a clear answer to a specific issue. **Polar questions** are a subset of the open/closed category, also referred to as yes/no questions. They have two answers, typically a yes/no, but some have a different pair of alternate answers like black/white, tea/coffee, or good/evil.

You can have a closed question that offers a set of alternatives, such as a multiple-choice question in an exam:

Which of these are noble gases?
A) Helium
B) Argon
C) Xenon
D) All of the above

Rhetorical

A rhetorical question is one that doesn't need an answer because the questioner already knows the information and is purely making a point. It is used for effect, or as a stylistic approach to language. Rhetorical questions generate a little drama, by making it seem as though there's a dialogue, even when there's only one speaker. We often see them used as literary devices. Speakers or presenters use rhetorical questions in the same way, especially as it's hard to have a dialogue with hundreds of people at once. However, these questions are not exclusively used in monologues. They're quite common in other spoken and written language, aren't they?

Do bears poop in the woods?
Do you think money grows on trees?
Are you crazy?

Shakespeare used rhetorical questions to good effect, as in this example from *The Merchant of Venice*, when Shylock is talking about Jews.

"If you prick us, do we not bleed? If you tickle us, do we not laugh? If you poison us, do we not die?"

Leading

'Were you in the Mission Viejo mall on Friday morning at 11am?' would be considered a poor question in a court of law. It suggests where the person was at a certain date and time, rather than asking a fairer question like: "Where were you on Friday morning?" The first question 'leads' the person to the response that the questioner would like to hear. You may be surprised to learn that, apart from in certain specific situations; leading questions are illegal both in UK and US courts—more on that later.

Loaded

"Have you stopped beating your wife?" is the most famous example of a loaded question. It presupposes that you're married, and if combined with 'please answer only yes or no', the question leaves the responder with a dilemma. Either answer confirms they have, at some time or other, beaten their wife. The standard defence is to challenge the underlying assumptions: 'That's a ridiculous suggestion, I've never beaten..." to which the opposition will counter that the person is avoiding a direct answer, and may repeat, 'Yes or no please.' Loaded questions contain implicit assumptions and represent traps in which even experienced people can be caught, possibly wrecking someone's career. It's a favourite structure in political interviewing. A loaded question differs from a leading question, in that it makes additional assumptions—such as the fact that a criminal was at a particular location and *did* commit a particular crime. The question 'Why did you smash the window at the jewellers, instead of using the unlocked door?' includes a couple of embedded assumptions, for example.

Suggestive

These are tricky questions that have been shown to result in false testimony. In the 1970s, a cognitive psychologist called Elizabeth Loftus demonstrated how witnesses could be made to testify to false memories, depending upon the wording of the 'suggestive' questions. She had a group of students watch some car-crash videos, and then interviewed them about the incidents, using an alternative key verb for each group. One of the questions was: "About how fast were the cars going when they (smashed / collided / bumped / hit / contacted) each other?" The average speed response from those who were asked the question with the verb *smashed* was 40.8mph. For those who were asked the same question using the term *contacted* the average speed was 31.8mph. It gets worse. Loftus was able to show that this was not simply a short-term effect, but a long-term influence on memory. In a second test, 150 students were shown a film featuring a car involved in another crash. One third of the group were asked "How fast were the cars going when they hit each other?"; one third was asked "How fast were the cars going when they smashed into each other?"; and the control group weren't asked any questions at all. A week later, all three groups were asked if they had seen any broken glass in the video—yes or no. Only 6 people in the control group said yes, plus another 7 people who'd been asked with the word *hit* in the previous week's question. In the group that had heard the word *smashed*, 16 people recalled seeing glass. There was no glass in the video.

There are other approaches that fit within the *Suggestive* category, too. For example, the use of repeated questioning to deliberately make people feel their first answer was incorrect.

"What colour was the car?"

"Red."

"What colour?"

"Red, with, like, some yellow."
"What would you call that colour?"
"Orange?"

This is known as confabulation; the production of a false or distorted memory about yourself or the world, without a conscious intent to deceive. It can occur through mental illness, or as a symptom of Alzheimer's or aneurysm. It can also be provoked via questions. For this reason, police guidance is very clear on how to gather information. A paper published by the US Dept. of Justice as guidance on collecting eyewitness evidence, gives the following pointers for conducting interviews:

- Ask open-ended questions, e.g. 'What can you tell me about the car?'

- Avoid leading questions, e.g. 'Was the car red?'

- Ask the witness to mentally recreate the circumstances of the event, e.g. 'What were you feeling, doing', etc. This helps to evoke the 'true' memory.

- Encourage non-verbal communication, e.g. ask them to draw or show an object involved—again, accessing the 'true' memory.

- Advise the witness to avoid talking to other witnesses and avoid any contact with the media or exposure to media accounts of the event.

Let's take a moment to reflect on two facts we've discovered here. Number one: the way somebody phrases questions can change your memory of an event. Two: certain categories of questions are banned in court. Those two facts are astonishing to me. If I'm not in court, who stops me using questions to change people's ideas and memories? Who has changed your perception of the world today?

Purpose-driven categories

Purpose-driven categorisations involve grouping questions that are related to something we're trying to achieve, such as educating a young mind, for example; persuading someone to buy a product, or gathering evidence for a court of law. Salespeople, for instance might place questions into the categories: **Understand** a problem, **Control** the conversation, **Label** another question, e.g. 'Do you mind if I ask you a personal question?' or ask for **Evidence**. They might have a separate category for **Buying** questions, such as 'Can we schedule the launch for next week?' By putting questions into these types of groups, we can observe meetings or perform roleplays, see how many questions of each type we ask, and also look for patterns to help us improve.

A very different categorisation of questions is used in Human Intelligence, or Humint, which is the gathering of information via interpersonal contact. Humint incorporates spying, interviews with political asylum seekers, interrogation of prisoners, and other aspects of human interaction. Here's a taxonomy of questions for Humint, from Wikipedia:

- **Initial questions:** directed towards obtaining the basic information on the topic. They often use the interrogative form of the direct questions below.
- **Direct questions:** basic interrogative questions normally beginning with one of the words: who, what, where, when, how, or why, and requiring a narrative answer. These are brief, precise, and worded simply to avoid confusion.
- **Follow-up questions:** used to expand on and complete

the information obtained from the initial questions.

- **Non-pertinent questions:** questions that do not relate to the collection objectives. They are used either to conceal these objectives or to strengthen rapport with the source.

- **Repeat questions:** ask the source for the same information obtained in response to earlier questions, usually to test for any deviations from earlier answers – i.e. to spot lying!

- **Control questions:** developed from recently confirmed information from other sources that is not likely to have changed.

- **Prepared questions #1:** developed by the Humint collector, usually in writing, prior to the questioning.

- **Prepared questions #2:** used primarily when dealing with a specific topic or information of a technical nature.

- **Negative questions:** questions that contain a negative word in the question itself such as, 'Didn't you go to the pick-up point?'

- **Compound questions:** consist of two questions asked in one sentence; for example, 'Where were you going after work and who did you meet there?'

- **Vague questions:** do not have enough information for the source to understand exactly what the Humint collector is asking. They may be incomplete, general, or otherwise nonspecific.

- **Elicitation:** is the gaining of information through direct interaction with a human source where the source is not aware of the specific purpose of the conversation.

- **Softball question:** a question that's easy or is on a topic that's not serious or important. Can be used to put a subject off guard, before a more challenging question.

- **Hardball question:** a confrontational question that presses the answerer to explain, e.g. inconsistencies or discrepancies with their previous stances.

- **Gotcha question:** a journalistic term used for a question or approach that entraps a person, so they make a statement that is damaging to themselves or their cause.

There's a whole chapter on professions later, but it's safe to say that every major industry appears to have at least one purpose-categorisation of questions that is used within that group. If you haven't been trained in a specific approach for the role you do, you might ask, why not? If nobody has defined such an approach, there might be an opening!

Hooks

When somebody is speaking to you, they will often indicate what they would like to talk about. I call these hooks, because people dangle them like bait on a fishing-line. It's your choice whether to take the bait and ask them the follow-on question. There are a few examples in the sidebar. I'm often amazed at how many people seem oblivious to these hooks. Here's a snippet from a telesales call, with some missed hooks:

SALLY   "Hello, is that Mr Anderson?"
Mr A   "Yes"
SALLY   "Oh, good afternoon sir, it's Sally calling from ManicSolutions. Can I confirm that you are the right person to speak to regarding marketing? Are you actually aware of my ManicSolutions at all?"

Two questions already, without waiting for a reply.

Mr A   "I think I am."
SALLY   "Have you previously used any of our products?"

And now a closed question too! Not good...

Mr A   "No, just from the recent press items that were interesting."
SALLY   "Right, I see. Basically, I was calling to find out a little bit more about your marketing and what you are doing really?"

Missed a hook! What interested him in the press items? Note Sally has not asked a clear question either; let's see what happens.

UNCOMFORTABLE PAUSE

Mr A "Okay. Do you want to ask questions, or do you want me to tell you?"

SALLY "For example, are any campaigns running right now?"

Mr A "Okay, we are currently...it's quite a confusing situation at the minute; we're primarily running campaigns on CenterPiece."

SALLY "Right."

Missed another hook! Why is the situation confusing?

Mr A "And we have some manual projects. We're still considering what our future platform should be."

SALLY "Right."

Missed yet another hook! Mr A is clearly indicating he would like to talk about the future platform, but Sally sails right by.

This was a real call, and interestingly, Sally felt the conversation had been a success because she'd gained a lot of information. From her manager's perspective though, there were multiple missed hooks (far more than the three shown in this excerpt). In fact, Sally had missed the chance to have a great conversation and make a potential sale.

Once you start looking for hooks, you'll see them everywhere. People love to hint at what they'd like to talk about. Set yourself a challenge to see how many hooks you notice today!

P.S. Just because you spot them, it doesn't mean you have to swallow them all. Pick and choose as you see fit. You'll also get a great reputation as a good listener.

Hook examples

Did you do anything exciting this weekend?
Translation: I did, ask me, ask me!

Have you booked your summer holiday?
Translation: I have, and I can't wait to tell you.

Don't get me started on *that!* Let's talk about something else.
Translation: Give me a push because I really *do* want to discuss *that.*

We would have tried that already, if it wasn't for what happened last time.
Translation: We aren't meant to talk about it, but ask me and I'll tell you.

Lectures & verbal diarrhoea

Nobody likes to be told what they're doing wrong or listen to somebody tell them about a better job they did in a similar situation. Yet, we do this to each other all the time. People try to change behaviour by highlighting our mistakes and explaining how to do things differently. A few, open-minded people can take such criticism on board, filter out the negativity and take some useful nuggets from the advice that will help them improve. Those people have my utmost respect. Most of us think about why we disagree with the person talking at us, how our position is different, and why their advice is not right in our situation. Unfortunately, we're sometimes on the other side of the fence too, wanting to change someone's behaviour, and realising we've switched into lecture mode, which will not achieve the desired effect. There's another approach to helping people that's actually much more powerful. You can ask questions. This lets the other person think through the situation themselves, and come to a potentially different conclusion, and in a non-confrontational manner. They'll also believe the result because it comes from their own thought process. In other words, they'll feel ownership for the idea, and will probably take action to make it happen. It may hurt your ego a little if you don't get any credit (because they'll think it was their idea), but you can ask yourself whether you're trying to appear clever or really trying to help? Let's look at an example:

Don: "I think people who have affairs are weak."
Jake: "Don't you think you'd ever have one?"
Don: "Never. I wouldn't even consider it."

Jake: "Do you like chocolate cake?"

Don: "Love it."

Jake: "Do you never get tired of eating chocolate cake?"

Don: "Not really."

Jake: "Wouldn't you want to nibble some lemon drizzle cake or eat a bag of chips or a steak sometimes?"

Don: "You can't make a comparison like that; it's not the same."

Jake: "Your wife must be pretty amazing, right?"

Don: "Yep. All I need."

Jake: "When you first eat a chocolate cake, you're full, and you don't want to eat anything else. True?"

Don: "I guess so."

Jake: "How long have you been married...?"

Don: "Nearly a year... Ah."

This is a heavily paraphrased conversation that I witnessed between two guys. Ignoring the terrible morals, the change in perspective that Jake affected in Don was startling. He didn't do it by arguing, or with a monologue, but a few straightforward questions and a peculiar analogy. I've seen this technique used many times—thankfully in more useful scenarios—and it's incredibly powerful. The funny thing is that it still works even when you know someone is doing it.

On the other hand, too many questions can sometimes seem like an interrogation, especially if the questions come hot on each other's tail. In a conversation, it can be tempting to add a follow-on question as soon as it occurs to you. And maybe a third: Should we go to the cottage this weekend? And go skiing? Maybe we should try that restaurant we saw last time? What was it called? Or should we take some food and you can try that new recipe from your aunt?

Too many questions can reveal nervousness, along with

your inner thoughts or fears: 'Did you think he looked nervous? Or was it just me? Am I just useless at reading people from different cultures? That doesn't sound racist does it?'

The term *verbal diarrhoea* seems appropriate for these rapid-fire chunks. Yet I bet you know someone who talks like that, barely giving you time to answer. Don't you? You do, don't you? Who is it? Tell me?!

The golden rule is to ask your question and then listen while it's being answered. By giving signals to the other person that you're actively listening to their answer, you will help to keep the information flowing. Let's look at that next.

Active listening

Sigmund Freud, the founder of psychoanalysis, was reputedly a fabulous listener. His attention was focused exclusively on you, the patient. He didn't glance at an attractive woman walking past the window or gaze over your shoulder while lost in thought. He showed that he was listening with a series of sounds and body language indicators—nodding his head, smiling at the appropriate moments, wrinkling his brow with concern. He would use a few words to keep you moving forward; "I see", "Interesting", "Fascinating", and so on. He might repeat a short phrase you'd just used. When he asked his next question, it would be related to what you'd said, a natural follow-on, or he would include a direct reference to your thoughts, demonstrating that he was paying attention and listening.

Most of us know at least one person that is a very active listener. Someone that pays full attention to those they talk to. These people are sought out as friends and advisors, because we all love to be truly heard. On the other end of the scale, many people are so busy trying to make a specific point or ask a certain question, that they're constantly in interrupt mode. As they wait for a chance to talk, they hear nothing that the speaker or other people are saying.

When mastered, active listening is incredibly powerful. The process is said to involve the three 'A's: **Attention**, which means listening exclusively to the talker; **Attitude**: having a positive mental mindset—don't go in thinking that what they're going to say will be rubbish; and **Adjustment**—a willingness to change your assumptions or what you were going to say in response to the talker. It all takes practice and patience. Here are the top ten tips:

1. Decide to actively listen to a specific conversation or speakers at a meeting.
2. Do it. Really listen. Think about what they're saying, not what you want to say.
3. Look at the person speaking, in the eyes if possible—but don't stare—breaking eye contact occasionally.
4. Lean forward.
5. Respond to the talk with body signals. Nod, smile, laugh, grimace, as appropriate.
6. Throw in occasional words to encourage the speaker: 'Interesting', 'Wow!' etc.
7. Repeat some of the points to ensure you understood.
8. Ask questions to clarify: 'Do you think that when you said x it was caused by y that you mentioned earlier?' to show you're listening, and to help you better understand what they're saying.
9. Resist the urge to add your own anecdotes.
10. Thank them at the end for sharing their knowledge / insight / thoughts / memories with you.

Active listening sounds simple enough but it takes determination and practice to do it effectively. The results though, can be astounding—because so few people do it well. If you want to take active listening to an advanced level, you can begin to think about *how* you are listening. It may be enough, in some work or educational environments to consider the information being imparted by the speaker. In many situations though, it would benefit us to think about the emotional aspects behind the conversation. Imagine someone talking about a project that failed, and how their company is seeking a new solution to replace it. You can look at the requirements as pure information, but you can also empathise, and ask if the person sharing this information was involved in the previous project, and what their role was. Perhaps the previous project manager was fired, and the new person is nervous about taking on the role and wants reassurance that they won't 'mess it up'. Or maybe they were the manager and need to rectify the situation to bolster their position.

As well as the emotional aspects, we can think about social information. When somebody apologises for being late because 'the traffic coming back from the Hamptons was terrible', you may take that as pure information, or you may register that a certain social group visit the Hamptons at the weekends, and the person is signalling their membership of it and hence their social status. There may be rapport to be built by registering these signals or looking for connections within social groups. I had a colleague who worked with a team of specialists who liked to add as many *Star Wars* quotes as possible into the monthly management meetings. This was in the early days of *Star Wars*, before it had become today's huge cultural meme, and managers were largely oblivious to comments such as:

"These aren't the reports we're looking for."
"I find your lack of faith in the Midas system disturbing."
"In my experience, there's no such thing as luck."
"We should do this, or not. There is no *try*."

Those who picked up the dialogue were part of the 'in-group'. If you weren't a *Star Wars* fanatic, you had to listen out for these lines and really pay attention. If you observed body language though, you would certainly have seen the other specialists struggling to control their laughter as these well-known lines breezed past their unwitting managers.

Another effective approach to active listening is to visualise the scenario that the speaker is describing. Humans have a strong visual mindset, and it's amazing how much more context and empathy you can generate by building a mental image to accompany someone's words.

One last tip; beware distraction! I knew a guy who had the habit of drumming his fingers on the desk when he was listening. He'd begin by fidgeting, shuffling in his chair, and before you knew it, he'd be tapping out complex rhythms with pencils, pens, or with his fingers. He used to do this in customer meetings, and it was embarrassing for everyone. His manager talked to him, but he was unaware that he was doing it. Nothing will kill a talker's vibe more than trying to communicate with someone who appears distracted and uninterested. If the conversation really is that boring, it may be because you are not fully engaged—active listening could make those 'boring' meetings far more interesting. I confess that I have a low boredom threshold myself. I've forced myself to be a better active listener because if I don't join in, I fall asleep.

Throwing combinations

Adam, a senior executive from a major organisation, has come to visit a small company. Because of his significance, a big team has gathered to meet him. After introductions, Adam gives an overview of his organisation. While everyone knows his company's name, they're not familiar with its current issues and challenges. Adam begins to talk in a way that is both entertaining and informative. Naturally, with so many talented and experienced people in the room, they question him about the areas he mentions, partly out of curiosity, but largely to identify ways they might partner together.

First, the senior executive asks Adam his questions, and drives the conversation down one line of thought. Before this executive has finished to his satisfaction though, the head of consultancy leaps in to ask a question that has been burning a hole in *his* mind, and subsequently follows up with several related topics. Next, the technical guru wants clarity on some points left hanging by Adam's explanation of his company's technology. A completely different line of discussion opens, but at the next pause one of the salespeople snatches their opportunity to ask about another topic. Just as they start to get somewhere, the senior executive comes back in to further pursue his original question. The proverb: 'Too many cooks spoil the broth' comes to mind. While the questions are intelligent and valuable, the meeting is failing because:

- it's taking too long—the meeting is running over schedule
- Adam must feel that he's under interrogation
- the team hasn't gained the critical understanding they need because each line of questions has been interrupted

Ultimately, the team failed to get the result they wanted. They captured a lot of data but didn't succeed in persuading Adam they had anything of value for him. A clearer definition of roles and responsibilities would have helped in this meeting. The key point, though, is that questioning is not about asking a single good question. There are patterns in the questions we ask. Like a boxer, none of the team were looking for a killer blow at the outset, they were putting together combinations to put themselves in a better position, so they could land a knock-out later. Unfortunately, nobody finished a combination, as somebody else has come into the fray from a different direction. When you think about questions, consider them as a sequence, like a boxer—a combination of left jab, left jab, right kidney punch, left uppercut. Here are a few common patterns for successful questioning:

Cascading: follows a line of thinking to a specific goal:
How do you make use of sensors in your shops?
How do you collect that data?
Can your network handle that much traffic?
Even from a remote region like Korea?
Have you considered compressing the data before sending it?

Levelling: picks one subject and keeps going deeper to gauge knowledge:
How many languages do you speak?
Which languages are they?
How confident are you with your Italian?
Could you cope if we conducted the rest of this interview in Italian?
Allora, si può descrivere...

Listening-led: open question to start, strongly driven by phrases of talker:

How was your weekend?

Sounds great, have you ever done it before?

I didn't know you were so into diving, have you done all the PADI exams?

Where was that?

Wow, Australia? You never told me you went around the world after college. Which other countries did you visit...?

Industry specific: these are based on the purpose-driven categorisations we looked at earlier in this chapter. Let's stick with the Huthwaite Research Group sales approach, SPIN. The name of this methodology is an acronym for the question pattern:

Situation: Tell me about the warehouse.

Problem: Do you sometimes run out of space?

Implications: How many new warehouses will you have to build? How much does each warehouse cost?

Need-Payoff: If we reduced slow moving stock by 50 percent so you only had to open one more warehouse this year, what would your cost savings be?

There are as many patterns as you can imagine. If you think about it, you may already have some favourite patterns that you use today. The key is to intentionally think about the questioning approach to use in a specific situation. If you have an important meeting, you may want to spend a few minutes thinking about your question patterns beforehand. If you use recurring patterns that are not effective, you can choose to change. If you've never thought about them before, try one of the templates above. Whatever you do, remember that patterns are important—so much so, that the UK government randomises the sequence of questions that can be asked in parliament (see the chapter on Professions).

Purpose

Imagine you're walking down the street when you bump into an acquaintance. You immediately recognise them but can't remember their name or where you know them from. Did you work together once? Are they in your fitness class? Did you meet them at that party a month ago? They say hello, use your name, and ask how you're doing. Your brain is scrambling but rather than ask a socially embarrassing question like: 'Who are you?' what you might do is use a question to buy some time, and hunt for a clue to their identity.

"Hey, it's good to see you! How are you?"

Of course, that closed question won't buy you very long. A better question might be:

"What have you been up to lately?" or even "How are things?"

That should give you more time to crank-start your mind, and may even give you some hints as to how you're connected. The interesting aspect of this, from our perspective in this book, is that the purpose of your question is not to get a direct answer or to learn. In this case, the question is a tool to give you space to think, and a kind of detective tool. You can't ask the question you want without appearing rude. Some readers may shrug and claim they'd be happy to ask a direct question, perhaps with a label to soften the blow:

"I'm really sorry, I can't place your face out of context— can you remind me how we know each other?" or some such direct question. If you have that confidence, and are happy doing this, then go ahead. One word of caution, though. No matter how kindly you do it, the message the other person will receive is that they're not very important to you.

There are many other situations where the purpose of our question is not to seek a direct answer. For example, I was once told that if I was acting as a presenter and someone's attention was drifting away, I should ask the person *next* to them a question, as this draws focus to that section of the room, and everyone suddenly sits straighter in their chairs. If you ask the daydreamer a question directly, it may be embarrassing as they won't be able to answer properly if they weren't listening. You'll have seen mean teachers doing exactly that in a hundred TV shows and movies, seemingly with a goal of humiliating the child. Hopefully this is a false stereotype. I once saw a trainer use this technique in a clever and funny way. He saw a man nodding off in a post-lunch slump, and turned to the person next to him and said:

"Do you think Steve is still awake?"

Roars of laughter ensued, waking Steve, who looked around frantically to see what he'd missed.

We should keep in mind that not all questions serve the same purpose. Questions are primarily used for learning—both in gathering knowledge and testing it, but they can also buy time, display credibility, wound, deliver praise, be used for humour or irony, and as we have seen, to deliberately change memories. When asking or answering a question, it can be a good idea to consider the purpose of the question, both the direct, observable purpose and the underlying, indirect goals. As with any type of action, it can often be hard to discern the motive, but that shouldn't stop us from considering it. If you're asking that question to show how clever you are, do you really need to ask it? Is there any point in responding angrily to a question that was asked in a deliberate attempt to provoke you? The purpose of a question can be at least as important as the content.

The $120 T-shirt

Before we finish this first look at techniques, we should explore how cognitive behaviour informs questions, especially in the combinations we've reviewed. Let's say you want to buy a new T-shirt from the hottest internet fashion site, called Rip-u-off. Everyone at your office, school, or club is raving about these clothes. You browse the site, and the first thing you see is a plain white T-shirt with a tiny embroidered Rip-u-off logo, and it costs $1000. You nearly fall off your chair. It's made from organic long-thread cotton weaved on ancient Japanese looms, but wow, that's a lot of money. You scroll through the next few items, priced in the range $600–$1500. Then you find a blue T-shirt, with the Rip-u-off logo, that's only $120. It's still organic, but not long-thread and it was made on modern looms. There are only a few in stock. You snap one up. Bargain! You just paid $120 for a T-shirt... are you crazy? No, you succumbed to good marketing and a cognitive theory known as anchor bias. Much of the early research and popularisation of anchor bias came from Daniel Kahneman and Amos Tversky, starting in the 1970s. They showed that people's numerical decisions were affected by the first piece of data they received, known as the anchor. In our example, the $120 T-shirt appears cheap because the price is significantly lower than the anchor price you encountered at $1000. This anchor bias, which has been the subject of multiple research papers, is applied in many situations, e.g.:

Forex trading is notorious for being anchored around certain prices for pairs of currency. I still feel that a British pound,

GBP, should be about $1.65 USD, and so it pains me to see it at $1.21 because for many years, $1.65 was the anchor around which the pair of currencies fluctuated. There was even a brief, exciting period where I could get $2 for every pound, but I always knew the price would sink back down to $1.65 eventually. What I didn't predict was Brexit, and the way the pound plummeted. Now when I need to exchange currency, I feel short-changed because my mental anchor is still set at $1.65. Slowly, I'm coming to terms with $1.25 as a possible new anchor, but if the market keeps going in the same way, we might soon see parity; a pound for a dollar. Apparently the 3-year average is $1.30, but with coronavirus raging the rate is presently $1.16.

Politics: In recent years, elections have come under increasing scrutiny regarding the use of social media accounts and the manipulation of news. None of this is new, it's just that the tools have got better. For years, people have manipulated poll results through anchor bias as well as question order bias, another cognitive tool that we'll explore later. Imagine a poll:

Question 1: Are you aware that the Red Party is planning a major healthcare initiative at a cost of $100 billion?

Question 2: The Blue party is planning a healthcare initiative that will cost $15 billion. Do you think this is enough money to support their plans?

By using an anchor to set a $100 billion spend as the 'standard' in the mind of the person being polled, the $15 billion now appears a small sum in comparison. It's likely that more people surveyed would respond with 'No' to Question 2, than if we'd asked the question without setting the anchor first.

This gives us three political problems. One is that a poll may not be an accurate reflection of how people feel. The second problem is that a manipulative pollster (or party) can design a survey this way, and use the results as evidence: '78% of voters in district x believe the Blue spending plans are not enough to fix the healthcare crisis—how did the Blue Party get so out of touch?' The third problem is that we've seen how asking questions can change people's minds. People may start to believe that $100 billion is the amount required, even though there's no evidence for this, and it could be a gross overspend.

Not everyone is as susceptible to anchor bias as the general population. People of high intelligence are less likely to be swayed, as are those with solid domain experience. The anchor number also needs to be reasonable to have the desired effect. If the T-shirt price had been $1 million, the anchor effect at Rip-u-off would not have worked. Certain character traits, such as agreeability, do make people more likely to conform to anchor bias. Don't leave this page believing that you're immune, because evidence suggests this is a very real, widespread behavioural trait. Another important point is that anchor bias not only affects numbers, it can also apply to concepts. If you're watching a political debate on TV and the first speaker sets out the stall by saying, 'this election is about universal healthcare and jobs', then the debate will probably focus on these issues, which have become the anchors. It may be that national debt or security are more pressing issues, but once the anchors have been dropped, anyone trying to move off the topics of universal healthcare and jobs will look as though they are trying to detract attention from the 'core' issues.

We may curse the marketeers and pollsters for manipulating us, but the situation is more complex, and this next point is scary: *If nobody gives us an anchor, our mind finds one anyway.* If we're not presented with an anchor, we'll latch on to the first reasonable value we see, and use that as our anchor, even if it is not correlated with the matter in hand. Here are a couple of examples you can test yourself with. Of course, you can't trust me—I might be manipulating you. See if you can answer each question honestly. The actual answers are on the next page.

1. The last value I saw for US debt is $22 trillion. How many websites are on the internet?

2. There are 52 weeks in a year and 60 seconds in a minute. How many people in the world are called Zhang Wei?

3. There are nearly 8 billion people on the planet. How many stars can you see by the naked eye in the sky at night?

4. My favourite number is 17. How many galaxies can be seen by the naked eye from Earth?

5. Scotland has a population of approximately 5 million. How many people are bitten by snakes each year?

Answers to anchor bias

1. There are 1.94 billion websites on the Internet (as of Jan 2019).

2. According to the 2007 census, Zhang Wei was the most common name in China, shared by 290,607 people. More than 270 million people in China share the surname Li, Wang, or Zhang, making these the world's most common last names.

3. There are about 5000 stars in the sky at night, but you can typically only see about 2000 because the Earth gets in the way—plus light pollution, weather, etc.

4. You can see 4 galaxies with the naked eye. That includes our own: the Milky Way, Andromeda, and the Magellanic clouds (small and large). Astronomers believe there are 200 billion galaxies in total, which have an average of 100 billion stars each.

5. The World Health Organisation estimates that 5.4 million people are bitten by snakes every year, and about half of those are envenomings. There are between 81,000–137,000 deaths each year—and three times as many amputations and permanent disabilities. That's more than 300 deaths every day, and yet sharks get a bad reputation for killing an average of 6 people per year, in a total of 60—100 attacks!

How did you do? Were you able to distance yourself from the misleading anchor numbers at the start of each question? If your answers were in the right order of magnitude each time, then you did well. Equally, you were prepared for this. Now look out for anchors in the real world and see if you can avoid bias when it really counts.

3. LANGUAGE

*The question is, said Alice, whether you can make words mean
so many different things. The question is, said Humpty Dumpty,
which is to be master, that's all.*

Lewis Carroll

Religion: part I

Once language and questions had emerged in our species, certain fundamental questions most probably arose, as they seem to in every culture:

> Where do we come from?
> What is our purpose here?
> Why does x happen? (the sun rise, the crops fail, etc.)
> What happens when we die?
> How should we live our life?

This is the realm of religion. In every human culture, religion has emerged to provide a belief system, a community, and an element of faith to help people deal with these questions. Religion asks believers to look at their motives and goals, and at how they relate to others. Throughout history, religious teaching has taken various forms, such as poetry, song, art, sermons, conversations, and stories. Many of these are filled with questions.

Let's take Christianity as a starting point, since it presently has the most followers in the world (followed by Islam, Hinduism and Buddhism, in that order; in case you wondered). Margaret Hunter—a mathematician who owns the organisation *Bible Charts and Maps*—has performed a series of analytic studies on the Bible. According to Margaret's statistics, there are 3,294 questions in the King James Authorised Bible. She also notes there are 3,157 question marks, giving us a total of 137 questions asked without a question mark—something we'll explore later when we look at grammar. Of course, it's hard to measure the number of questions accurately because the Bible is translated from Hebrew and Koine Greek, with different approaches to punctuation—and perhaps most importantly, no question marks; as this was a later invention.

When validating Margaret's statistics, I began searching through online versions of the Bible to compare the frequency of different words. Did you know the Bible contains 188 lambs and only 150 lions? I got different results depending on which system I used to ask the question, however. I'll come back to that in our Technology chapter, when we look at how to achieve a single version of the truth. The very first question in the Bible appears in Genesis when the Serpent asks Eve:

"Yea, hath God said, Ye shall not eat of every tree of the garden?"

The Serpent's cunning line of questions and discourse leads to Adam and Eve to make a fateful decision. There are several other very famous questions in the text of the Bible, such as Cain's response to God when asked about the location of his (murdered) brother Abel: "Am I my brother's keeper?" As far as Biblical questions go, the most famous sequence is found in the trials of Job when he experiences a series of terrible events designed to test his faith. The entire Book of Job is founded on the core question: *Will you still have faith when everything around you fails?* Religious scholars view this Book as an investigation into divine justice, and they phrase the central question as: *Why do the righteous suffer?* Interestingly, the story of Job begins with God and Satan having a little Q&A session:

And the LORD said unto Satan, Whence comest thou? Then Satan answered the LORD, and said, From going to and fro in the earth, and from walking up and down in it.

And the LORD said unto Satan, Hast thou considered my servant Job, that there is none like him in the earth, a perfect and an upright man, one that feareth God, and escheweth evil?

Then Satan answered the LORD, and said, Doth Job fear God for nought? Hast not thou made an hedge about him, and about his house, and about all that he hath on every side?

Notice how Satan answers a question with a question—a useful technique that should not be restricted to manipulators and fallen angels. God responds by sending a series of disasters to test Job's faith (strictly speaking he lets Satan do this, but He authorises it); decimating Job's business and livelihood, killing his children, and so on. When Job remains faithful, Satan is sent back to inflict boils and illness on Job. Yet it was not Job that began to question his faith, but his wife. She asked her husband: "Dost thou still retain thine integrity? curse God, and die."

Next, Job meets three friends and they debate whether Job has suffered because of his sin, as they can't conceive that a 'just' God would punish a righteous fellow so badly. While these questions are never answered directly, the Book of Job contains a poem to wisdom and two speeches by God, in which the debate centres around the question: 'Where is wisdom to be found?' God does not make a direct answer but responds with more questions that suggest He knows what He's doing and shouldn't be interrogated over His choices.

Where wast thou when I laid the foundations of the earth? Who shut up the sea with doors, when it brake forth, as if it had issued out of the womb? Have the gates of death been opened unto thee? Hast thou seen the doors of the shadow of death?

In fact, God piles questions onto Job, racking up at least 70 (some are compound questions). Clearly, the art of questioning has some divine backing. There is a fair amount of scholarly debate about the authorship of the various parts of the Book of Job, and it appears as there may have been multiple authors. What is fascinating is that there are similar tales of suffering and questioning of divine authority in other religions that pre-date Christianity, such as those in Egypt and Mesopotamia. This may point to a shared knowledge of these stories by the author/s of the Book of Job, but more likely, they are separate stories that emerged to answer the same underlying key questions, especially on why a just God would let a good person suffer—or at the very least, to open these subjects for debate, since there seems to be no clear answer that satisfies everyone.

Religion: part II

Unlike the monotheistic religions, the multi-deity religions such as the Greek, Roman, or Norse—each possessing a large pantheon of gods—have a strong argument to explain the suffering of individual worshippers. They believed that humans were caught in battles or jealousies between their gods. The mortals become collateral damage, in modern parlance. In the Trojan wars, for example, fleet-footed Achilles was largely indestructible because he was part-god, having been submerged in the river Styx as a baby. Ultimately, he is murdered via his one fatal flaw, the ankle that was left exposed when he was dipped into the river, although he would have survived had it not been for the meddling gods. The Trojan Wars feature many divine interventions that cause death and pain to the humans involved. The conflict traces its very beginnings to a golden apple inscribed with the words 'For the Fairest' that is tossed into a wedding feast attended by the gods. Hera, Aphrodite, and Athena argue about who should receive the gift, and the human hero Paris is chosen as the judge. Each goddess tries to influence his decision. Hera offers him the chance to be King of Europe and Asia. Athena offers wisdom and skill in war, but Paris chooses Aphrodite who offers him the world's most beautiful woman, Helen of Sparta. Never mind that Helen was already married to King Menelaus! From this inauspicious start, the gods continue to interfere with the heroes' lives, and with the lives of those caught in the conflict. From Zeus, Apollo, Athena, and Achilles's sea-nymph mother Thetis—the poor lady whose wedding feast was interrupted by the golden apple event—even down to the lowly river god Xanthus, it seems that every god gets mixed up in human affairs. While the gods tackle their relationships with humans in different ways, such multi-deity religions were concerned with raising fundamental questions for their believers to consider—in this case, which goddess should Paris have chosen to receive the golden apple? Is wisdom or power more valuable than love?

If we look at other sacred texts, we find them likewise filled with questions. We have the same problem as with the Bible though, when analysing these texts: How to find a single version of the truth? For example, most modern Islamic scholars agree that the Quran has 6236 verses, although many scholars have held different opinions over the years, with 6666 being a common belief in the thirteenth century. The Quran, as it is known today, is written in classical Arabic, although there is some dispute over whether it was originally written in an Aramaic dialect that predates Arabic. This is a delicate topic, as Muslims believe the Quran is the word of God to Muhammed directly transferred via the angel Gabriel. If it has been translated, then it has been corrupted. If we take the classical Arabic versions compiled by Abu Bakr, which is widely accepted by the majority of Muslims as the standard version of the text, then we find no question marks. This is because classical Arabic did not contain modern punctuation. The Quran does contain a lot of interrogative statements and rhetorical questions, however. There's also a passage where Allah specifically instructs:

"So ask those who possess knowledge if you do not know." (an-Nahl 16:43)

This is a clear piece of advice to ask questions in order to learn. There's a catch though, as the Quran also includes a warning against asking the wrong type of questions:

"Ask not about things which, if made plain to you, may cause you trouble. But if you ask about them while the Quran is being revealed, they will be made plain to you." (A-Maa'idah 5:101)

I've seen some interesting online debates by puzzled students trying to come to terms with these verses, which perhaps is one of the reasons that Islam, Christianity and (nearly) every other religion, also has trained specialists that go under a variety of names: mujtahid, vicar, priest, who can help answer such questions and guide those looking for clarity in their understanding.

Which brings me on to Judaism. The rabbi is the name of the teacher in this religion, and I was told an anecdote a few years back about how a new rabbi is appointed. Judaism differs from many other religions in not making a direct link between God and the religious teacher or leader. The rabbi is a knowledgeable person but does not have a special hotline to divine wisdom. Rabbis act as community leaders and historically, were involved in judging and legislating, as well as matchmaking, teaching about the faith, and performing duties at funerals and weddings; all while pursuing their lifelong studies of the Torah, meaning the core reference materials of Judaism, although the word is also used to encompass many of the other aspects of the Jewish culture in its totality. With all those tasks and responsibilities, the rabbi is clearly a critical person in the community. In other religions, there is often a central governing body that appoints the leader of a community. In Judaism, there may be recommendations, but the members of the congregation themselves select the rabbi. They do this via a search and interview process, as you might do for any senior role in a corporate organisation. Several years ago, my friend told me he'd been involved, over a period of five years, in the selection of a rabbi on three occasions; explaining how the primary characteristic his congregation valued was *the rabbi's ability to ask good questions.* Just think about that for a moment. In most interviews, the questions are firing in from the prospective employer, with a few minutes at the end for the candidate to ask a handful of questions. In the search for a rabbi though, the reverse is true (at least it was for my friend's congregation). They realised that as a leader, the rabbi needed to be able to ask good questions if they were to understand the complexities of the scenarios they would be faced with, so they made *questioning* a primary skill. I'm not sure if this is a common approach across Judaism, but I can say that the Rabbinical Assembly Organisation has a document on its website (written by Rabbi Elliot Salo Schoenberg) that helps congregations go through the process of selecting and nominating a new rabbi. It includes the following advice: "Good questions by the candidate are often just as important to understanding the candidate…[as] their answers to your questions." Well said.

There's also a wealth of other religions to explore; Buddhism, Hinduism, Confucianism, and Jainism, along with the traditional indigenous and folk religions with roots in animism or ancestor worship; or those led by shamans. We have modern examples too, such as Scientology. That's not to exclude a large percentage of the world population that identify themselves as agnostic (those that haven't decided the answer to the basic question: *does God exist?*) or atheist (who have answered that same question with a negative). While there are believed to be thousands of religions and a multitude of belief systems and values, they all focus on helping us answer the core questions we started with: Where did we come from? and What happens when we die? Religions have produced some wonderful tales and beliefs for answers, but around about 500 BC an influential group of philosophers adopted a different approach, using a new way of thinking.

Classical thinking

Ancient Greek scholars invested heavily in questions to better understand the world around them and their place within it. Socrates's approach, which was documented by his student Plato in *Dialogues,* has influenced thinking, science, psychology, teaching, and many other fields of knowledge for centuries. It's good that people like Plato and Xenophon recorded the thinking of Socrates, since the great philosopher was not a writer. Even his infamous death, when sentenced to drink a vial of the poisonous hemlock after a public trial, was captured for posterity by Plato. Of course, Plato was a great philosopher himself, and there is always a slight question about how much of his writing is an accurate rendition of Socrates' speech, and how much is Plato putting his own ideas into the mouth of another (can't trust authors!).

The Socratic Method consists of presenting an argument in the form of a dialogue. It allows us to explore a subject to find the hidden assumptions and contradictions, in order to test hypotheses. The dialogue involves one person asking a series of questions to another, who answers. Here's an example where Socrates is debating whether a life of pleasure is better than a life of wisdom:

> SOCRATES: Would you choose, Protarchus, to live all your life long in the enjoyment of the greatest pleasures?
> PROTARCHUS: Certainly I should.
> SOCRATES: Would you consider that there was still anything wanting [lacking] to you if you had perfect pleasure?
> PROTARCHUS: Certainly not.

SOCRATES: Reflect; would you not want wisdom and intelligence and forethought, and similar qualities? Would you not at any rate want [fore]sight?

PROTARCHUS: Why should I? Having pleasure I should have all things.

SOCRATES: Living thus, you would always throughout your life enjoy the greatest pleasures?

PROTARCHUS: I should.

SOCRATES: But if you had neither mind, nor memory, nor knowledge, nor true opinion, you would in the first place be utterly ignorant of whether you were pleased or not, because you would be entirely devoid of intelligence.

You can see here, that Socrates has set a hypothesis (if a life of pleasure is perfect, you don't need wisdom), and begins testing the idea by asking questions of his protagonist. At first, Protarchus thinks it would be a great way to live, but then Socrates shows his friend that it is not possible to have pleasure without a little wisdom. Socrates might then revise his hypothesis—perhaps to see if the reverse is true—that a life of wisdom would be better than one of pleasure. Rather than sink into this debate, the point here is to see the approach. The Socratic Method involves a pattern: first to form a mental model of a theory (a hypothesis), and then to test this via a series of questions—perhaps also seeking exceptions to the rule—to decide if your hypothesis is correct or not; revising if necessary; and then continuing to explore with further questions. It's no coincidence that this approach is the basis for the scientific method of inquiry too.

Socrates himself was interested in questions of morals and good living. He used his techniques to explore what it meant to live a good life, asking questions about how society should be structured; exploring values of justice, virtue, and character. This is still a common method of questioning for teachers and psychologists. Its value lies in putting the onus on the person answering the questions to think more deeply about their own ideas, challenging their assumptions, and potentially changing their perception.

Plato was clearly a believer in the value of asking questions, as we can see from his most famous quote: 'The unexamined life is not worth living.' The influence of these two philosophers has echoed on through our modern civilisation.

The scientific method

Modern science is based on the Latin injunction ignoramus—
'we do not know'. It assumes that we don't know everything.
Even more critically, it accepts that the things that we think we
know could be proven wrong as we gain more knowledge. No
concept, idea or theory is sacred and beyond challenge.

Yuval Noah Harari,
Sapiens: A Brief History of Humankind

The patterns of questioning and thinking that emerged from Socrates, Plato, and later by Plato's student Aristotle are largely considered to be the basis of the modern scientific approach. Together, these philosophers laid out the distinction between deductive, inductive, and abductive reasoning, along with the use of analogy. This approach was advanced in the thirteenth century by Roger Bacon, who was well ahead of his generation in wanting maths to form the basis of science, and by another Bacon in the 1600s, Francis this time (no relation); along with growing contributions from a roll-call of philosophers: Descartes, Hume, John Stuart Mill, Kuhn, and more. As science became more specialised, thinkers and theorists in each niche formed their own views, approaches, and hypotheses—think of Karl Marx, John Maynard Keynes, or Milton Friedman, for example. All their ideas emerged from a rigorous approach to questions. This modern scientific approach can be summarised as:

Start with a question: *Is the Earth flat?*

All good science comes from a key question. See the sidebar for some well-known examples.

Gather information: *Look at maps, collect data such as how far everyone has sailed in each direction, make measurements, consider whether you can see that tall Church spire across the flat plain, and measure how far away you can still see it.*

This is the observational stage of science, sometimes called characterisation, where we make initial measurements, capture existing data, and make some definitions related to the subject.

Create a hypothesis: *The Earth is not flat.*

A hypothesis is a theory (although mathematicians like to call it a conjecture) that explains some aspect of the subject in question and is worded in such a way that allows people to prove if the theory is true or false. Typically, scientists construct hypotheses so that they can be proven *wrong* by performing experiments (this is known as the null hypothesis). For example, rather than stating *the earth is a sphere,* we set our initial (null) hypothesis to say that *the earth is not flat.* There are several good reasons for this approach; one is that it helps us avoid bias, as it's easy to find evidence to support your favourite theory, so instead we take a sceptical stance and try to prove things wrong—humans seem to be pretty good at that—and it is often simpler to gather meaningful statistics to support a negative. This is the famous black swan scenario: if you hypothesise that all swans are white, you can inspect thousands of swans and see they are white, but does that prove your hypothesis? It only takes one black swan to disprove your theory.

Develop validation experiments: *If the Earth is flat, standing at the top of a tall tower should not affect how far you can see.*

This step involves making predictions, based on your hypothesis and some deductive reasoning; then devising experiments that could be performed to test the prediction. The tests should be repeatable, as free from bias as possible, and should isolate the key prediction so that no other factor could influence the results.

Perform experiments and capture results: *Have a series of test subjects stand at ground level next to Tower x on a day with clear visibility, and note the furthest object they can see, while a similar group stand on the top of the tower and list the furthest objects they can see.*

The experimental stage may suffer from issues and might need to be repeated. The tower may overlook a plain with no discernible objects in the distance, for example, so we'd need to find a location with a more varied landscape; or the test may be invalid in some way—perhaps those at the top of the tower had poor eyesight, whereas those on the ground had better general vision.

Question the results: *Did they prove or disprove the hypothesis? Are the results valid? What can we infer or deduce from them?*

We started with a question, and we finish with more. We analyse the results in great detail and check to see how it has altered our perception of the hypothesis. A false result can often be as exciting as a positive one, as all the results contribute to a better model; a more advanced theory about the subject of our initial question. We may return to an earlier stage in the process, develop better experiments, more advanced tests. We may alter our hypothesis and create new experimental ideas. The whole process is iterative, but this is often the point for skipping back to an earlier stage to adjust, and restart.

Publish: *The Earth is not flat!*
Before any academic paper is published, it goes through a process of peer review, where it is checked and inspected by other scientists, who rigorously question the conclusions. Higher-profile journals will have the most distinguished scientists on their review panel, making it harder to be published without a strong hypothesis, test approach, and results.

There is yet another stage beyond this, where specific hypotheses are pulled together into general theories. These attempt to simplify prior results and express a law or rule that fits with evidence from multiple hypotheses. Once formulated, these general theories are subject to questioning and experimentation in order to prove their value. Often, we find theories supplementing or enhancing prior laws. Although Isaac Newton's laws of gravity are valid in most situations, or instance, we now understand (or think we do) that these laws do not operate on very small scales—in quantum mechanics—or on very large scales, where Einstein's relativity 'rules'.

One of the interesting aspects of science is the way that knowledge builds on prior knowledge, letting our questions get deeper and more sophisticated over time. At first we may wonder what the sun is, and why it revolves around us, then through a process of asking increasingly more advanced questions, and testing our assumptions and beliefs, we reach a point where we understand the composition of the sun, and can prove that objects in the solar system are in constant motion in a large vacuum, exerting gravitational effects on each other, and that the earth revolves around the sun.

Almost every major technological advance you can imagine, and the step-changes we see in science, philosophy and medicine, have come from individuals asking themselves questions, and following a standard approach to answering them. The power of questions layered upon questions is phenomenal. It's like compound interest for ideas.

Scientific questions
that have changed our world

Why did the apple fall perpendicular to the floor?
Isaac Newton, *theory of gravity.*

Instead of calculating numbers for navigators, what if there was a way to make a general-purpose mechanical machine?
Charles Babbage, *designing the analytical engine—the first computer.*

What would I see if I chased a beam of light?
Albert Einstein, *Special Theory of Relativity.*

Is the Earth really at the centre of the universe?
Nicolaus Copernicus, *heliocentric theory, which put the sun in the centre of our universe model, allowing us to evolve our modern understanding of the universe and our place in it.*

Why has mould prevented the bacteria from growing in this petri dish that was accidentally left open?
Alexander Fleming, *discovery of penicillin, a group of antibiotics that have saved millions of lives.*

What can I do to stop the local wines tasting so acidic?
Louis Pasteur, *inventing pasteurisation while on his summer holiday. It was nearly 40 years until the process began to be applied to milk—it was used for wine and beer at first.*

Why don't we organise the elements by atomic weight?
Dimitri Mendeleev, *The Periodic Table. It took science nearly 100 years to find an effective way to group and organise the elements, following the first attempts by Lavoisier in 1789.*

Question marks

You can tell how important the question is to human language by looking at the way we construct our sentences in print. Apart from the letters that make up the basic sounds, there are only a handful of symbols used in everyday text, commonly referred to as punctuation marks. These include speech marks to show dialogue, commas, apostrophes, full-stops (known as periods in American English) and colons / semi-colons to help clarify meaning and show where the emphasis and pauses should occur, plus hyphens, and brackets; joined relatively recently by the ubiquitous @ symbol. Then there are two special symbols: the Question Mark '?' and the Exclamation Mark '!'

The exclamation mark is used to indicate either strong emotion, surprise, sometimes shouting, or an imperative:

"You don't mean that!"
"So *you* were the masked man all along!"
"I told you he was a liar!"
"Don't move!"
"Wham! Bam!"

Or as a warning:
Danger!
Keep out!

There's a definite view that the exclamation mark gets over-used, and also a perspective that serious writers should avoid using it. F. Scott Fitzgerald said "Cut out all those exclamation points. An exclamation point is like laughing at your own jokes."

On my Twitter account, my most popular tweet was a one-liner about exclamation marks that I posted without much thought, which has been retweeted and favourited by many people who were unconnected with me. It said: *Just noticed! I keep using exclamation marks! Must stop now!!!*

If there's a genre that's more closely associated with the exclamation mark, it's the comic. This is typified in the classic Roy Lichtenstein image of two dogfighting planes, with one exploding along with the word *Whaam!* The exclamation goes by several slang names too—the bang, pling, screamer, shriek or slammer. The French, Germans, and Turks like to use it to punctuate commands and orders, and in various places—such as France—it's used with a space between the preceding word and the mark. The Spanish are keen to flag what's happening in advance and like to put an upside-down exclamation mark at the start of a sentence, as well as the standard symbol at the end. They do the same with the question mark. ¿Do you think that's strange, or useful?

You may be wondering why we're studying the exclamation mark, when this is a book on questions (good question!). The answer is the *interrobang*, which we'll come on to soon.

First let's explore the slightly murky history of the question mark. In her book *Eats, Shoots & Leaves,* Lynne Truss suggests Alcuin of York, who lived in the late 700s, as the possible inventor; although the original symbol bears little resemblance to the one used today. It wasn't until several hundred years later that the burgeoning book industry began to standardise punctuation. It's been suggested that the symbol itself came from the Latin QVAESTIO which was often abbreviated to qo, and the letters were then written above each other, gradually (or perhaps rapidly) evolving into the symbol we see today. However, there don't appear to be many examples of Q over O in the Medieval Latin texts that are preserved.

The use of the question mark varies across different languages and cultures. In Arabic it appears as a mirror image of its usual form, which makes perfect sense since the writing flows from right to left. Yet in Hebrew, which is also a right to left language, the question mark appears in the traditional form and position. Rather surprisingly, the question mark is used in modern Chinese and Japanese writing. The way questions are phrased in these languages means that question marks are not absolutely required, but they're in common use anyway. In fact, these languages also use the question mark to indicate an indirect question, such as: 'I wonder if you could help me?'

Of course, the question mark can only be used in text. It's never actually pronounced, although it affects intonation, which makes it a rather strange character. It does have other uses, though. As a symbol, it has been seized by the technology industry, just like @, where it has specific uses that we'll look at in the Technology chapter. What I find most striking is how the question mark is so widely used across disparate cultures and languages. Along with the exclamation mark, it is a fundamental building block of written and spoken language, and one might argue, thought.

Given the importance of the exclamation and question mark symbols, it's not entirely surprising that someone decided to combine the two. In 1962, Martin Speckter, the head of an American advertising agency, decided that adverts would look better by using one combined symbol to convey a rhetorical question. Publishing an article on the subject in a printer's magazine, he asked readers to suggest names for the new punctuation mark. He chose 'interrobang' as the winning name from the suggestions. Speckter wasn't the first person to propose this symbol, however. In the sixteenth century, English printer Henry Denham created an inverted question mark: ؟ for use with rhetorical questions. Although Denham ran a successful printing business, the symbol never quite caught on. Spectker had a little more success with the interrobang, partly because it was picked up by a few typeface designers and included on some typewriters in the late 1960s and early 1970s and became a fad fashion. While the interrobang was intended for rhetorical questions (i.e. those that don't require an answer), combining the exclamation and question mark does give the symbol a wider range of uses, such as expressing excitement or disbelief. For example:

What were you thinking‽

You said what‽

What the...‽

Of course, there is also an upside-down version of the interrobang, so that rhetorical questions can also be asked in Spanish. I'm not sure that everyone needs to learn about rhetorical questions either. It's bad enough teaching apostrophes, and they seem to lead to debates and style arguments. What most writers do is put an appropriate balance of ? and ! into their sentence endings to show feeling, rather than using the interrobang. Of course, this is a grammatical style-guide faux-pas, but I suspect that most readers, unless they are editors or English schoolteachers, don't care. For example:

You said what?!?

[puzzled and a little confused, mildly surprised]

You said what?!!!

[shocked]

Ultimately, it's all a matter of choice. Questions have so much depth and complexity, I'm not sure that flagging just one type is of value. If we have a character for rhetorical questions, why not one for loaded questions, and a special mark to indicate if a question is open or closed?

Grammar

Wait—don't skip this section! Only a very small number of people are grammar-geeks so I'm going to make this section short. There's no test to worry about, either. It's a useful background for some of the later material, but we won't go too deep. Here's the simple overview: questions are generally classified into **declarative** statements, 'Are you here to kill me?' and **interrogative** phrases, 'Why are you here?' To form questions, languages use a combination of syntax—those horrible rules and structures you had to memorise when learning a foreign language—plus tonality, pitch, and rhythm. Let's start with a quick look at the handful of ways in which a question is formed.

Inverting the verb and subject
This is the standard approach to indicate a question in many languages, and was once far more common in English, but is now restricted to a few special cases. Here's an example:

He can sing.
[a nice declarative statement]
Can he sing?
[inverted verb and subject]

This also works with negative questions, i.e. 'He cannot sing' or 'Can he not sing?' The same applies to negative questions that contain contractions, like 'He can't sing' or 'Can't he sing?' Meanwhile, here's a different example:

The lion roars.
[another declarative statement]

Does the lion roar?
[we added an auxiliary verb to make it work]

We won't go too deep into this, but if you really want to know more you should research auxiliary verbs and the use of the verb 'to do'.

Intonation

This is where the question is formed purely by the tone of voice, usually a rising pitch at the end of the sentence, or on a key word. If you read the previous questions aloud, you probably found it hard to resist altering your pitch or enunciation in the inverted version. *Does the lion roar?* Here are more examples, with the rising intonation underlined:

The dog ate your <u>sister</u>?
His cat <u>decorated</u> your wedding cake?
His cat decorated your <u>wedding</u> cake?

Use a tag

A question tag is an additional word or phrase added to a declarative statement in order to turn it into a question. Often, a tag question will be expressed as a negative if the person expects a positive answer, and vice versa (unless someone is trying to be sarcastic—which you may have to work out from the intonation):

You broke the glass, correct?
['correct' is the tag]

She's crazy, isn't she?
[expects a positive answer, using a negative framing]

They did a great job, right?
[positive answer, using a positive framing]

He should win this, shouldn't he?
[positive answer, negative framing]

We aren't rich yet are we?
[negative answer, negative framing]

Do you love me, still?
[negative answer, positive framing]

You're so smart, aren't you?
[sarcasm! negative framing, negative answer]

Wh-words

For interrogative phrases we normally use the wh-words: who, why, what, where, when, how (it may not start with wh, but how contains both letters). Interestingly, these words largely start with the letters qu in Latin... as of course does 'question'. These make up the bulk of most questioners' tools. You can see the sidebar for Rudyard Kipling's famous take on these words.

Where were you last night?
Why didn't you call me?
Who were you with?
What were you doing?
When did you get home?
How do you expect me to believe that?

Indirect questions

This one is a bit trickier. An indirect question is normally embedded inside other sentence structures, and they don't always follow standard rules for question construction. I think they were deliberately constructed this way to increase fees for English-as-a foreign-language tutors. They follow phrases like *Do you know*, or *Can I ask*, or *I wonder if...* If this sounds like gobbledegook, you might be better reading some examples:

Do you remember where the car is?
[indirect, and note the verb order]
instead of: Where is the car?

Can you tell me what time you close?
[indirect]
instead of: What time do you close?

This form of indirect questioning is also known as labelling, and is very common for consultants, as it comes across as a polite way of asking a tough question such as: 'Do you mind if I ask about your present financial situation?'

No question mark required
There are also a few question types that do not require a question mark as punctuation. Certain indirect questions fall into this camp:

He wondered how he could ever thank her.
The audience considered whether it was an impossible feat.
They had to decide the wheres and whens of the secret mission.

Also, certain types of formal, courteous ways of addressing people and making requests are typically written without a question mark:

How do you do.
[That one still causes some debate, but would you ever put a question mark after Howdy, which has the same meaning?]

Would the Lords and Ladies please arise for His Majesty, King of England.

Two last things, and then we can forget about grammar for now. Here we go: the question mark does not need to be followed by a full-stop. You can only put an exclamation mark behind it, which really turns it into an interrobang, as we have discovered. Now for my last and most cardinal grammar rule: never put a space between the last letter of the sentence and the question mark (unless you happen to be writing in French. Please refrain if you're writing in English). I'm not entirely sure which style guides still teach this, but it drives me crazy when I'm editing short stories from other authors. I've been told that it's more prevalent with Indians who were taught from a common schoolbook written by two Englishmen (Wren and Martin) who recommended a space before question and exclamation marks, full stops, colons, em dashes, and semi-colons. They may also be the people behind the two spaces after a full stop/period which drives me crazy. Take a look:

Does this look right ?
Don't you think this looks better?   Me too :)

Six honest serving men

I keep six honest serving-men
(They taught me all I knew);
Their names are What and Why and When
And How and Where and Who.
I send them over land and sea,
I send them east and west;
But after they have worked for me,
I give them all a rest.

I let them rest from nine till five,
For I am busy then,
As well as breakfast, lunch, and tea,
For they are hungry men.
But different folk have different views;
I know a person small—
She keeps ten million serving-men,
Who get no rest at all!
She sends'em abroad on her own affairs,
From the second she opens her eyes—
One million Hows, two million Wheres,
And seven million Whys!

By Rudyard Kipling

Foreign tangles

Business guides to Japan recommend you avoid yes/no questions because it's more polite to say 'yes' in their society and therefore, you may get the wrong answer. e.g.

'Is this the right way to the Golden Temple?'
'Yes' [even though it isn't, it would be impolite to say no]
A simple rephrasing might have avoided this dilemma.
'Which way is the Golden Temple?'
'You need to turn right, over there.'

The Japanese use the symbol -**か** (pronounced *ka)* , along with a rising tone, to indicate a question at the end of what would otherwise be a statement:

You're crazy   [statement of fact]
You're crazy ka   [question: Are you crazy?]

When they're talking informally amongst friends though, they may leave out the 'ka' and use intonation to highlight the question. The Japanese also have a full range of question words, equivalent to the English who, what, why, where, and how. One thing the Japanese don't officially have, is the equivalent of a question mark. They use the full stop instead. I should clarify, that is a Japanese full stop, which differs slightly in use and meaning from the western equivalent. Nothing is ever easy, eh? As mentioned earlier in this chapter, the question mark has proved so valuable that it has rapidly found its way into Japanese writing, appearing in manga, novels, texts, and less formal versions of writing, along with the standard technology uses (where it indicates missing data).

How about Chinese? In Mandarin, you can add the glyph

吗 (pronounced *ma)* to change a sentence into a question. Easy! You can also find a list of specific question glyphs—the equivalent of who, what, where, when, which, and how. There are a few extra specific symbols for questions like how many, or when the answer is a number under ten. Now it's starting to sound a little more complex. The key thing you need to understand though is where in the sentence to place the question symbol/s. Unlike in English, where you change the word order, add a tag word, and so on, in Mandarin you must place the question words next to the word in the sentence you are asking about. Nothing else in the sentence changes. Of course, China is a gigantic country with many regional dialects. Some of the question words differ from north to south, for example. I won't recreate the symbols here, but to ask 'Where?' in Beijing, you would be saying 'nar' while in Shanghai you would be more likely to ask 'nali'.

Of course, the same is true across the UK. Accents can make for a difficult time in translating both questions and answers, even though the language is theoretically the same. A scouser, a geordie, and an eastender have distinct accents and phraseology. We don't have to travel very far to feel like a foreigner. I recall many trips to Edinburgh in the 1990s, and as an English businessman I was often asked 'Where do you stay?' My instinctive response was to name the hotel, but in Scottish vernacular, stay = live, so they were really asking me which part of England I was from. This was not an accidental question, either. If you answered your hotel name, it showed that you didn't spend much time in Edinburgh and didn't understand the cultural differences. It was a question used by locals to see which salespeople were committed to doing business with them. Clever. The Scottish have some different phrasing of questions, which can sometimes be found in the north of England, too. 'Why not?' can be phrased as 'How no?', as one example, and you might be asked, 'What age are you?' instead of the traditional English phrase of 'How old are you?' That's an interesting pair of questions—they appear to be asking the same thing, but the Scottish one is more precise, asking for a specific number, while the English approach is broad inviting a general answer like, 'Too old to dance!' These subtleties in language make a difference in the perception of the questions, and perhaps explain some of the cultural misunderstanding between different groups. Language is one more barrier we must contend with when asking questions, and it means we need to think carefully about the structure and type of approach we take.

4. SCENARIOS

All that non-fiction can do is answer questions.
It's fiction's business to ask them.

Richard Hughes

Top ten interview questions

These are not the best questions to ask, but the best ones to prepare for, because managers seem to love them. Make sure you are ready to answer these, before any interview.

1. Why should I hire you?
2. What would your current manager most like to change about your behaviour?
3. Who's your hero, and why?
4. What do you do in your leisure time?
5. What do you know about our organisation?
6. What's the best way to motivate you?
7. What type of manager do you like?
8. Where do you want to be in 5 years' time?
9. What are your strengths / weaknesses?
10. Why do you want to leave your current job?

Interviews

When people imagine a scenario where they're forced to answer difficult questions, they often picture a job interview. Everyone has a story about the nightmare interview they attended. Stuck in my mind is a harrowing time where an interviewer asked me to describe myself in three adjectives, and my brain spent seconds trying to recall what type of word an adjective might be. In panic, I spluttered "handsome, intelligent, liar". I was aiming for humour, and if you'd seen me that day—a gawky teenager, you'd probably have guessed my intentions from the first word. The interviewer wrote down one word, which I suspect was 'delusional'. Many people have said far worse things in the stressful situation of an interview. I know this because I've sat on both sides of the table. Here are my favourites:

Me: "What are your weaknesses?"
Woman: "Just the usual feminine ones (bats eyelashes)"

I have to say, apart from being a scary answer on many levels, this was even more peculiar because I was interviewing in partnership with my female boss, who was sitting immediately to my right. I'm not sure which one of us was more shocked by this answer.

Me: "Can you tell me some of your strengths?"
Man: "I'm quick-thinking."
Me: "Can you give me an example of where this helped you?"
Man: "Urrrr......."

Caught in his own trap! A bit of mental preparation before the interview could have helped this candidate.

This next one might need a warning. It came from an attractive Persian lady, who had good English, but it was her second language. I'm not sure if she got the implication of her sentence, and the problem was mine and not hers, but I narrowly avoided collapsing into hysterical laughter. I should say, in my vague defence, that this happened an hour after the first example. At this point, my female boss and I were on high alert for odd answers.

Me: "The agency bio was very formal and didn't tell us anything about your pastimes. What do you like to do to relax?"

Woman: "I play with my organ."

There are a few questions I've heard during interviews that are so awful (i.e. racist or sexist) that I can't reproduce them here. The female boss I mentioned previously was a dream to work with, but I was often paired with other interviewers that were not so easy to work alongside. A tough question to ask yourself, is what you would do if your boss asked an obnoxious (possibly illegal) question when you were interviewing together? The interviewee would have the option to:

- make a joke of it
- walk out
- make a formal complaint
- ignore the comment
- let the interviewer know the question is inappropriate
- a combination of the above

Sitting alongside the interviewer, you have similar options. If you choose to handle it after the event rather than during the interview, that leaves you open to an accusation of prejudice by not dealing with it immediately. Your livelihood is on the line though, since you have a job in the organisation, and not many bosses like to be publicly contradicted and/or corrected. I can't give you too much guidance because it depends on the question, the situation, your relationship to the boss, the culture, and so forth. I would say that you need to be able to live with yourself, and we all need to ask tough questions sometimes, no matter how uncomfortable it is. If a few more assistants to film producers and celebrities had been doing that, we might have avoided some terrible abuses of power, although we'd undoubtedly have seen a lot of fired assistants at first. Let's look at some tips. For the interviewee:

- be ready to answer the 'standard' questions (see the sidebar on the top 10 interview questions)

- make sure you can run through your career history to date, succinctly, and answer any questions about gaps / short-term jobs

- be prepared to briefly explain your key achievements in each role (and how they might help you in this new job)

- have your own questions ready for the interviewer and make sure they're not on anything you could have discovered on their website (otherwise it looks as though you haven't bothered to do any research)

- use questions to ask for the job—you can do this easily, towards the end; 'Do you think I have the skills and experience you're looking for in this role?'; 'Do you have any concerns about me in the role?' (good chance to pull out any final objections, and try to handle them)

To the interviewer, I would say:

- do your research; read the bio and prepare questions in advance
- if you're interviewing a team for multiple hires (e.g. five electricians), have a 'standard' set of questions to ask each person involved in the interview process, making it easier to compare answers across the pool of candidates
- always do some levelling to gauge an interviewee's depth of knowledge (see Throwing Combinations in the Techniques chapter)
- Be clear about the skills, attitude, and experience you're looking for

I've encountered many organisations that believe in the Patrick Lencioni books as a tool to set their culture, *The Four Temptations of a CEO*, *Death by Meeting*, and so on. In *The Five Dysfunctions of a Team*, Lencioni highlights three essential virtues that good team members need: humility, hunger, and people smarts or EQ (emotional intelligence, as it is known). Lencioni has suggested questions to help identify the requisite virtues:

"What was the most embarrassing moment in your career?"
Humble people generally aren't afraid to tell their unflattering stories because they're comfortable with being imperfect.

"How did you handle that embarrassment?"
Has this candidate learned anything from that experience?

"What is the hardest you've ever worked on something?"
Look for specific examples of real, but joyful sacrifice. Do they have hunger?

"What do you do that others might find annoying?"
People with emotional intelligence are generally aware of their behaviours, able to articulate them, and moderate them at work.

Sometimes, interviewers like to throw in a curveball. If you ever get asked one of the quirky interview questions (see sidebar), remember that your answer is not critical. The interviewer wants to understand how you react and get insight into your thought processes. You should remain calm, demonstrate energy and enthusiasm, talk through your ideas, and ask some questions to clarify what they're looking for. That will buy you time, and make you look smart. Questions can do that, even more than the answers.

Quirky interview questions

1. Why is a tennis ball fuzzy?
2. How many golf balls can you fit into a shipping container?
3. What is the funniest thing that has happened to you recently?
4. If you could remove one city in the world, which would it be and why?
5. Name five people that you think should lead a project to set up humanity on Mars.
6. What song best describes your personality? Can you sing it for me?
7. If I gave you $5 million to launch a new business, what would it be?
8. A cow walks through that door with a rifle. What does he say?
9. What prize would you most like to win?
10. Why are manhole covers round?

Battlefield

The battlefield is one of the most extreme scenarios a person can find themselves in, especially as it stretches normal human interactions into different forms. Historically, the battlefield has been a place where questions are pushed aside; military training and best practice means obeying orders unflinchingly. There are far too many sad examples, such as the infamous Charge of the Light Brigade by the British cavalry in 1854 during the Battle of Balaclava in the Crimea War. The British were fighting the Russians, and from his high ground, the commander Lord Raglan could see that the enemy forces were going to try and remove some naval guns from a fortified position that was being overrun. The British light cavalry were fast, and they could outrun the defenders trying to make off with the heavy artillery, to either kill or capture them, or force the Russians to retreat without the guns. Lord Raglan sent a handwritten note with his instructions to the commander of the cavalry, Lieutenant General Bingham. The note was carried to Bingham by Captain Nolan. Bingham asked for clarification from Nolan as to which guns Raglan was referring to, and Nolan waved his arm in the direction, not of the naval guns, but to others at the far end of the valley. Bingham then instructed the head of the light cavalry, the Earl of Cardigan, who happened to be his disliked brother-in-law, to make an attack. This meant charging down a mile-long valley towards artillery in a strongly defended position, with defenders and crossfire on both sides. It was suicidal, and both men knew this, but they followed the orders without question. Of the 670 cavalry, more than half the men were killed, wounded or taken prisoner. Interestingly, the Earl of Cardigan, who had led from the front, somehow survived. At the very beginning of the charge, he was overtaken by Captain Nolan, who was hit by an artillery shell and killed. Some people believe Nolan had realised his mistake and was trying to redirect the charge. Cardigan was of the view that Nolan was trying to steal the glory by leading the charge. Remarkably, Cardigan not only reached the guns and fought the enemy, but also rode back down the valley, and returned to his yacht where he ate a champagne dinner! The charge was made famous by a Tennyson poem, published a few weeks after the incident. The poem highlighted the valour of the troops, but the true story was one of miscommunication, incompetence, and a willingness to follow orders without question.

The First World War was filled with brutal battles and staggering casualties, where men were given instructions to go 'over the top' of the trenches into a no-man's land of barbed wire, artillery, mud, and machine guns. Questioning orders was grounds for a court-martial. In the army, troops and officers are not rewarded for asking questions. The military follows certain approaches to achieve obedience and to discourage soldiers from asking questions in the field of conflict. Nobody wants to willingly put themselves in the line of fire. Troops are trained to follow orders, asking questions only for clarification (rather than questioning the underlying assumptions), and to follow leaders, who regard their troops as family that they would die for.

Joseph Heller's masterpiece *Catch-22* is a story based on an American World War II air-force captain called Yossarian, who wants to leave the war behind and return home. There are two ways to be sent home, alive. The first is to complete a set number of missions, but the number continually rises, so nobody ever achieves it; the second way is to be declared insane. The catch referred to in the title, is that to be declared insane you must complete a form, but by doing so you prove you are sane—and therefore remain in combat. The book is an exploration of the madness of war. Yossarian frequently questions his orders and the war in general. One day, the crews are told they must bomb a city where they have flown before, and the flak was heavy. Yossarian refuses, and is asked why:

"They're trying to kill me," Yossarian told him calmly.

"No one's trying to kill you," Clevinger cried.

"Then why are they shooting at me?" Yossarian asked.

"They're shooting at everyone," Clevinger answered. "They're trying to kill everyone."

"And what difference does that make?"

Joseph Heller knew his subject. He'd been a bombardier in Italy for the US air force during the Second World War. In his own description of the book, he stated: "Everyone in my book accuses everyone else of being crazy. Frankly, I think the whole society is nuts—and the question is: What does a sane man do in an insane society?"

Undoubtedly, many soldiers question what they are fighting for, or why they are being asked to obey what must seem—and sometimes are—crazy commands from their officers. To prevent the armed forces from disintegrating, military training focuses not just on physical fitness and the ability to wield the tools of the job, but also on leadership and team spirit. To help avoid any awkward or complex questions from being asked in the field, the teams are trained as follows:

- Leaders work hard to earn the respect of their teams before they go into conflict situations. It's easier to obey someone you respect.

- Expectations are set in advance. Each person's role is defined. John is the radio operator, Steve is the Squad

Leader, and Dave keeps a lookout from the left flank. If John is taken out, then Steve is trained to use the radio and he will assume that role. No questions need to be asked. The expectations have been set already.

- Leaders are trained to be direct and unambiguous. Have you ever noticed how ex-military people talk in short, sharp sentences?

- Leaders don't shout unless they must, because of noise levels. People yell orders in films, true leaders are calm.

- Once a decision is made, the team act on it. Teams don't change their mind halfway through. They execute to the best of their ability. If new information becomes available—a sniper in the tower—the leader will re-assess and adjust the plan. Then the team switches back to action. However tough the plan, they push ahead.

- The leader will lead, from the front. Nobody will follow a leader anymore who is not prepared to do what he's asking others to do.

Underlying this approach is a strong team ethic that means members look after each other; it rewards—with medals, honours, or promotions—those who follow orders effectively and bravely, and it punishes—through demotion or court-martial—those that do not.

It would be unfair to state that the military does not like questions. The military is always asking questions; changing, adapting, testing new strategies and tools, and questioning in order to improve effectiveness and efficiency. The battlefield, though, is a different scenario. There, questions are relegated to second place; swift action and following the agreed plan are paramount.

Music: call and response

A pattern of question and answer, sometimes called call and response, is very common in music. Essentially, it is a sequence of paired musical phrases, with the first phrase posing a 'question' and the second answering, or providing a musically satisfying response. In classical music, this was often achieved by using different instruments, so the two voices had a different tone and timbre. Think of Beethoven's famous Fifth Symphony, with its dramatic and ominous da-da-da-dum opening. As the first theme in the symphony develops, there is a call and response between the strings and wind instruments of the orchestra, perceived not simply from the melody, but the actual voice of the instruments chosen to play each phrase. This call and response is also widely used in modern culture, having flowed through African music into jazz, blues, rock, and pop. Of course, it has been popular in the military for a long time too, where it works well; especially since no instruments are required other than voice, alongside the rhythm of the activity—typically running or marching:

Instructor:	I don't know but I've been told
Cadets:	I don't know but I've been told
Instructor:	Air Force wings are made of gold
Cadets:	Air Force wings are made of gold
Instructor:	I don't know but it's been said
Cadets:	I don't know but it's been said
Instructor:	Army wings are made of lead
Cadets:	Army wings are made of lead

These type of cadence songs have featured in movies such as

An Officer and a Gentleman and *Full Metal Jacket*, although the movie version, and many sung in real training, have—or used to have—bawdier lyrics (before they were banned):

If I die on the Russian Front...
Up jumped the monkey from the coconut grove...
Captain's got a girl with a rubber head...

I'll leave you to imagine how those songs might pan out. In US military parlance these call and response songs are sometimes known as Jodies, since there was a civilian character called Jody in many of the songs, enjoying an easy life while his army buddies worked, e.g.:

Your baby was lonely, as lonely could be
Til Jody provided the company
Ain't it great to have a pal
Who works so hard just to keep up morale

It may seem strange to consider these as the question and answer style, since in many of them the same line is repeated both as call and response, sung back to the leader by the group. Requiring only a limited short-term memory, these are easy to perform—which might be helpful on a 12-mile run with full military kit. There are plenty of examples that use different phrases for the call and response though. Here's a British sea shanty about Napoleon:

Boney was a warrior
Wey, hay, yah
A warrior, a tarrier
John François

Boney went to school in France
Wey, hay, yah
He learnt to make the people dance
John François
Boney fought the... you get the idea!

Sea shanties thrived in the age of sailing ships, from around the fifteenth to the twentieth century. Typically, a shanty man would lead the singing, providing the call to which the rest of the crew would respond. Because the work was tedious and physical, the singing served multiple functions of making time pass, giving pleasure, and helping co-ordinate the physical work. There were also songs where each sailor would make up their own line, and everyone would sing it, such as 'Roll the old Chariot', which might have a variety of lines based on the whims of the singers, such as:

Oh, we'd be alright if the wind was in our sails
Oh, a drop of Nelson's blood wouldn't do us any harm
[Nelson's body was supposedly preserved in brandy]
Oh, a night with the gals wouldn't do us any harm
Oh, a nice fat cook wouldn't do us any harm
Oh, a roll in the clover wouldn't do us any harm

Interestingly, this song seems to have originated as an American Negro spiritual song and was included in a songbook made by Laura Ingalls Wilder, author of *The Little House on the Prairie*. It seems like question and answer singing patterns were common for soldiers, sailors, slaves and workmen for several centuries, and possibly reached back into antiquity.

The call and response style still finds its way into the very latest music. Naming a few current hits as examples would rapidly date this book, so I'd encourage you to listen carefully to your preferred music. You might find a duet—which is a classic question and answer form. Sometimes a duet will be broken into individual lines from each singer, so that we get a highly interactive play of call and response. At other times, you'll find each singer getting an entire verse to present their case—or question—to be answered by the other singer.

While there are many talented songwriters, it is interesting how frequently writers work in pairs. Songs written in this way are replete with questions and answers. There's an interview with Paul McCartney where he describes the origin of the song *Getting Better,* which illustrates the use of question and answer, and shows why writing in a pair can be so successful. McCartney had written the line "It's getting better all the time," with his typical optimism. When he played it to John Lennon he sang, without a pause, the reply "it couldn't get much worse." The hit song shows a different attitude in a musical question and answer. Paul McCartney said he could never have brought in that type of interplay into many of the Beatles songs if he'd written them by himself. It takes two, in other words, for a good question and answer.

Questionnaires

A local school recently sent out a survey about drugs and alcohol that included the question: 'How accessible is alcohol in your home?'

I heard one student discussing her answers with some friends. In her home, wine was stored in the pantry. The alcohol was easy to reach, and therefore easily accessible, but if a bottle of wine disappeared it would be obvious to her parents, who would certainly not approve. In her mind, the alcohol was not accessible because she knew she couldn't just take it as easily as that. Many of her friends had answered 'Yes', even though they were in a similar position. In essence, the question was ambiguous, and therefore the data collected in the survey would be largely meaningless. There are many other ways this could have been tackled to avoid such ambiguity. The survey could have asked if alcohol was kept under lock and key, or if the child could consume alcohol at home only with parental supervision. The questions really depend upon the intentions of the question-setter. I'm not certain if the question aimed to discover whether children could easily steal alcohol if they chose to, or if they were allowed to drink responsibly at home.

Questionnaires and surveys make me laugh, when I'm not crying in frustration. The design is often so bad it can be shocking; but creating a balanced, valid questionnaire is harder than you probably think. The primary question that anyone setting a survey should ask is *Why?* Why are we doing this, and what do we want to achieve? The questions—as few as possible please, and the information you want to collect— will flow more naturally if you know what the goal is, rather than meandering across a wide-ranging interview. To preserve the sanity of millions; if you must design an online questionnaire (paper surveys are just as bad, but at least people can scrawl comments in the margins), please consider the following points:

Don't use mandatory fields with values that exclude some people

Are you a: US citizen / illegal alien?

[Can't I be a legal alien?]

Please enter all 5 lines of your address:

[What if I have only 4 lines?]

Multiple choice questions need an 'other' field

This is nearly always true, but especially so if you're going to make a question mandatory. To truly interpret the answers, you should include a text box for other, as well, which would solve the problem in the question above:

Are you a: US citizen / illegal alien / other _____ ?

Answers must give mutually exclusive choices

Unless you let the user tick several answers, you need to make sure the options provided don't overlap. As a 21, 30, or 50 year-old, what should I choose here? I'd also be in trouble if I were an 80 year-old.

Please indicate your age:
  5-21 years
  21 - 30 years
  30 - 50 years
  50 - 75 years

Not all countries use the same telephone numbering

When you ask me to enter my telephone number and then use a validation rule based on American telephone formatting, it's going to fail. Please use validation rules that take international codes into account and can match numbers with the right formatting rules, or alternatively give me a blank text field where I can type in any number.

Don't tell me that I don't know my own date of birth

Although this happens more frequently on password login forms, it still applies to surveys. Please don't ask for something like my date of birth, my name, or my mother's name, and then tell me the answer is wrong. I can assure you I do know the answers to those questions. Feel free to tell me that I may have mis-spelt the answer, or I may not have set up security yet, but don't tell me the answer is wrong. It isn't. It's your system that's wrong!

Use comment boxes consistently

I don't mind how you achieve this. You can include a comment box after every question: 'What else should we know about these colour choices?' If you prefer, you can dispense with comment boxes in the main part of the survey, and include a catch-all box at the end: 'Do you have any other comments to share with us?' Whatever you do though, don't include comment boxes on a bunch of features, and then forget to include one on performance or price, or anything we're bound to care about and are keen to comment on. Be consistent.

Make comment boxes big enough to write in

If you want the feedback, give me enough space to write a decent reply. Asking for comments on your customer support service and providing 24 characters in which to respond will

make me rant. Let me try now: 'Your service is total cr'.
Damn! Out of letters.

Don't ask me stuff you already know

If you send me a personalised email with my name, and you have my credit card details, address, purchase history, and basically all my demographic information, I don't expect to fill in that data again in your survey. Give me a link where that stuff is prepopulated, and I can validate this, or use some hidden code to link it all up. Technology can do some cool stuff. Use it. This goes for you too, banking call centre. Don't make me type my account number and code into an automated system and then ask for it again when I reach a real person.

Give me enough choices to supply you with a valid answer

I hate those questions that ask you to ring the word that most closely fits the question, especially if the range is too limited. Help me out here.

'My personality can best be described as: crazy / aggressive / stupid / violent.'

One question at a time please

How will you understand the answer if you give us one choice in responding to a question with two parts?

'Is this the smoothest car you have ever driven, with the best satnav? Y/N'

Don't treat us like idiots if you want our respect (and honest answers)

If you ask the same question with slightly altered adjectives or phrasing, we'll give the same answer, unless we decide to mess with you for wasting our time.

'Do you get a thrill from trying extreme sports? Y/N'

'Would you stand in the middle of a field in a thunderstorm? Y/N'

'Would you describe yourself as risk-averse? Y/N'

[At least they had the decency to switch this to a negative response, unlike the next option...]

Don't attempt to trick us into answering in a certain way

We aren't stupid. Many of us understand that a pattern of questions can be dishonest. In the chapter Right & Wrong, we'll see how question order bias is often manipulated in surveys. For example:

'Do you live on planet earth? Y/N'

'Have you ever drunk water? Y/N'

'Can you read? Y/N'

'Do you agree with smart people that PopCola is the greatest drink ever? Y/N'

We're also utterly unimpressed by leading questions:

'Do you agree that our restaurant has excellent food? Y/N'

My local garage has started calling me after my car has been serviced. They tell me I'll receive a survey about the work they've done. If I don't give them a 5-star rating, they want me to give the reason. They've sent me letters with the same message. I can understand the motivation here; the questionnaire probably comes from a central group or an independent survey firm, and the results may impact financial benefits to the individuals or dealership. If there's a problem, the local team want to deal with it and make me happy (to keep their scores high). Unfortunately, it feels like the mafia asking if I'd like to insure my home because it would be 'very easy for something to happen to these windows, if you know what I mean' If you want an honest response from a customer survey, don't pressurise us.

Finally: anonymous surveys. These can be incredibly useful, and the theory is that they allow people to be more open and honest than they'd be otherwise. How relaxed and truthful are you going to be completing a sexual preferences questionnaire if it will be posted online with your name attached? Yet the underlying data can be incredibly valuable in helping determine a policy or course of action. Companies use anonymous surveys to understand employee morale and identify areas for improvement. The information can shed light on changing attitudes, concerns, and areas where the company is doing great work. Here are two points on anonymous surveys, gained from my years spent learning valuable life lessons:

For leaders and marketers
If you tell people a study is anonymous, make sure it really is.

For the rest of us
Don't believe that surveys, especially in the workplace, really are anonymous.

Jokes

What's big and red and eats rocks? Wait for it…a big, red, rock-eater! Not the world's greatest joke, but many young kids love it. The answer is so obvious and logical, which is the opposite of how we think. Everyone hearing that joke for the first time assumes there is some clever answer or payoff, but can't find it, so they have to shrug their shoulders and ask for the punchline. When it comes, it's a sucker punch. Many jokes, especially the oldest ones with the most well-known structures, are based on questions:

> Knock, knock!
> *Who's there?*
> Europe
> *Europe who?*
> No, you're a poo!
>
> Knock, knock!
> *Who's there?*
> Little old lady
> *Little old lady who?*
> I didn't know you could yodel.

Admittedly, these are a favourite for children, who love word games, fixed patterns, and the silly nature of these jokes. Another favourite is: *What's black and white and red all over?* The traditional answer is 'a newspaper' but there are variants:

> An embarrassed zebra.
> A penguin with a rash.

The original joke is making a pun based on the identical sound of red and read, while the subsequent jokes rely on us expecting the standard answer and are a trick because we know the original answer is 'too obvious'. There's a good story about a man asking the editor of the New York Times this joke, who immediately replied, 'your balance sheet'.

Sometimes, a single structure can accommodate a whole range of jokes, encompassing many categories—from crazy to political. 'Why did the chicken cross the road?' is a prime example (look at the sidebar for a selection of answers). We can even get joke mash-ups:

Why did the chicken cross the road?
To get to the idiot's house.
Knock, knock!
Who's there?
The chicken.

There are plenty of other common, question-based structures for jokes:
What do you get if your cross a duck with a firework?
A firequacker.

This 'crossing x with y' approach is popular in humour both for kids and adults. Here's an example that you're unlikely to find in the playground:

What do you get when you cross an insomniac, an agnostic, and a dyslexic?
Someone who stays up all night wondering if there's a Dog.

Another common structure frequently used for adult humour is the lightbulb joke. Traditionally, these were derogatory statements targeted at national stereotypes. These days, they tend to focus on professions, and are often created or repeated by those in that industry, almost as a badge of honour.

How many mystery writers does it take to change a lightbulb?
Two. One to screw it most of the way in, and another to give it a surprising twist at the end.

How many politicians does it take to change a lightbulb?
Five. One to change the bulb, one to pull the ladder from under them, two more to stab them both in the back, and one from the opposing party, to tell them they're doing it all the wrong way.

How many programmers does it take to change a light bulb?
None. It's a hardware problem.

How many mice does it take to screw in a lightbulb?
Two, but it's pretty cramped.

How many Germans does it take to change a lightbulb?
One.
[Okay, so that plays on the national stereotype of Germans being highly efficient and having no sense of humour, which I know isn't true. Couldn't resist it though.]

We also have jokes formed in a more complex interrogative fashion, like this:
What can a goose do that a duck can't and a lawyer should?
Stick his bill up his ass.

There are sometimes whole jokes based on a series of questions. Here's one, which I've seen on multiple golf websites (apologies to the author, who I haven't been able to identify):

"Dear," said the wife "what would you do if I died?"
"Why, dear, I would be extremely upset", said the husband.
"Why do you ask such a question?"
"Would you remarry?" persevered the wife.
"No, of course not, dear", said the husband.
"Don't you like being married?" said the wife.
"Of course I do, dear", he said.
"Then why wouldn't you remarry?"
"Alright," said the husband, "I'd remarry."
"You would?" said the wife, looking vaguely hurt.
"Yes", said the husband.
"Would you sleep with her in our bed?" said the wife after a long pause.
"Well yes, I suppose I would, "replied the husband.
"I see", said the wife indignantly. "And would you let her wear my old clothes?"
"I suppose, if she wanted to", said the husband.
"Really!" said the wife icily. "And would you take down the pictures of me and replace them with pictures of her?"
"Yes. I think that would be the correct thing to do."
"Is that so?" said the wife, leaping to her feet. "And I suppose you'd let her play with my golf clubs, too."
"Of course not dear," said the husband, "she's left-handed."

Given what we've discovered about the nature of asking questions, and considering what we'll explore later about how this connects to the meaning of being human, it's probably not surprising that many jokes are formed around questions.

Humour must also, surely, be a critical aspect of our species. We even have a distinct category of crossover between jokes and questions that has deep historical roots: the riddle. Tolkien's wonderful children's book, *The Hobbit*, has one of the most famous examples, with our hero Bilbo Baggins trapped in a dark cave with the scary creature Gollum, playing a game of riddles to save his life.

> What has roots as nobody sees,
> Is taller than trees,
> Up, up it goes,
> And yet never grows?
> "Easy!" said Bilbo. "Mountain, I suppose."

The pair trade riddles for a while, with Gollum promising to lead Bilbo out of the cave under the mountain if he wins, or to eat him if he loses. With such high stakes, Bilbo is incredibly stressed, and begins to run out of riddles to ask. With Gollum demanding the next riddle, Bilbo puts his hand in a pocket and discovers a ring he found earlier.

"What have I got in my pocket?" he says aloud, to himself.

Gollum is incredibly upset, because this is not a true riddle. We instinctively agree with Gollum's assessment. "Not fair! Not fair!" the creature cries, but he continues to play. However, the definition of a riddle is hard to come by. Various academics have debated this, but seemingly without coming to a clear conclusion. All riddles form a question, but the language is disguised so that the answer referred to is hidden in some fashion. There are many famous historical examples, such as the riddle of the Sphinx:

"Which creature has one voice, is four-footed, then two-footed, then three-footed?" (Man. He walks on all fours as a baby, on two feet as an adult, then uses a walking stick in old age.)

As with questions, we can trace riddles back to the very beginning of language. Our first examples are from Babylon where a few have been captured in old school texts. Sadly, we don't have the answers:

"Who becomes pregnant without conceiving, who becomes fat without eating?"
"My knees hasten, my feet do not rest, a shepherd without pity drives me to pasture."

Again, our historical trail runs cold. What is clear is that jokes, riddles, and questions are an intrinsic part of what makes us human.

Why did the chicken cross the road?

The answer, as any small child can tell you, is 'To get to the other side.' This is actually an anti-joke—it's only funny because it's logical and has no punchline. In reality, this is now one of the best-known jokes in the world. Part of its power is the potential for thousands of variants. In fact, this is one of the characteristics that we see in viral videos, which also tend to involve things that others can imitate—think of Gangnam Style and the deluge of alternate YouTube versions showing people doing the dance at work, as policemen or wedding guests, and so on. The number of variations on the chicken joke is fascinating.

From slight variations:
Why did the rubber chicken cross the road?
To stretch her legs.

Why did the chicken cross the Mobius strip?
Because there was no other side.

To political answers:
To get to a less challenging society where people don't question your motives.

Or alternate creatures:
Why did the dinosaur cross the road?
Because chickens didn't exist then.

Why did the cow cross the road?
To get to the udder side.

Why did the duck cross the road?
He was playing chicken.

Why did the turkey cross the road?
It was the chicken's day off.

Why didn't the skeleton cross the road?
Because it had no guts.

My favourites are based on imaginary answers by celebrities:
Martin Luther King: It had a dream.
James T Kirk: To boldly go where no chicken had gone before.
Darth Vader: It couldn't resist the power of the dark side.

Telling stories

For many people, Frank Herbert's book *Dune* is the greatest sci-fi novel ever written. Undoubtedly, it also had a significant influence on music, as well as on many novels, and movies, and even on Star Wars. So much has been written by and about Frank Herbert that it can be hard to separate fact from fiction. In one interview, Frank said he decided to write a story set in a desert landscape, and the question he wanted to answer was "Would you get the perfect society if you had the perfect leader?" For anyone who has read the book (or watched world politics), it becomes clear that there's no such thing as the perfect leader. Even so, it's a great premise for a novel. Many wonderful pieces of fiction are based on a single, central question. It's not always easy to discover if the writer came up with the question first, or whether the question bubbled up out of the creative process. See how many of these you recognise:

What if you could only remember the last 5 minutes?
[*Memento*]

Could we build an android that doesn't realise it isn't human?
[*Blade Runner*—more on that soon]

Could a single member of a jury convince all the others they were wrong?
[*12 angry men*]

How would it feel to wake up transformed into a huge insect?
[*Metamorphosis*]

What would happen if a spaceship full of malnourished aliens arrived in South Africa?
[*District-9*]

How would a group of boys cope, stranded on an island with no adults?
[*Lord of the Flies*]

Would the world be different if one person had never existed?
[*It's a wonderful life*]

What if fertility rates fell, so only a few women could have children?
[*A Handmaid's Tale*]

Can you change someone's accent so they can pass as highly educated?
[*My Fair Lady*]

What would happen if we recreated dinosaurs?
[The entire *Jurassic Park* series]

The short story is a great genre for a writer to experiment, and many authors have used this format to explore intriguing questions. The same is true for readers. You may not want to read an entire sci-fi novel about a policeman predicting when a person might commit a future crime, but it can be fun to imagine the concept in a short story (e.g. *Minority Report* by Philip K. Dick. You could watch the movie, although that takes longer). Many writers keep a journal and jot down story ideas whenever they occur:

- What would it be like to wake up in a pitch-black room, with no idea of how you got there?
- Being lost is a state of mind, not related to geography. So what does it feel like to be (mentally) lost, in New York?
- How would the world be different if we got a replacement body every time we died?
- What would I do if the man kindly taking our family photo ran off with my camera?
- What happens if a robot with facial recognition technology spots a face in the random swirls of a tree bark?
- Could someone build paradise in a west London tower block?
- Would it be possible to breed a black tiger?
- How would it feel to hide in a priest hole while soldiers searched the manor house?
- Could someone be a serial killer, and not know it?

I bet you could add more questions to this list. Maybe you want to know: 'Why don't sharks roar?' or: 'What would I do if my reflection in the mirror didn't look like me?'

For many writers, the creative process often involves experimenting with questions like those above. A writer may place people they know or have met, such as their last Uber driver, a friend from school, the quirky waiter in a local restaurant, or an ex-girlfriend, into a specific environment—the woods they grew up in, the back streets of Venice, a deserted beach, or the Paris metro—and let the characters try to resolve the question. Writers like to leave readers with questions—about how they'd have acted differently, or how the narrator could have been so stupid. It is very rare to read a book where each loose end is tied up. Not everything in literature is a question. Yet some of the most popular and successful movies, books, and TV series, have underlying themes based around fundamental questions. The best ones don't give us answers but offer alternative perspectives and let us make our own choice. Next time you go to the cinema or read a novel, try to identify the question they were asking!

Group dynamics

Strange things happen when you place people in groups. Behaviours change, dynamics evolve, and people can act very differently to when they're alone. An individual within a group may take on a specific role that can vary depending on the situation, on their confidence, and on their perception of the others. Someone will become the leader, or perhaps several will vie for this role; another person may record the actions and tasks, while a third person may become the devil's advocate, and so on. For groups that meet frequently in a formal structure, such as a school governor's meeting, or a scheduled team event at work, the roles may already be known and established. In more fluid situations, like a group of survivors from a plane crash, however; the roles emerge through actions, personality and skills. While people can, and do, change roles, their roles tend to stay fixed for a certain period, and can become locked in place. One of the clear ways that people signal the role they're playing to others is via questions. In fact, there's an expectation that certain roles will involve asking certain questions. Which of these people would you follow, after a plane crash, and what do you understand from their first statements?

"Someone is going to get sued to the ends of the earth for this!"
"Is anyone badly hurt?"
"Does anybody have a signal on their cellphone?"
"What the hell was the pilot doing?"
"Has anyone seen Susie? She's only this tall."
"Can everyone move away from the wreckage? That engine looks like it's going to explode."

"Where's my bag?"

"Do we have any doctors or nurses here?"

Nobody wants to make a snap judgement on a person, but in a life or death situation, that's exactly what you may have to do. The questions are revealing. We can see who is still coming to terms with the crash, those looking out for others, and a one or two people taking a leadership stance to help the group. This scenario opened the TV Series *Lost,* and we rapidly discover who will lead, who will follow, and who will be a pain in the backside. Their questions signal their intent.

For a couple of years, I was selling a software product to teams of technology professionals. I would frequently visit potential customers to engage them in a conversation about their challenges and explain how my company might help. In the room, there would be a mix of job titles and responsibilities, but over time, I learnt that in nearly every case, the following roles were being played:

- **decision maker**: typically, the most senior person in the room

- **technical expert**: attending to understand (or poke holes in) the technology

- **niche technical expert**: with a specialist skill

- **business expert**: to provide a different perspective on the value and applicability

- **consultant**: the trusted advisor to the decision maker; could be an internal or external person

After nine months of these meetings, I knew my company and product pitch inside out, and I had learnt the places—even down to the specific PowerPoint slides—where people were most likely to ask questions, and I'd also figured out the most common questions. What shocked me was that after the team had introduced themselves, I knew precisely which person would ask which question. This wasn't because I'd developed some peculiar psychic ability though. I believe that most people who regularly deliver the same message or sales pitch reach this level of understanding. Quite simply, we see people as playing a part, 'acting' their role, if you like, and that means that when there's a gap in the narrative structure of the story (the sales pitch, in my case), the relevant person will ask the question to fill that gap. Almost as though we were all acting out a scene from a play, without having ever seen the lines. That's crazy, you say. Oh no it isn't! Oh yes it is, you shout back—if you've ever been to a pantomime, and learnt your triggered response.

Let's say I'm presenting an aspect of my company's Artificial Intelligence capabilities, and I mention that we support Machine Learning. If there's a niche technical expert for this domain in the room, they'll ask,

"What type of Machine Learning approach do you use?"

If there's nobody in that role, then the consultant/advisor may step in with the same question. They'll ask in a different way, however; because one of the consultant's goals is to justify their knowledge and value, so they might say:

"Do you use reinforcement learning or neural nets for your machine learning, or is this just a basic support-vector machine?"

Alternatively, I might talk about the value our product delivers, leaving an obvious hook for someone to ask about the price. If there's a procurement person in the meeting or someone from finance, they'll inquire about the cost. Alternatively, this question could be left for the decision maker, although, they'll ask for a ballpark number, with details to be provided later, as they don't want to take decisions on the spot.

You could argue that what we see in groups is cohesive social behaviour. I'm not going to ask a question about price if my speciality is in the technology, as this might be perceived as encroaching on my boss's responsibility and authority. I agree that we are conditioned to act and respond in certain ways, depending upon the environment and social structure. If the Queen sneezes on a state visit to your organisation, are you going to step forward, say 'Bless you', and offer a tissue? She might be pleased if you did, but social conventions suggest that you should let one of her attendants deal with the situation. Although, you might find yourself saying 'Bless you' anyway, as it has become semi-programmed into many people. We all play roles in established group settings, and we do this through our choice of questions. In new groups, we define our roles *by the questions we ask* and the actions we take. It pays to listen carefully to see who asks which questions. Consider the reason for a person asking a specific question and you'll understand their role, or at least the role they'd like to take. Likewise, if you want to be perceived in a certain way, think about the questions you're asking, and decide your motives. Are you really curious to know the answer, or are you just trying to impress your manager?

Philip K. Dick and the movies

Trivia question for you: which movie had the longest gap between the original and its sequel? The answer is *Bambi* and *Bambi II* (63-year gap), although since the sequel was a direct-to-video release, you might argue that it doesn't count. There was a 54-year gap between *Gone with the Wind* and the sequel *Scarlett*, but that was a TV sequel. *Fantasia* is our winner, with *Fantasia 2000* coming out 59 years after the original. To explore the use of questions in Hollywood, I'm going to delve into a pair of movies separated by only 35 years, although the book was written 14 years before the first movie, giving a 49-year span in total. The title of the novel was phrased as a question: *Do Androids Dream of Electric Sheep?* later to be immortalised as *Blade Runner* by the director Ridley Scott, starring Harrison Ford. The novel was written by Philip K. Dick, a writer who was ahead of his time, and whose work is strewn with questions about the nature of the world, very often revolving around a dual state—Am I a human or an android? Am I in a dream or in the real world? Am I alive or dead? Which version of me is the real one? In the past few years there have been four seasons on Amazon based on Dick's book *The Man in the High Castle*, as well as a collection of his short stories *Electric Dreams* adapted for television. Additional Hollywood adaptations include the films *Minority Report, Total Recall, Screamers, A Scanner Darkly, Paycheck,* and *The Adjustment Bureau*. The cultural impact of his work has been enormous, although to the wider public he is best-known for *Blade Runner*.

The fundamental premise of the movie is based on the androids—called replicants—that look identical to humans, and are manufactured to work off-world in human colonies. The replicants are forbidden to visit Earth, and certain policemen—called blade runners—are employed to hunt down rogue replicants for 'retirement'; i.e. to kill them. Because the replicants look like humans, the Voight-Kampff identification test has been developed to differentiate between them. The test requires a piece of apparatus that displays an enlarged version of the suspect's eye and measures the dilation of the pupil while the suspect is being interrogated. The questions are deliberately designed to provoke a measurable emotional response. In the film, we see a blade runner called Deckard hunting a group of replicants. The film is full of questions, both those spoken and the ones we form in our minds as we track the narrative:

- Why have the replicants risked returning to Earth?
- Is this character a replicant or a human?

We see the Voight-Kampff questions used to provoke responses, and also counter-questions used in an attempt to disrupt the results, as in this exchange:

Policeman: You're in a desert, walking along in the sand when all...
Leon: Is this the test now?
Policeman: Yes. You're in a desert, walking along in the sand when all of a sudden you look down...
Leon: What one?
Policeman: What?
Leon: What desert?
Policeman: Doesn't make any difference what desert, it's completely hypothetical.
Leon: But how come I'd be there?

As the story develops, we discover it's possible for a replicant to be made so well, with implanted memories, that they don't know they're not human. We ask ourselves:

- What does it mean to be human?
- Is Deckard human?
- Are my memories real?
- How can you tell if memories are real?

We learn that the replicants returned to Earth because of a question. They were built to expire after four years, with a sell-by expiry date like a perishable food product. They have come to meet the man who designed them, their personal god in human form, to ask: *Why can't we live longer?* (The actual question used is "Can the maker repair what he makes?").

At the climax of the movie (spoiler alert) the leader of the replicants saves Deckard from death, even as the replicant's four years run out and he dies. Deckard summarises his emotions: "All he wanted were the same answers the rest of us want. Where do I come from? Where am I going? How long have I got?"

As our hero, Deckard, departs with the female replicant he has fallen in love with, attempting to evade the police that may be pursuing her (and/or him), he reveals that his companion was made differently, without an expiration date. The movie ends with a final, voiceover question: "I didn't know how long we'd have together, but who does?"

There are even visual questions posed to the audience throughout the movie. One character repeatedly makes small origami characters and leaves them behind at key locations, making us wonder about the meaning and implications of his paper statements. They're never fully explained.

Blade Runner has been the subject of numerous books and university theses—on topics as diverse as redemption, race, the illusion of free action, class, and dystopian society—with many funny and illuminating facts emerging. Even the petty disputes between actors and film-crew members have been poured over and debated. At its heart though, this is a movie that forces us to consider big questions, and without answering them for us. It is often more powerful to pose a question than to answer one. Indeed, there was a fan backlash when a Director's Cut was first released, in which Ridley Scott added a couple of extra scenes that nudged us towards a specific answer for one of the most contested questions—Is Deckard a replicant?

Critics' reviews of the sequel, *Blade Runner 2049*, were mixed, but it captured the essence and atmosphere of the first movie, hurled a few new questions into the fray, and also left the audience to make their own decisions. As I type this, early in 2020, the original movie has an 8.1 rating on the IMDb film enthusiast website, and the sequel scores 8.0, with both having hundreds of thousands of votes. People care about these movies. It's important that people make intelligent, thoughtful films that ask us profound questions. This is one of the primary functions of art, in my opinion. For any aspiring writer or film maker, or anyone trying to sell or advertise a product, Blade Runner illustrates a critical lesson: if you want to truly engage people, tell them a story that poses a question, but let them answer it for themselves.

5. RIGHT & WRONG

To be, or not to be, that is the question.

Hamlet, by William Shakespeare

Ethics

The Oxford English Dictionary defines ethics as the branch of knowledge that deals with moral principles. I rather like the expanded definition given by Wikipedia: "Ethics seeks to resolve **questions** of human morality by defining concepts such as good and evil, right and wrong, virtue and vice, justice and crime."

The actual word 'ethics' is derived from a Greek word êthikos, or "relating to one's character". In plain prose, ethics is about how you live your life; the way you respond to the questions the world throws at you. While we may start life with the idealistic viewpoint that every situation has a right and wrong, over time most of us begin to see that the world as coloured with many shades of grey. Ethical questions frequently do not have a 'correct' answer, but alternatives with advantages and disadvantages. Here are some examples:

- Are all humans equal?
- Why should animals not have the same rights as humans?
- Should a chimpanzee have the same rights as a snail?
- What about trees?
- Do robots with Artificial Intelligence have rights?
- Sticking to humans, should euthanasia be legal?
- Is it okay to 'design' a baby?
- Should alcohol be made an illegal drug?
- Now that cannabis is legal in some places, should people in prison in those locations for prior crimes relating to the drug, be freed?
- Would we still do the 'right' thing if nobody was watching?

Let's take the first question in the list above. After the second world war, the United Nations elected a commission on human rights, and began work on a document which evolved into the Universal Declaration of Human Rights. The commission was chaired by that remarkable woman, Eleanor Roosevelt, and after two years, they had pulled together the Universal Declaration. Here are the first two articles:

Article 1: All human beings are born free and equal in dignity and rights. They are endowed with reason and conscience and should act towards one another in a spirit of brotherhood.

Article 2: Everyone is entitled to all the rights and freedoms set forth in this Declaration, without distinction of any kind, such as race, colour, sex, language, religion, political or other opinion, national or social origin, property, birth or other status.

The Declaration was voted on by the 58 member nations (there are 193 members today, as the organisation has grown significantly since the 1940s). While the vast majority voted in favour of the Declaration, two countries did not vote, and eight others abstained. You would think that something as basic as human rights would be simple to agree, but in practice it proved hard. There were still plenty of countries in the 1940s who were not giving equal rights to women, and/or to certain social classes or racial groups. Of the countries that abstained, six were communist, and while officially, their objection was that the Declaration did not oppose fascism strongly enough; some believed it was Article 13, which states that "everyone has a right to leave any country, including his own". The South African government was opposed, on the basis that several articles challenged their apartheid system, and Saudi Arabia abstained because of Article 18, which gives the individual the freedom to 'change his or her religion or belief', and the articles related to equal marriage rights. The Saudi delegation was concerned that the Declaration violated Sharia law, a position that other Muslim countries, such as Pakistan and Turkey, disagreed with, however. A more general point, made at various times, is that the Declaration is a construct based on Western/Christian thinking, and that alternative human rights systems, potentially based on different religions, could be created with equally valid rights.

Some countries, including Britain, were unhappy with the Declaration because it did not go far enough, not being enshrined in law. While many countries have since embedded the articles into their legal systems, and international lawyers have claimed that the Declaration is a de facto legal standard, others accept its moral guidance but do not necessarily hold the document as a legal standard. Subsequently, organisations such as Amnesty International have campaigned for additions to the Declaration, such as 'the right to refuse to kill', which would be useful for conscientious objectors or even soldiers that are placed in difficult circumstances. In 1993 the so-called Bangkok Declaration was adopted by many Asian countries, which agreed with the core Universal Declaration, but supplemented this with more emphasis on non-interference, sovereignty, and cultural rights.

The harsh reality is that while the Universal Declaration of Human Rights has provided a beacon and has been a useful visionary tool, governments have tended to pick and choose the aspects they adhere to. While America was often perceived (in the West) as the guardian of human rights, it suffered a major blow in this perception following the use of torture in Guantanamo Bay, which is strictly against the Declaration. It is not alone in breaching this specific article, as 150 of the current 193 member states have been known to use torture. Eric Posner, professor at the University of Chicago Law School, wrote a fascinating article published in The Guardian in 2014 against human rights, arguing that they are the equivalent of western missionary and colonial escapades of the previous centuries, and represent an attempt to control developing countries. Too often, economics and world influence have stood in the way of securing human rights, while on other occasions politicians have used human rights as justifications for strategic moves of warfare. Posner highlights the fact that there were deep splits between the approaches of the United States and Russia, for example, on whether the rights should be political (free speech, right to vote, etc.) or social (the right for healthcare, education, and to work). More critically, he notes many examples of where countries flagrantly ignore the rights they have ratified, or that they don't, or can't enforce. In Brazil, the Human Rights Watch group believes there are more than 1,000 summary executions perpetrated by the police each year in Rio de Janeiro alone. Yet Brazil is one of the world's larger democracies and supports the human rights agreements. It is not alone in struggling to enforce agreed policies; and similar issues have occurred recently in countries like South Africa and India. Other countries, such as China, have actively campaigned against certain rights, and possess a perspective on rights that is markedly different from western democracies. Posner argues that it is time to start afresh by promoting wellbeing in foreign countries using an approach that is empirical rather than ideological.

If the world's experts find it hard to agree and act on the most basic of questions—*what are the fundamental human rights?*—how hard will it be to answer the question for animals or intelligent androids?

Let's take a simple scenario and see how questions can help (or hinder) us in making an ethical decision. Imagine you are a film censor deciding whether to approve a movie, and then allocating a rating. On your first viewing you notice a few swear words. There is a single mild sex scene and two murders, with a certain amount of violence but this is not very graphic. You might elect to give it a rating suitable for teenagers or alternatively, for adults only. Would your view change if your friends asked you these questions?

- Isn't this based on a true story?
- Shouldn't this be a general release as it's based on a children's book?
- Isn't this the director who shoots the scenes for real—so isn't the violence real?
- How many countries have outlawed that sexual practice?
- Did you notice all the murdered characters were Asian?
- Is it true that the actress was traumatised by the murder scene?

If ethical issues are some of the biggest, deepest, and perhaps most important challenges we face in building a society, it makes sense that we should explore ethical scenarios. The best way we know of doing that is by asking questions.

Times NOT to ask questions

Instinct is often a critical factor in sports activities—but that doesn't mean questions are not of value. A team planning a game against a major rival will want to understand their tactics, who plays which position, what choices they have made recently, which side they favour, which shot is their preference, and how that changes under pressure. In fact, most sports with large winnings at stake now use software applications that perform analytics based on historical databases to help teams prepare for each game. A goalkeeper in a soccer penalty shootout for a major tournament will have studied the opposing players previous penalty kicks, and will know which side they prefer, and where they hit their last shots. In the heat of the game though, players rely on instinct, experience, and intuition. The fractional seconds that may be required to make a decision mean that questioning would inhibit their reactions.

Miyamoto Musashi had a slightly different approach. Born in 1584, he became one of the most famous samurai, becoming a master swordsman despite his humble beginnings, and remaining undefeated across at least 60 duels. Musashi used a wooden sword, while his wealthier, noble opponents would wield more costly forged-metal blades. He founded schools of swordsmanship, and towards the end of his life in 1645 he wrote a book on his philosophy of fighting called *The Book of Five Rings*. He has been the subject of many TV shows, movies, and novels. I read a well-known fictional retelling of his story by Eiji Yoshikawa. One passage from the novel has always stayed with me. It explains how Musashi fought best by standing perfectly still, carefully emptying his mind, and waiting for his opponent to make a move. In the instant the opponent began an attack, they typically exposed a weakness during the shift from a defensive stance. Musashi's fast reactions and years of training enabled him to exploit that gap. His body could react more quickly than his mind. There was no time to think in mortal combat.

The book made such an impression on me because it rang true from the competitive badminton I used to play. A badminton shuttlecock can travel at 306 miles per hour—that's compared to a squash ball at 176 mph, an ice hockey puck at 114 mph, a cricket or baseball at just over 100mph, or a tennis ball which is a comparatively slow 155 mph and bounces before you hit it; unlike badminton where you have to hit the shuttlecock before it reaches the ground! Of course, the shuttlecock—or birdie, as the Americans call it—decelerates faster than those other projectiles, but the players stand closer to their opponent. A badminton smash is made from the mid-court, and the defensive position is also mid-court; so the players may be 22 feet apart on average, rather than the 80 or so feet that separates tennis players, or the 60 feet between a baseball pitcher and the home plate. That's a lot of numbers, but I can tell you what it means in practice. When somebody is about to smash in badminton, you take up a certain defensive stance, you observe their body, the racket face, and shuttle. Your brain calculates how many times this player has hit the shot to your right, left, or middle, and whether they have a preference on key points. All of that sifts through your head, and then... your body reacts, using all that data and your training. You don't exactly see a fast smash, but somehow, you return it. There's no time to consider the shot, just as Musashi didn't have time to think through his opponents' motives or moves. The questions take place long before you reach that critical moment, whether you're playing a competitive sport or fighting for your life.

One more anecdote—this one from an experienced pilot. Something went wrong when he was launching in a fast jet from an aircraft carrier. There wasn't full power from one engine, and in a split second the plane was off the deck, and into the ocean. The pilot ejected the instant before his plane tilted towards the water and he was safely recovered. At the speed at which these take-offs happen there's only a fraction of a second to react. In the messroom later, one of the younger pilots asked the man when he had decided to eject. "Twenty years ago", he replied. "I made a decision that if I reached that point in the take-off run without full thrust, I would eject."

Of course, there are plenty of other times where we shouldn't ask questions. Sometimes that decision is valid, and at other times we're just making excuses. Look at the sidebar for a few examples. Having some constraints is probably a good thing though. Children must learn that they can't ask any question at any time. I remember my horror when a child walking past the checkout queue at a grocery store turned to her mother and said, blending two socially unacceptable statements into one short sentence: "Did you hear that fat woman fart?" A world in which everyone asked any question they wanted, uninhibited, would be a challenging place to live.

We don't ask questions because we:

- don't want to look stupid
- are frightened to hear the answer
- don't want to appear like a troublemaker
- feel the social pressure (too many people in the room)
- feel the peer pressure (too many people at your level, in the room)
- know there's a gap in the hierarchy/position between you and them
- daren't breach a taboo subject
- don't have enough time either to ask or to hear the answer
- live in a culture of obedience where asking a question just isn't 'done'
- fear how the recipient will react—they may hate to be challenged
- are too shy / introverted
- don't want to expose our perceived weakness
- lack confidence in our language skills— especially in a foreign language
- are not sure the question is relevant or important enough
- don't believe the person knows the answer
- want to spare the person the embarrassment of answering this question
- have nothing to ask, because we weren't paying attention
- have forgotten our question by the time the chance came to ask it
- were daydreaming, and not sure if our question has already been asked
- have asked more than our fair share of questions

The wrong question

I once met a woman who ran a European sales team; she had smart people who were experienced, knowledgeable, and enthusiastic. In terms of sales achievement vs target, her team were well ahead of her peers in Asia and America by halfway through the fiscal year. On a trip to the company's headquarters, I noticed she was frequently asked variants of the following questions: *Why is your team so successful? What best practices can you share?* She gave various answers and tried to think of all the positive things they were doing. Yet the more she thought about it, and the more she talked to her counterparts in different regions, she realised they were asking her all the wrong questions. She told me a better approach might have been for her colleagues to ask: *Why do you think the American and Asian sales teams are under-performing?* Unfortunately, this was an unacceptable question since it focused on the negative (what's going wrong?), and implied criticism of other teams. You could also argue that since her jurisdiction was Europe, her direct experience elsewhere was insufficient to make any valid comments about their issues, which was a reasonable concern, but also an assumption. The main point was that she was being asked why her team was over-performing, when the reality was, they were on target, and the other teams were under-performing. The questions being asked of her were therefore not going to uncover any valuable insights.

I've seen many examples where culture forces us to ask only positive questions. I understand why this happens, but we need to look for the negatives too, because we do want to identify and fix problems. Hidden within this conundrum is the assumption that a positive question is simply a different phrasing of a negative one. Often the questions themselves are fundamentally different. It is, however, quite possible to ask a negative question in a positive fashion. Let's look at a worked example before we get lost in this meta-language.

The beautiful Cinderella lives with her plainer stepsisters Viv and Sharon. A Prince has met the three sisters at a ball and told his friend that Viv was the most attractive. His friend, who knows all three women, questions him about this, believing that Cinderella is the most attractive in every respect—personality, intelligence, and looks. If his friend takes a positive approach to questioning, focusing only on Viv, what will he learn?

Friend: What did you like about Viv?

Prince: She's a good dancer, friendly, outgoing, great company.

Interesting, but it doesn't help our friend who feels sure that Cinderella is a better match for the Prince. His question has not got to the root cause of the issue. He can ask more questions about Viv but is unlikely to learn much more. Alternatively, he could be direct, and ask: *'What's wrong with Cinderella?'* but that negative question would be politically insensitive in the polite circle of the Court. Instead of focusing on the positive aspects of Viv, the friend could try to uncover negative information on Cinderella using positive phrasing, which might help the Prince to find the right match.

Friend: What did you think of Cinderella?

[open, positive question]

Prince: The girl in rags with her face covered in soot?!

Ah! Now the friend has learnt something. Perhaps the Fairy Godmother was late. Whatever the issue, the friend knows what needs to be done to help Cinderella win the Prince's heart. Had the friend pursued a line of questions on why Viv was fabulous, he wouldn't have got far. Had he used a negative question about Cinderella, it may have offended the Prince. Instead, by using a different phrasing, the friend has drastically improved his chance of helping the Prince.

For a variety of reasons, there are often certain questions we cannot ask. Some of these questions are permissible if you're careful about phrasing though, while others are genuinely wrong. As part of my research, I spoke to many different types of professionals about the way they use questions, including hairdressers. They're often very socially aware and spend their time in conversation with folks from different walks of life. I asked several hairdressers what question they most dreaded being asked. Demographically, they were largely women and men in their twenties. I was expecting to hear: *How was your holiday?* or *What did you do for Christmas?* which I guessed they heard ten times a day. The answer they consistently gave surprised me. The one question hairdressers do not want you to ask is: *Would you like to go for a drink tonight?* Why is this such a terrible question? First, it's embarrassing you've asked them for a date because it means you've misinterpreted their friendliness for flirting. Second, the hairdresser can't run away; they must finish cutting your hair after a suitably gentle putdown. When they refuse, no matter how nicely, you feel embarrassed, and you can't leave immediately, either. The result is that both sides suffer embarrassment and you probably won't go back, which means the hairdresser will lose a client.

With some careful thought though, you can ask this type of question without embarrassment. You could ask an indirect question about your hairdresser's social life, such as: *What did you get up to last weekend?*

It's very easy for someone with good social skills to identify this type of question and reply: *Last weekend we went to my boyfriend/girlfriend's wedding...* sending a signal to you.

Or you can ask questions about group activities: *Does everyone at the salon go for a drink together at Christmas?* for instance; and if they're interested in you, the person might respond with something like: *We don't have a party, but Julie and I often go to The Escape on a Thursday night. We'll probably be there tomorrow.* Questions are great tools for signalling intent and interest without having to be direct. Rather than ask the wrong question, see if you can use questions with more subtlety to achieve the same goal.

Never ask this in casual conversation*

If you're easily offended, you may want to skip this section!

Too personal:
- Are you pregnant?
- When are you getting married?
- How much do you earn?

Sexual bias:
- Are you gay/lesbian/straight?
- How many sexual partners have you had?

Gender bias:
- Are men/women better at [fill in the blank]?
- Why are women such terrible drivers?

Racial bias:
- Is there a genetically superior race?
- Why are [insert ethnic group] so stupid?

Questionable legality:
- Would you prefer to be tortured physically or mentally?
- Where can I get heroin? Will I need my fake ID?

Breaking cultural taboos:
- Which aspects of Hitler should we admire?

Corporate and/or legal regulations:
- How old are you? is illegal in interviews, in some places

Expressing vanity:
- Do you think I'm incredibly good-looking?

Offensive:
- Are you stupid?
- What made you marry an ugly guy like him?

This sidebar was originally titled 'Never ask this', but in some circumstances these questions are valid, e.g. a financial analyst may be entitled to ask, How much do you earn? In normal circumstances, anyone asking these questions will be insulted, assaulted, or even sued—and quite rightly too.

Politically correct tangles

I once walked into an unfamiliar office building to deliver an urgent document to a man called Derek. There was no receptionist. I asked someone I met in the hallway where I could find Derek and how to recognise him. They told me he was on the third floor, and was slightly above average height, smartly dressed, and had a northern twang to his accent. They thought he might be wearing a red tie. I wandered around the third floor in vain, however; desperately looking for someone who matched the description and listening to every snatch of conversation to try and pick up the right accent. In the end, I had to ask someone else for help. It turned out Derek was sitting just a few feet away. He was the only black person on the floor. In fact, he was the only non-Caucasian I'd seen in the building. I could have found him in seconds if the first person had told me that Derek's distinguishing feature—for identification purposes—was his colour. It's very easy to understand how this happened. I must admit I'd have provided a similar answer myself if Derek had been my colleague. There are three good reasons for this:

- When we think of a colleague, we think about who they are, their personality and experience, not their skin colour.
- In most scenarios, it's considered racist to highlight skin colour.
- By considering colour as an aspect of someone's identity we may be contributing to a racist culture even if we aren't racist ourselves.

So, what should we do? I think the answer is to look deeper than the surface question. What the questioner wanted, in this scenario, was to find Derek. There were several ways this could have been accomplished:

- They could have been led to Derek
- They could have been asked to wait in the lobby, and Derek could have been informed that a guest was waiting for him there
- The person could have shown them a photo on their phone (if they had one)
- They could have checked Derek's social media profile (and photo) before the meeting
- I'm sure there must be other solutions here, too—use your imagination!

Of course, racism is only one of the politically correct tangles we can find ourselves in. Similar challenges spring up around sexuality, religion, politics, and even security. If we want to understand the issues in this area, and how our questions can offend certain groups, we need look no further than the American Library Association, which maintains a list of the books that have either been banned or challenged (where a group tries to get it removed from the public education system). The list includes well known classics like *Brave New World,* the *Harry Potter* series, *Catch 22, The Decameron, To Kill a Mockingbird, Of Mice and Men, The Catcher in the Rye,* both *The Adventures of Tom Sawyer* and *The Adventures of Huckleberry Finn, Animal Farm, Brideshead Revisited, The Call of the Wild, Captain Underpants*—okay, maybe that one isn't a literary classic—*Fight Club, The Hunger Games, James and the Giant Peach, Fahrenheit 451, The Lord of the Rings, Fifty Shades of Grey, Ulysses, Women in Love, The Lovely Bones, Lord of the Flies*, and the list goes on. Many of these books pose challenging questions that some sections of society find offensive or threatening. Whether censorship is an effective remedy is highly debatable and is not a topic to explore here. I think the key is whether or not people care enough about these fundamental questions—of race, society, sexuality, etc.—to fight to have them banned.

When we're asking questions, we clearly need to be aware of the cultural and societal backdrop to ensure that our approach will have the desired effect without igniting an issue. Life might be simpler if we could ask and answer questions directly, but we must consider the impact of our words. We should strive to avoid politically inflammatory questions, unless, of course, that is exactly the desired effect of our question.

Let me ask you this first...

If humans were logical, rational creatures, we would answer questions truthfully and accurately. Since we're emotional and passionate, as well as subject to influence from a variety of sources, it turns out that—surprise, surprise—we can be easily influenced in how we answer questions, by factors such as the attractiveness of the person asking the question, through to the weather, and even the question sequence. This last factor, which has been briefly mentioned earlier, is known as *question order bias*. It's so powerful that many software survey tools will automatically randomise a set of questions— if they genuinely want quality data and aren't trying to influence you, that is. Even governments have systems to prevent question order bias, as we'll see later in our chapter on professions. Activists and pollsters, who gather data to support a cause, are also very aware of question order bias. Let's say you've been paid to deliver statistics that support the current leader of your country, who has a strong anti-immigration policy. Your survey may start by mentioning immigration to place this topic as a key issue in the mind of the voter.

Do you believe immigration is a critical issue for the nation?
Will you vote for President [x] at the next election?

In 1948, a fantastic piece of research by Herbert Hyman and Paul Sheatsley asked Americans if they thought it acceptable for communist reporters to be admitted to the USA to report on the news. Only 33 percent of respondents thought it was acceptable, but if respondents were asked first whether it was acceptable for US reporters to be admitted to the Soviet Union, priming the topic in their mind, then the subsequent number of respondents who agreed that communists should be permitted to report on US news jumped to 73 percent. That's a phenomenal change in perception, made by asking another question first. These tests have been repeated more recently, and the results were not quite as dramatic, partly because the general public is better educated on certain topics such as freedom of the press, but question order bias has been shown for other topics, such as abortion. While education can help reduce bias, it doesn't eliminate the effect completely.

In another famous survey from the 1980s, respondents in the General Social Survey were asked to select three qualities from a list of attributes it was important for a child to possess. When the word 'honest' was listed towards the top of the list, it was chosen by 66 percent of respondents. When the same word was moved towards the end of the list though, it was picked by only 48 percent of people. This tendency for people to choose items near the top of a list—technically, known as *response order bias*—is reversed when the survey is done by phone or in person, however. In those scenarios, a respondent is more likely to pick something they hear later in the list.

Another bias frequently used with question order is the assimilation effect. This is where somebody is more likely to respond in a fashion similar to earlier answers, than if the question were asked in isolation. Imagine, for example, interviewing two families of passengers getting off flight UA12 to discover how well the cabin-crew service had performed on the flight:

Family 1
Were you on flight AA67?
No. I was on a United flight.

Were you travelling on your own?
No, with my family.
Did it land on time?
No. We were ten minutes late.
Was the service good?
No, not really. It was slow.

Family 2
Were you on flight UA12?
Yes, that's right.
Were you travelling with your family?
Yes, with my wife and daughter.
Did it land within 15 mins of schedule?
Yes, just ten minutes late.
Was the service good?
Yes, very good.

This example also makes use of the acquiescence bias, which is the tendency for people to say yes, and be agreeable. If you get people saying yes to a sequence of questions, they're more likely to say yes to the critical question later in the survey. There are many other biases and tricks; such as the contrast effect. If someone scores one answer very highly in a survey to say they really like something, there is a tendency to score another item much lower to contrast—and balance—the results.

One of my favourite aspects of surveys is the way we get to second guess the questioner. This frequently happens in job-specific surveys. I came across a psychological questionnaire for screening potential fighter pilots. One question asked what you would do in an open field during a thunderstorm (with options like run, lie flat, stand under a tree, etc.). If you wanted to pass the test, your answer would not be driven by the 'right' thing to do, or even what you might do in practice, but by what type of personality you believed they were seeking. We might imagine that fighter pilots are not risk-averse, cautious people who would lie down in a field. In this way, surveys rapidly become a test of intelligence between the person who set the test, and those that take it. I've lost track of the number of forms that start with a phrase like 'Please answer this questionnaire as honestly as you can'. This shows a serious misconception about the way many people think. Try answering these, aloud:

Can you read?
Have you read other books, before this one?
Would you recommend this book to others?

If you answered yes to this last question, thank you. If you answered no, then realise this response shows a bias against question-order psychological tricks, and you should reconsider your answer :)

To be or not to be

As we saw in our Scenarios chapter, the better authors ask questions of their readers. The best writers ask big questions of the right/wrong, black/white kind, with various shades between. Classic works of literature are often inspired, or at the very least can be summarised, by a critical question. In George Orwell's *1984* there are many big questions at play: *What happens if the state has total power? Does language control our thought?* Different genres ask different questions, which can be simple or deep:

> Who killed Samuel Ratchett?
> [*Murder on the Orient Express*]
> Will Elizabeth Bennet and Mr Darcy ever marry?
> [*Pride and Prejudice*]
> Incidentally, the fundamental questions in Jane Austen's novel are about personal identity: *Who am I? What are my values? What do I want from life?*

Science fiction writers love to use technology as a mechanism to pose questions, and seek to examine the repercussions that come from the answer. Many novels and movies have explored the theme of what it means to be human, especially in the realm of robots and Artificial Intelligence, such as *Blade Runner*, which we outlined before. Earlier writers, such as Jules Verne, were asking questions like: *What lies at the centre of the earth?* or *What lives at the bottom of the sea?* Dinosaurs are a common theme, with questions such as *What if dinosaurs had survived?* recurring in books such as *The Lost World* by Arthur Conan Doyle and updated into: *What if we could recreate dinosaurs?* by Michael Crichton in *Jurassic Park*. Underneath these themes are questions of how we perceive monsters, how we play at god, and the damage humanity is wreaking on the environment—and how it may come back to bite us, literally!

In fact, the list of questions inspiring literature, both modern and classic, is huge. Some writers have been able to stretch a single question into an entire series of books. Kim Stanley Robinson did this in the Mars series: *What will happen when we try to establish a community on another planet?* Additionally, the six seasons of *Lost* by J.J. Abrams had most viewers asking questions like: *Where the hell are they?* or *What on earth is going on?!* The popular movie *Contact* with Jodie Foster in 1997 was based on the question: *What would happen if we received a message from outer space?* and the 2016 movie *Arrival*, starring Amy Adams asked: *How will we communicate with an alien species?*—a question we'll explore later.

Authors don't adopt deep themes purely as an inspiration or motif in their work, but instead, use questions for more practical reasons. The underlying questions can progress the narrative, reveal the feelings and perspectives of characters, and provide background information without making it too obvious (nobody likes a big information dump). Screenplay writers talk about exposition, which is how they cunningly give us the background to the tale and our characters. They try to hide it with humour, conversation, conflict, and questions. Here's an example, written by James Cameron, who before *Titanic*, wrote the screenplay for the original *Terminator* movie. The character Reese has saved Sarah Connor from being killed by the Terminator (played by Arnold Schwarzenegger), but Sarah, like us, the audience, doesn't know what a Terminator is yet. She asks Reese:

"How could that man get up after you... [shot him]?"

"Not a man. A Terminator. Cyber Dynamics Model 101."
[Exposition starting! Next, we see the police chasing Reese, and the Terminator following them too; the tension builds. The police are radioing the location of Reese and Sarah, and the Terminator responds using a fake accent, so we know he's in pursuit.]

Sarah says: "A machine? You mean, like a robot?"

Reese: "Not a robot. Cyborg. Cybernetic Organism."
[They have to yell over the roar of air through the broken windshield of their car, where the Terminator had smashed his fist.]

Sarah: "But...he was bleeding...?"
[More action. A police cruiser gets near them, while the helicopter flies overhead. Reese squeezes between a big truck and the ramp exit.]

Reese: "Alright. Listen. The Terminator's an infiltration unit. Part man, part machine. Underneath it is a hyper-alloy combat chassis, micro-processor-controlled, fully armoured. Very tough..."
[More action as he slides the car around a curve.]

Reese: "But outside, it's living human tissue. Flesh, skin, hair...blood. Grown for the cyborgs."
[As the scene progresses, we learn more about the setting, and Sarah asks the questions we want to ask.]

Sarah: "It's from the future, is that right?... And you're from the future too?... Can you stop it?"

This is a great example of using a character to ask the questions so we understand the premise, while mixing in enough action that it doesn't feel like a brain dump. Here's a very different example of question usage, taken from one of the first short stories I published, called *Appetite*.

Susan stood at the butcher's block, adrift in the middle of the kitchen. She slid a large knife from its slot and sliced a pepper. After discarding the top and tail she held the knife at both ends and chopped the slices into tiny pieces.

"If it works out, the money should follow." I said.

"Why can't you get a normal job?"

"Providing the reviews are OK," I added.

"Instead of chasing rainbows."

The point of this opening scene is to show both the disconnection and the tension between the two characters. There's some foreshadowing in the use of the knife, and the choice of vegetable, and the chopping into tiny pieces. Yet the real dysfunction is on display in the question. It is direct but remains ignored. Each character is locked in their own position, holding a dialogue to which the other is not responding properly. It's immediately obvious that there's conflict between them. These are typical of the tricks and techniques writers use in constructing their story. Questions are another part of their toolbox and are rarely used for the single purpose of providing information. Authors love to make a few words do several things at once. They might use questions as a mechanism to distinguish characters. Perhaps one person frequently says "Umm, like...' before they ask any question; as a way of revealing something about their dialect or intellect. Another common trick is to have a character verbalise a question to themselves (i.e. to the audience).

"To be or not to be, that is the question."

Shakespeare frequently used questions, and in the play Hamlet, he puts them to a multitude of uses—as insults, jibes, internal narratives, or as exposition. Of course, the writer has one huge advantage in forming questions. An author has time to think, to craft exactly the right sentence, instead of having to deliver their questions to the intended target in real-time. It's this extra thought-time that potentially allows writers to think of critical issues, and to explore them in their work, while also using questions for tactical reasons. The best writing tackles ethical and philosophical themes in a way that makes these big questions relevant and relatable for everyone.

You have the right to remain silent

The police are one group that really have to know right and wrong, ethics, and the use of questions. When you see someone arrested on TV, the police officer will read them their rights. You know the phrase:

"You have the right to remain silent. Anything you say can and will be used against you in a court of law. You have the right to a lawyer. If you cannot afford a lawyer, one will be provided for you. Do you understand the rights I have just read to you? With these rights in mind, do you wish to speak to me?"

'The right to remain silent' as the police call it, dates back to the 17th century in the UK, and is meant to prevent anyone from incriminating themselves. The same right applies in the US, where it is known as 'the Miranda warning'; a term introduced following the trial of a 23-year-old Mexican, named Ernesto Miranda, in 1963. He had abducted and raped a young girl, and after police interrogation—and a line-up— he confessed his crimes and signed a confession. He was unaware of his rights under the US Constitutions 5th Amendment, which includes the right to remain silent, and therefore incriminated himself. Because of this, the evidence was overturned, although he was still found guilty at the retrial. What the case showed was that the police must let suspects know their rights prior to an interrogation, or risk the case being thrown out of court. The US Constitution's 6th amendment provides for suspects to be represented by counsel, hence the wording of the second half of the Miranda warning statement. In drama, the police officer runs through the warning when making the arrest, but this doesn't typically happen in real life. Often, a detainee is 'Mirandarised' immediately prior to interrogation, but not before they are bundled into a police vehicle.

The next question is, what constitutes an interrogation? Officially, an interrogation involves direct or indirect questioning, or police actions, related to a specific crime. Note that indirect questions and actions are considered functionally equivalent to direct questions. In other words, anything that may incriminate the suspect before the warning statement is given, is out of bounds. If the officer has a reasonable expectation that the suspect may incriminate themselves, has an intent to incriminate the suspect, or even has knowledge that certain questions or actions will elicit a certain type of response from a suspect—like taking someone with vertigo to the top of a tall building, for example—then this is not permitted without a Miranda warning statement. Making any kind of accusation is also forbidden. If a police officer reads out a statement from another witness that provides incriminating evidence, this is also considered an accusation—and without a Miranda warning—is a breach of the suspect's rights. If you're wondering how police actions could be used against a suspect, imagine a fake line-up, where the suspect is included and the people walking the line all pick the suspect. He may be induced to confess to a crime, even though the 'witnesses' were actually police stooges.

Here are a couple of hints in case you find yourself in police custody. A Miranda warning statement is not required if you're talking to your wife in the presence of a police officer, or if you're on a long, but necessary, journey with an officer. First, keep your lips sealed! Also, the police can ask a whole batch of what they term 'neutral questions' without a Miranda warning. These include basic police procedural questions, such as your name and address, or general questions unrelated to the crime—"Have you ever been to Napa?", "Oh my god, I was going to hide out there after I shot Nancy"—no Miranda warning was required there, as the crime wasn't linked to Napa, but the murderer still managed to incriminate themselves. The police can also answer questions from a suspect, without a Miranda warning. It sounds strange, but there are cases when a suspect has asked a question about a crime, heard a factual response from the officer, and then broken down and confessed the crime. A police officer answering a question in a short, straightforward way is not considered as interrogation.

As you can see, the police have some interesting red-tape to get through before they even start to ask questions. What else do they do? Well, they like to separate the people they are going to question. This helps on many levels. It applies psychological pressure—setting up the prisoner's dilemma: "Has my partner confessed?"—and allows them to take the learnings from one suspect and apply them to the other. The separation also means the officer can pretend to have evidence from one suspect to prompt another to start talking.

"How's Joe doing?" he asked.

"Singing like a nightingale", said Officer Smith.

Another police questioning technique is to ask the suspect to write information down. They start with the basics: name, address, etc. and then progress to written statements. This can be a powerful technique. A friend of mine (who shall remain nameless for obvious reasons!), once told me how one night, when he was very young, he and two friends had gone on a drunken spree in a city centre. They stole shopping trolleys and raced them around; they urinated from the top of a parking structure; and lifted a parking barrier to help some attractive foreign tourists, breaking the barrier in the process.

Eventually, they were picked up by the police and interviewed separately. They were each told that their friends were talking and asked to write down a statement of the night's activities. A month later, the statements were read out aloud in court. Each of the three men had decided to tell a partial version of the truth but had left out certain aspects of the night's events. Unfortunately, they had each omitted different misdemeanours. By the end of the statements, not only had the 'true' story emerged, but it looked even worse—who knows how many more activities they had got up to that nobody had confessed to? The judge was not especially lenient.

It would be remiss of me to omit the good cop/bad cop as a questioning strategy too, since we've all seen it in a range of melodramatic productions. However, it doesn't have to be quite so blatant. A two-person strategy could involve a translator and a 'simple' cop who doesn't speak the language. After the translator has left without any solid info, the suspects remain in the room with the simple cop guarding the door. They may have seen the translator drive away—nobody trusts that mirrored glass in a police interview room. They start to talk freely among themselves, unaware that the 'simple' cop is a fluent speaker of their native language. There are many other approaches that two people can take to manipulate others and get answers to their questions.

Law enforcement agencies also have opportunities to use more nefarious questioning techniques. I'm not talking about waterboarding here, but more basic approaches such as *response framing*, which limits the answers to incriminating options:

"Did you see Colin in the bar, or did you meet him at the house?

"Was that before or after you had lost your gun?"

The police may try to paint a bad image of an associate, with questions:

"You know Colin has done this several times before?"
"Did you know his last driver got ten years when Colin said he told him not to ram the police car?"

As we've discovered, questioning about a particular event can also change someone's mental recall, replacing their original memories with suggested ones. That can lead to many dark consequences. Language is a complex, nuanced tool, with plenty of scope for ambiguity. In the hands of responsible people, it can be wonderful, but like any tool, it can be manipulated. I'll leave you to think about the case of Derek Bentley, a British teenager with learning difficulties who fell in with a London gang during the 1950s. While on a warehouse robbery, Derek and his friend Craig were cornered by police officers. Bentley was captured, but Craig was still free and wielding a shotgun. A policeman instructed Craig to surrender his weapon, and Derek shouted, "Let him have it, Craig." It was unclear whether this was an instruction for his friend to hand over the weapon, or to fire it. Craig chose to fire, killing one officer and wounding another. As Craig was only 16-years-old, he was spared the death penalty. At the trial, Derek was bombarded by questions from smart, aggressive lawyers. As a young adult with learning disabilities, Derek was out of his depth. He was convicted and hung, although this was eventually quashed nearly 50 years later, in 1998. We may never know for sure what somebody means by their words. Language is ambiguous. Questions, used appropriately, are one of the best tools for discovering intent. Used incorrectly, they can become a weapon.

The police have a challenging job, and good questioning techniques are among the primary tools in their kitbag. If you'd like to understand the techniques of questioning strategies, I recommend you read some Tana French novels. Her *Dublin Murder Squad* series is remarkable. What makes the novels compelling is the way she inhabits the thoughts of her characters, especially the police narrators, and shows them working to interview suspects—often sending signals to each other at the same time—through their questions or body language. The sophisticated psychology used is fascinating and goes many levels beyond the good cop / bad cop approach we encounter in films. Tana has built a big following with her work, and it's easy to see why. Her books are fascinating insights into the way people think, and act, in extreme situations; and how questions can be used to uncover information from unwilling participants.

Cautionary Tales #1

Every year or so a story hits the news about a celebrity or someone in authority abusing their position of trust. These news stories are heart-breaking. Whether it's a school sports team coach, a film director, or a DJ, the human damage they can cause is immense. Typically, they prey on teens, and the parents are left with terrible feelings of anger and guilt over how they could have prevented this from happening. Sometimes the stories are about finance; with one person making a series of decisions that cost their company, or the employees, huge sums of money. Other stakeholders in the business shake their head and wonder how this disaster and scandal could have been averted. In all cases, somebody is left thinking: *Why didn't I ask them _____?* In a surprising number of situations, somebody did ask, but was rebuffed by someone who should have been pursuing the concerns rather than becoming an accomplice to a cover-up. A few simple questions, and not taking 'no' for an answer, could have prevented countless problems. This lesson is easy to understand, but hard to put into practice. If you apprehensive about a situation or person, then ask questions. If you're not happy with the answers, keep asking. If you're still not happy, then don't get involved.

Our biggest regrets may be the questions we didn't ask.
Don't keep your questions to yourself.

6. ANSWERS

*Sometimes the questions are complicated
and the answers are simple.*

Dr Seuss

*The brain is a question-answering machine. If you ask good
questions, you get good answers. If you ask lousy questions you
get lousy answers.*

Tony Robbins

*I would rather have questions that can't be answered than
answers that can't be questioned.*

Richard Feynman

Understanding answers

A few years ago, I bumped into a friend of mine called Simon. At the time, he was working as an executive at a financial services company, with a dedicated group of data scientists in his team. They specialised in asking and answering complex questions about their business. I described my journey to learn more about questions and wanted to understand the difference between his best scientists, and the more average ones. He told me the main benefit of experienced data scientists was not so much the capacity to ask good questions (although this was a key part of the role), but rather *the ability to spot a meaningful answer and recognise its value.* That's such an important point. While we can't all be experts able to spot subtle nuances in the information we receive, there's little point in asking a question if you aren't prepared to listen carefully to the answer.

I'm tempted to immediately argue with myself here, because there are some exceptions; you can ask a question for other reasons, such as a delaying tactic, or to provoke an emotional response. There are other occasions where you may not be interested in the answer at all. In general, though, if you have asked a question, you owe it to yourself—and to the person responding—to listen to the answer.

Of course, not all questions have an answer. To be more precise, I mean that not every question we ask will generate an answer as a response. Consider these pairings, for example:

"Are you going to clean that up?"
Silence [no response]

"Why are you late?"
"Why are you always asking me that?"
[question as response]

"How do we cure Alzheimer's?"
"We don't know, yet."
[the knowledge to answer the question is not available]

"Can you help me with this history homework?"
"I'm just taking the dog out for a quick walk."
[diversion, not answering the question]

Strictly speaking, a question generates a response—even if it's silence. A subset of those responses will be answers, and we may categorise these as true or false—based on the perspective of the person answering—since truth is an awkward concept, as we'll soon see, and we may want to categorise answers into factually correct or incorrect, but even that is a murky zone. Someone might answer with a half-truth:

"Were you in the bar again with that girl from accounts?"
"No!"
[We went for a meal last time, so this is the first time we've been to the bar]

Alternatively, they may answer in a way that is completely true from their understanding, but which is factually incorrect. In this chapter we'll explore truth, lie-detection, and what happens when you become a guru. We'll also look at what happens when people ask questions of those who don't know the answers. If you want to get better at asking questions, you're only doing half the job if you don't pay attention to the answers.

Salespeople have a notorious reputation for talking over people, and not listening properly. Telesales people are the worst, and I've recently been receiving automated telesales calls, where I'm fed an automated spiel by a robo-system. Not much chance of a conversation there, or a good Q&A session. This does the sales profession a disservice, though. Many salespeople have been trained in the philosophy that we have one mouth and two ears, and therefore should spend twice as much time listening as talking. It's not a bad rule of thumb. In the Techniques chapter we talked about active listening. If you want to get the most out of the information being given in response to your question, I would encourage you to consider the following points regarding each answer:

- What's the context?
- Is it true? [or is it a half-truth, or outright lie?]
- How accurate is the answer?
- What assumptions, values, perspective, and bias are tied into the answer?
- Is there enough data available to answer this question?
- Does the person I'm asking have the knowledge to answer?

We'll look at these points in more detail in this chapter.

Cautionary Tales #2

Mirror, mirror on the wall, who is the fairest one of all?

There are some questions that you're better off not asking. The evil queen's question in the story of Snow White is a good example. She uses her magic mirror to appeal to her own vanity, repeatedly asking it who is the fairest, because she believes the mirror will answer, as it has done previously, that she is the most beautiful in the land. She knows the mirror cannot lie. [Let's avoid the whole question of the ambiguous choice of the word 'fairest'—does this refer to skin colour, ability to judge between right and wrong, or the most attractive?] By asking a question to which she already knows the answer (or thinks she does), the Queen is courting disaster. When the mirror replies that Snow White is the fairest, the Queen is at first envious and jealous, and later— when Snow White is supposedly dead—flies into a rage and sets off on a course of action that will ultimately destroy her. There's a clear lesson here.

Don't ask a question if you're not prepared
to hear the answer.

Context

Imagine you're presenting the results of your latest project in front of a large audience. You invite questions. A hand shoots up. You point at the person and wait for the question.

"How many times did you have sex last week?" they ask.

Most people would be shocked at this question, reacting with humour, anger, or simply ignoring the question to look for a more valuable contribution elsewhere. And yet, in a private meeting at an infertility clinic a few days before, the same question would illicit a straightforward, honest answer. The difference is the context; by which we mean the environment, the language, and the objects, as well as the other people surrounding the focal point of the question. Context also includes the historical and temporal juxtaposition of the question—in terms of what has just been said, for example. Context is a something we instinctively understand in our own conversations, but which computers find hard to master, and often make amusing—or dangerous—assumptions.

Imagine a student doing her Spanish/Mexican homework and looking up 'well done' using a search engine. The answer they receive would probably be 'bien hecho', which means 'well done, you did a great job!' What if the student was trying to describe how she likes her steak cooked though? If she preferred her steak to be cooked 'rare' and looked that up in a translation tool the answer may also be misleading—you need to understand the context is cooking meat. If you ask for a 'rare steak' with the wrong context, you may end up with a fillet of llama, or perhaps an ancient stick with a sharp end that could be used to impale a vampire—that is, if the system in question uses voice recognition, and can't tell the difference between 'steak' and 'stake'. Context is everything. Some of the key contextual factors for questions are:

- **Person:** If the queen asks you: Is that a banana in your pocket? you may answer differently than when your girlfriend throws you the same classic line.

- **Location:** If the question above took place in (a) your bedroom, or (b) the Hampton Court Fruit Festival, it may change the way you respond, although what the Queen would be doing in your bedroom is a mystery.

- **Prior conversation:** This often provides the context and allows for subsequent questions to be abbreviated. In a trial, a prosecuting lawyer may lead a defendant through a sequence of questions that establish context: 'Where were you on the night of December 13?', 'Did you see Mr Smith at the Sweet Shop on the corner of Old Fife Street and the Strand?' and 'Were you still carrying the metal pipe from the scaffolding job you were completing?'. By establishing context, the critical question 'Did you hit him with it?' has meaning. Although in a court of law, it might be wiser to be unambiguous and ask, 'Did you hit Mr Smith with the pipe you were holding?' In normal conversation though, we would take the abbreviated form of the question, and assume the person understood the context.

- **Social environment:** Gender, race, diversity, and class, or hierarchical structures, are all critical factors to consider. 'Do you want to come to my hotel room and work on this after dinner?' may be a normal question between two colleagues of the same gender—and sexual preferences—but may not be considered appropriate between a manager and an employee of different genders. That's a whole kettle of complexity and political correctness. I'm not advocating what should or shouldn't be permissible, but rather that social context needs to be considered.

- **Historical setting:** As already mentioned, there's a trend to ban certain books that were created in previous time periods because they're no longer considered politically correct. We can all understand why a book with homophobic language would not be welcome in a modern classroom. At the same time, we must look at the time and place where the book was written and judge it by that context. In a world where Christianity has become a minority belief, would we suddenly ban the works of art created in earlier centuries, and stop people seeing the Sistine Chapel because we no longer considered it valid? Art needs to be judged in the context of the time and place it was created.

There are other contexts to consider, too. We'll look at Technology in that specific chapter, but it's interesting to see that Google has an Awareness API, which is a programming interface that lets applications gather context on a user, so applications can make relevant choices about how to interact with the user. The Awareness API offers seven aspects of context:

Context type	Example
Time	Current local time
Location	Latitude and longitude
Place (Deprecated)	Place, including place type
Activity	Detected user activity (walking, running, biking)
Beacons	Nearby beacons matching the specified namespace
Headphones	Are headphones plugged in?
Weather (Deprecated)	Current weather conditions

Two of the functions—place and weather—have been switched off (deprecated). Typically, this happens because there's a better solution, or because these functions were misused. I'm not entirely surprised to see that *place* has been deprecated. It's easy to see how people would be unhappy if they discovered that apps on their phone were tracking exactly where they were at all times. These days, there's an increasing trend for apps to ask for permission to share contextual data—they're being forced to do so by governments, privacy groups, and software platform vendors—and to inform you how much data, with what frequency, is being shared.

One of my favourite snippets around technology is on Artificial Intelligence and the complexity of teaching computers to understand language, which is dependent on both context and concepts, not just grammar. This is beautifully illustrated by these two statements, which humans find easy enough to figure out:

Time flies like an arrow
Fruit flies like a banana

Natural Language Processing in technology is getting better all the time, and many of these challenges are being solved, so that the systems we interact with are better at grasping both concepts and context. In dealing with each other, we still need to remember the critical importance of context in both questions and answers. Making assumptions about context is a dangerous game.

Slippery as an eel

Truth is one of those seemingly simple concepts that gets more complex the more you think about it. Truth is as slippery as an eel. Consider these statements. True or false?

- The glass on your table is stationary.
- I'm a good person.
- My height is 5'11".
- I 'm 34-years-old.
- Ghosts do not exist.
- Aliens control the prime minister.
- It's impossible to teleport to Dallas from London in the blink of an eye.
- I can read English.
- Anne Boleyn was beheaded by Henry VIII.
- Coke Zero is targeted at a predominantly male audience.
- You've stopped taking drugs.
- Reincarnation happens frequently.

Hopefully, you'll have struggled to answer at least a few, if not all these questions, with a confident 'true' or 'false'. I don't believe any of these questions are easy to answer. There are different underlying challenges. Let's look at the issues:

Context
Fresh from our last section, we learnt that context is critical. Here we see it in action: Is the glass on the table truly stationary if we consider that our planet is rotating at several

hundred miles per hour? Never mind that the planet is also rushing through the Universe at 67,000 miles per hour... if the glass were not moving, it would have been left far behind. The real question (may be): *Is the glass stationary relative to other objects in the kitchen?* We don't always give context when asking a question, and most of the time that's fine as it is implied or understood. There are times, though, when specifying the context is critical.

Time
Several statements have answers that will change over time, as in 1, 2, 3, 4, for example. Clearly your age changes over time, but so does your height (as an adult, you start to shrink at some point), and you could certainly alter your behaviour from good to bad or vice versa, perhaps even from one minute to the next. The glass may be moved to the dishwasher or be knocked off the table. We've only skimmed the possible answers here: it's feasible—if unlikely—that we could teleport in the future, or that aliens will control the prime minister, or we may discover that he was under their control today, but we weren't aware of it. You may believe that point 9 is fixed, because the past doesn't change. Unfortunately, even that's not always true. Historians and politicians have a regrettable habit of changing the past. It only takes a different context, a new interpretation, or a new shred of historical evidence to invalidate our previous beliefs.

Granularity
When the doctor asks how tall you are, the context is now, not when you were a baby or your height in the future when you have shrunk by an inch or two. You may answer confidently that you are 5'11" tall, but wait! Doesn't your height change during the day as gravity pulls your spine down? Might you be

5'10.998" inches tall now that it's late evening? Since you're standing in high-heeled boots, your height could be boosted by an extra 1.5", making you more than 6' tall. And when did you last measure your height? Many people stick with the height they were measured at in their late teens or early twenties. There's a chance your measurement may have altered since. There's also a good chance that it wasn't carelessly measured in the first place and was never correct. Answering a question accurately requires knowledge of the granularity that is meaningful. If the doctor is comparing your height and weight on a chart for a BMI reading to gauge your general health, then the margins of error caused by the reasons we've listed are largely irrelevant. Yet if the measurements were being made for a skintight spacesuit to keep you alive on a lunar mission, then you might ask for new measurements. Likewise, statement 4, 'I'm 34-years-old' may be fine in a casual conversation, but perhaps not in a detailed census or a survey of the differences between people aged 34–36. Granularity is particularly important in science.

Ambiguity

Language, especially English, is often ambiguous. Meaning can sometimes be hard to define. This is an advantage, in so far as much of our daily wordplay, jokes and double-entendres stem from this fact. With this in mind, let's examine statement 8: 'I can read English'. Are we talking about UK or American English? How about the English dialect spoken in the Caribbean, in Pakistan, or in China? Modern or Old English? I'd also be interested to know if we're taking the word 'read' to mean 'make appropriate sounds for the words' or 'comprehend the meaning of the words, sentences, and paragraphs'. If you answered 'yes' to this question, and feel confident you can read English, have a look at Beowulf (written around the year 1000) without a translation, and see how you get on:

> II Gewat ða neosian, syþðan niht becom,
> hean huses, hu hit Hring-Dene
> æfter beorþege gebun hæfdon.

Again, the context is key. If you're filling in an application form for an office job, and it has a checklist of languages that you can read, you may feel confident in ticking the checkbox for English, as you'll assume this is not referring to a dialect or Old English. You might think twice if the application were for a role as a scholar in medieval literature at a University, however.

The ambiguity so often present in language can make true/false distinctions hard to assess. Incidentally, did you think statement 9 was a trick? You may recall that Anne Boleyn was executed by a French swordsman (brought over at her request, since she'd seen the mess usually made by the English axe-wielding executioners), and therefore she was not literally executed by Henry VIII. In essence though, he was the person that instigated and commanded the execution, so to all intents and purposes she was beheaded by Henry VIII, even if the physical act was performed by an official representative of the crown. We might also debate whether Thomas Cromwell or others in the court influenced Henry, and whether he was manipulated into making the decision, meaning that, in effect, it was Cromwell or another court figure that killed Anne Boleyn. The truth gets messier the more we probe, like a pond that we poke with a stick.

Faith

Some questions, like reincarnation, are simply a matter of belief or faith. You may not believe that such a thing occurs, especially if you were brought up in mainstream Christianity, Judaism, or Islam. Yet it's a central tenet of Hinduism, Sikhism and Buddhism. The Buddhist view of reincarnation is significantly different from the classical western view, with no consciousness passed between reincarnated selves. However, with a combined following of more than 1.5 billion people, you would have to say that a large percentage of the world population consider reincarnation to be a distinct possibility and may well answer this question as true. There are also several academic papers that explore the 'previous-life' memories of small children that may add credence to this belief. If a large percentage of the population believe a statement to be true, and you have no counter-evidence to disprove it, can you be sure that the answer is false?

False positive

It's a common belief that you cannot prove a negative, only a positive. This isn't entirely true—there are ways to prove a negative, such as by demonstrating that other known facts would be inconsistent with the truth. Most science operates on the principle of creating a hypothesis and seeing if it supports the results of tests and experiments. Essentially, scientists look for evidence to prove that a model is false. If they cannot find any, then the hypothesis stands. Note that proof of a theory is simply a set of evidence that supports the hypothesis, it does not actually make the theory true. So in our statements above, it's difficult to prove statements such as 5, 6 and 7. We can build a case to show that the prime minister is not being controlled by aliens, but it's hard to prove, so we may be better off searching for evidence that aliens have been behind the prime minister's every move—attempting to prove a positive rather than a negative.

Perception

'Perception is truth' is another popular view. Hmm. There was a wonderful television advert for *The Guardian* newspaper during the 1990s that showed a young, muscular punk charging down the street towards an old businessman in a suit. A lady watched from her doorstep as the punk hurtled into the businessman, sending him crashing to the floor. In a court of law, the lady would no doubt have stated that the punk had attacked the businessman, which certainly appeared to be true from her perspective. Yet when the camera panned out, the viewers could see a hob of bricks falling out of control directly above the businessman's head. The punk ran down the street and knocked the businessman out of the path of the falling bricks, saving his life. The advert suggested that unless you had all the facts, you were getting a skewed perspective. Of course, who's to say that the punk had seen the bricks himself—he may simply have been attacking the man anyway?! The point is that perception is simply that; perception. It does not imply any particular truth.

Confidence

That brings us to a key concept, perfectly demonstrated by the Coke Zero statement (10). Unless you were part of the Coca-Cola marketing team, or have read a specific article on their marketing strategy—and if you have, was it based on fact? — then your decision on the veracity of this statement will be based on experience plus guesswork. You may recall that Pepsi launched a successful Pepsi Max product that was specifically targeted at male drinkers who were embarrassed to order diet products, and so the colouring and advertising

179

were deliberately aimed at a male demographic. With that knowledge, you may have a high degree of confidence that Coke Zero was marketed in the same way, to the same demographic. The colour scheme seems to support this hypothesis. However, if you didn't know about the Pepsi Max case, then you may still have decided that this statement was true, but with a lower level of confidence. Increasingly, our software tools will begin to highlight answers for our questions, which they believe to be correct—I won't say 'true'—based on a *level of confidence*. This confidence-factor may be reported to us, to help in our decision making.

When considering answers to our questions, we automatically filter through our own personal experience, and determine our own level of confidence in the answer. While I cannot discount the possibility that there may be ghosts, I have a high degree of confidence they are not real. My view is based on:

- the fact that I've never seen one
- no 'hard' evidence for their existence has been put forward, as far as I know.
- there are some strong logical arguments to show their existence would be incompatible with our known world, and we should be seeing more and more ghosts, given the number of people that have lived and died in the past century for example

Don't be too quick to decide whether an answer is true or false—identify which filters you're applying and determine your confidence by considering the evidence.

Truth & lies

Multiple theories on truth have been proposed and debated by philosophers, masters of logic, and religious leaders. Yet there is still no agreed definition of truth itself. The most common theories state that truth involves consensus, correspondence, coherence, and semantics; and is pragmatic, constructivist, deflationary, and pluralist. If you are interested in the subtle distinctions, I would encourage you to become a philosopher! For now, let's look at a few quotes, which have given rise to some of the theories:

"There are no whole truths; all truths are half-truths."
Alfred Whitehead, British mathematician and philosopher

"To say of what is that it is not, or of what is not that it is, is false, while to say of what is that it is, and of what is not that it is not, is true."
Aristotle. [If you can figure that one out, you're probably a philosopher already!]

"If you tell the truth, you don't have to remember anything."
Mark Twain

"The truth is rarely pure and never simple."
Oscar Wilde

"Men occasionally stumble over the truth, but most of them pick themselves up and hurry off as if nothing ever happened."
Winston Churchill

"In a time of deceit telling the truth is a revolutionary act."
George Orwell

"Art is the lie that enables us to realize the truth."
Pablo Picasso

"The truth knocks on the door and you say, "Go away, I'm looking for the truth," and so it goes away. Puzzling."
Robert M. Pirsig, Zen and the Art of Motorcycle Maintenance

"We do not know—neither the sophists, nor the orators, nor the artists, nor I—what the True, the Good, and the Beautiful are."
Socrates

Lies, on the other hand, are much easier to define. They are untrue statements made with the intent to deceive. Under normal circumstances, when we receive an answer to a question, we might have a fair expectation that the information will be true, at least from the perspective of the person providing the answer. There are scenarios, though, where we suspect that the person we're questioning may be lying. Here are some situational questions where we may be especially wary of the answer:

Did you murder him?
Are you having an affair?
Will the project be finished on time?
Are there any known health risks to this expensive product?

In all these cases, there is an incentive for someone to lie; they don't want to go to prison, taking the first example. As humans, we naturally look for ways to detect if someone is telling us a lie. Many people are aware of the common body language signals, which they will look for when listening to an answer:

- scratching the nose (i.e. covering the mouth)
- fidgeting during an answer
- lack of eye contact
- providing too much detail
- blushing
- hesitation

Let's examine that last one, hesitation. A manager took a new consultant to a sales meeting. The consultant's role was to demonstrate a product and answer any technical questions. At a certain point in the meeting the prospect asked,

"Does your product do _____?"

[the feature isn't relevant]

The manager knew the product had this feature, and confidently waited for the consultant to confirm this. There was a pause, a very long pause. Just as the manager was about to step in, the consultant answered:

"Yeessss," he said uncertainly, "it *can* do that." and he went on to explain the options.

Afterwards, when the consultant and the manager were sitting in a cafe reviewing the meeting, the manager wanted to show him how timeliness can be critical in answering a question. Out of the blue, the manager told the consultant to ask him if he was sleeping with his wife. The consultant was taken aback but asked the question, as requested. The manager paused, for a long time and then said:

"Noooooo, I'm not."

He then asked the consultant how he felt about the reply.

Most importantly, did he feel the manager was telling the truth? He laughed, and immediately realised the manager was referring to his answer in the customer meeting. The consultant agreed that a pregnant pause before an answer can become very uncomfortable, and makes you doubt the eventual answer. The questioner wonders why it's taking so long to get an answer, and what the other person is considering. It feels like they're either constructing a lie or deciding whether to tell the truth or not. The consultant explained that he'd taken a long time to answer the client's question because while he knew the answer was yes, he wasn't sure which of the two methods by which the product could accomplish this task was the best one for the client to use. A better approach would have been to: answer yes (or no) immediately, and then explain the hows and whys. It can also help to use a labelling statement, e.g.

"Yes, it does that. There are a couple of ways to achieve that result. Let me think which might be the best approach in your scenario."

This kind of answer breaks any tension that can develop between the questioner and answerer, it provides time to think, and reduces the risk of the answer being perceived as a lie. Interestingly, in practice it's been shown that habitual liars rarely hesitate; they tend to move rapidly forward with their answers. Which means you should answer appropriately, but perhaps not too quickly!

Technology has been deployed, with mixed results, to help law enforcement agencies detect lies. From the infamous polygraph, through to modern experiments on micro-emotions, functional magnetic resonance imaging, EEG tests, functional near-infrared spectroscopy, and truth drugs such as sodium thiopental, technology has been deployed to spot lies. Tests have tended to focus both on physiological factors, such as eye dilation, along with psychological factors, such as the use of word patterns and certain sentence structures. Proponents of these approaches claim, with a certain amount of evidence, that the techniques show a higher rate of detecting deception than trained professionals such as police detectives or lawyers. The challenge is that these tests do have weaknesses, however. Typically, the results can be distorted or invalidated by the emotional state of the person being questioned, as the very fact that someone is taking such a test is a stressful situation that can skew results. Other factors, namely the psychological conditions, the environment, training in lie-detection avoidance (countermeasures), and in some cases, the expert's interpretation; can all strongly affect the results.

When we consider that it's not always easy to discern what is true or false, there's also the philosophical question concerning the efficacy of any lie-detection test. At its most simple, the matter of whether you're telling a lie or not boils down to whether you aim to deceive, rather than whether your answer is factually correct; especially when the truth is as slippery as we discovered earlier in this chapter.

While there's a government and possibly corporate-driven desire to be able to detect deception, it's fair to say that a reliable scientific method is yet to be developed. Remarkably few countries have legislation that makes lie-detection admissible in court, although it may be permitted in limited circumstances. Witnesses and defendants in court are typically questioned on past events, and memory has several important limitations. There's a great quote by C.J. Brainerd in his 2013 article *Murder must memorize,* which says "The science of memory is as central to the law as biology is to medicine." Memory is not recorded like a video but encoded and integrated with other memories by the brain—it's subject to bias, illusions, false creation, and can be changed at a later stage by various techniques, such as questioning, as we've seen.

Before we disappear into a rabbit hole here—or is it a rat-hole?—the takeaway is that detecting a lie is perhaps not as straightforward as we might imagine. Truth can be subjective, and is certainly hard to define, while lies are simpler to pigeon-hole but not always easy to catch. It's interesting to consider whether we'd even want a lie-test that was completely accurate. Imagine if a future website or phone app sprang up that could accurately tell if you were lying, and could be used by your partner, children, the police, the tax office, your boss, the government, and so on. How would that change your world?

The fork in the road

You died, and now you're walking down a road. You remember a trusted friend telling you there's a fork in this road, and that one way leads to heaven and the other to hell. There are no signs, though. You must decide which way to go. Once you've made a choice, you can't turn back. Two brothers take turns to guide people in their decision, and on any day, you may find one or the other at the road's split. One brother is a devil who would like to send you to hell, and the other is an angel who would direct you to heaven. You cannot tell them apart because they appear identical, but there is one difference: the angel always tells the truth, and the devil always lies.

As you approach the fork, you see one brother standing there. He greets you and explains that you can ask only one question. Then you must choose which path to follow. The fork on the right, or to the left. What question should you ask to ensure you follow the path to heaven?

Don't peek! Here's the answer...

You should ask: "If you were your brother, and I asked you which way I should go to reach heaven, what would you say?"
You should then take the opposite direction, in order to reach heaven.

How to be a guru

Mark was lucky to learn a critical lesson early in his career, more by accident than planning. He discovered how to become an expert in a subject. In the space of a couple of years, Mark became known as 'the Mantis guru', which sounds like a Kung-Fu Panda character, but Mantis was an esoteric computer programming language. I'm not sure how a spiritual term from Hinduism and Buddhism became associated with technology, but for some reason, any expert in a particular technology is referred to as the 'guru'.

Mark was working on a project that used Mantis. He was a decent programmer in Mantis, but not an expert. Luckily, his team had three hired Mantis contractors who worked alongside him and could answer his questions. They'd worked on multiple Mantis projects before, and were willing to share their experience. After absorbing as much as he could from the contractors over nine months, Mark accepted another job, and moved to the big city. Happily, his new firm also used Mantis, so he didn't have to learn anything new. When Mark started there, he was surprised to discover that Mantis was quite new to the company, and that he had more Mantis experience than anyone, except for one relatively senior guy who was very busy. When people realised that Mark had this experience, they started asking him questions. These were basic questions that were easy to answer as a moderately experienced programmer in that language. Of course, by answering their questions Mark was encouraging them to come back with more, and they did. Unfortunately, as their experience developed, their questions got harder, and Mark no longer knew the answers. At this point, he could have sent them away and let them figure it out for themselves. However, he knew this might take a long time, and many of them were working on projects with tight deadlines. Mark also knew that nobody else in his organisation could answer the questions. Realising that someone had to work out the answers, Mark saw no reason why he couldn't do it. Instead of turning people away he would tell them: *let me look into that.*

Mark soon discovered ways he could test answers himself. He found additional books and resources to reference. He built a strong relationship with the Mantis customer support team. He even built a network of other Mantis experts in different companies, including the contractors he'd worked with before, who could help with tricky problems. Within a few months, Mark realised with amazement that he'd become a Mantis expert with a reputation as a guru. When he considered how it had happened, the answer was simple. Mark had set himself up as the person who would help, and then *had been educated by other people's questions.* The first few 'tough' questions had been really difficult, but after a while he saw patterns and common themes, and learnt strategies for answering the most intractable issues.

To become an expert, be like Mark. Set yourself up as the person who will answer questions on a topic and encourage others to approach you for help. You'll also make a lot of friends. Mark found this position by default, since there was nobody else to take the role, but it doesn't mean you can't do this more purposefully, even if there are existing experts. The real lesson is that answering other people's questions is a fabulous way to learn.

They don't know the answer

You must have seen one of those interviews on television with a person that has recently hit the magical age of 100. The interviewer will inevitably ask them about the secret of their longevity. Here are the answers I've seen, and collated, so that you too can reach a century:

- lots of swimming—it's a great way to stay healthy
- gin and tonic every day
- everything in moderation
- a glass of red wine per day [funny how often alcohol crops up]
- keeping active—it doesn't matter what you do
- treat people well; be kind
- no alcohol [damn! I thought I'd found a pattern here]
- never wear make-up
- choose your parents carefully—it's all in the genetics
- bacon, eggs, and porridge for breakfast every day
- good luck
- ice cream
- eight hours sleep every night
- a diet rich in olive oil (or sushi)
- laughter
- don't retire

Interesting list, but here's the big problem. None of these people know why they've lived such a long time. They probably had plenty of friends with a similar upbringing and outlook, who died many years before them. In fact, less than half a percent of men (in America) make it to 100, although 1.66 percent of women achieve this milestone. Therefore, your best chance of surviving to be a centenarian is to be female.

The people who answer the question are unreliable on several counts: they are at the extreme edge of human longevity and may not have full command of their faculties (i.e. they may be senile). More importantly, how can they identify the one aspect of their life that has resulted in their age? Longevity is a complex thing, and the causality is extremely hard to determine because of the large number of factors and the mesh of their interactions. Being very curious, though, we still like to ask people: How? These are good questions, no doubt, but asking the person that has reached the milestone may not be the best way to determine the truth. In many cases, the better answer is to be found in the data—if it exists.

Data is always a great place to start if we want to get the facts (I won't say the truth, given what we learnt earlier). We have a whole chapter on technology later, and how that can help us with questions. We should recognise, though, that there are entire categories of questions for which data does not exist or is unreliable—asking people why they made a certain decision, like who they chose to marry, is notoriously unreliable, as we tell ourselves stories. We are narrative engines.

Before we ask a question then, we should consider whether the person being questioned knows the answer. We may still ask the question anyway, because questions are not only to gather information, as we've discovered. I may ask my grandma how she got to be 103 because I want her to feel that she's sharing her life lessons, and because I know she enjoys talking about these things—not because I plan to follow her strict regime of "no alcohol and a spoonful of olive oil every day".

I should add a quick note about politicians here. It seems to me that most of the time, they don't know the answer. They tend to be generalists. However, they have access to teams of people who may know the answer. Therefore, if a politician is briefed about questions in advance, they can appear very knowledgeable and provide good responses to the topics they'd anticipated. On the other hand, opposition politicians will ask them questions to which they know the other side does not know (or possess) a good answer, in order to cast them in a bad light. Therefore, we can see that in some professions, knowing that the person you're questioning doesn't know the answer is a benefit!

Not enough data

Sometimes, there's just not enough data to produce a good answer. The data may be inaccessible, incomplete, or 'dirty' (see the Technology chapter). If someone is asking you a question, and a lack of data prevents you from answering properly, there are various strategies you can use.

1. Explain there's not enough data to answer the question.
2. Make an educated guess at the answer, based on the data you have.
3. Make a wild guess at the answer, with nothing to go on but your instinct.
4. Combine 1 with 2 or 3.
5. Lie.

We can debate whether there's much difference between some of these options other than a deliberate attempt to mislead. Sometimes a questioner may already know the answer and will use the question to determine the honesty and integrity of the person answering. Imagine, for example, a small child with a brown, sticky face, who has eaten a chocolate bar on the car journey home with his father. When he arrives home, unknown to him, the dog has stolen his sister's birthday cake. Seeing the missing cake and her son's sticky face, his mother might ask:

"Who ate the cake I left on the table?"

Let's see the child's answers aligned with our response categories.

1. "I don't know. I just got home with Dad."
2. "My sister. It's her cake."
3. "Aliens or dinosaurs. They're everywhere."
4. "I don't know, but it might have been my sister because it's her cake."
5. "Dad."

There are also scenarios where we appear to have enough data to answer a question, but we need to combine the information in so many ways that it can make the question too hard to answer, or will take too long to work out. I was recently working with a company that makes breakfast cereals. The product must be heart-healthy—which means it must include a minimum amount of beta-glucan, and gluten-free—which means eliminating any barley that's got mixed into the oats. This can happen when the same trucks and trains transport different grains, or simply by seeds blowing into adjacent fields and growing in the wrong place. Removing any barley seeds can be challenging as the shape and size is similar to oats. If we have 40 silos of grain, and have sampled the contents of each silo, we know the approximate percentage of each type of seed. We must then choose which are the best silos to blend together to give us a product that meets our quality targets. If we're blending 3 silos at a time, then this is:

40 silos, 3-way blend = 9,880 possible combinations

That's not too bad. We might not want to write them all down, but a spreadsheet or a computer could easily calculate the best option for us. What happens, though, if we have even more silos and we want to blend more of them together?

100 silos, 4-way blend =	3,921,225 combo's
200 silos, 6-way blend =	82,408,626,300 combo's
300 silos, 9-way blend =	48,052,241,692,154,700 combo's

This rapid growth of options is known as the combinatorial explosion. It happens in lots of common scenarios—such as planning routes for delivery trucks. Organisations can't send their data to a supercomputer and wait for weeks to get an answer as the decision is probably needed that day, perhaps even within a few minutes. Luckily, there are techniques using specialist algorithms for solving these combinatorial explosion problems that can identify good solutions in a reasonable timeframe.

Without data, it's hard to get answers to critical questions, but as combinatorial problems demonstrate, sometimes having the right data is still not enough. There are times when the speed of an answer is more important than finding the perfect solution.

"Is that a Bengal tiger or a Siberian one?"

The answer is: "Run!"

Cautionary Tales #3

Lance Armstrong was a competitive bike racer, who won the Tour de France on seven occasions after suffering testicular cancer in 1996. Following his first Tour de France win in 1999, allegations surfaced that he was using performance-enhancing drugs. The press, and even other riders were consistently asking the question: *Is Lance Armstrong a drug cheat?* Lance denied any wrong-doing, however, and aggressively defended all accusations against him. Although in fact guilty, he won libel cases against The Sunday Times, and had out-of-court settlements with various people (including an ex-employee) to cover up his activity. Finally a US Anti-Doping Agency (USADA) investigation discovered that over a ten-year period starting in 1996, he had secretly met and paid more than a million dollars to Dr Michele Ferrari (who had been banned by the Italian Cycling Federation) despite publicly stating that he had severed all professional relationships with the doctor from 2004. Ultimately, following the USADA investigation published in 2012, Lance admitted his use of drugs, essentially claiming that "everyone was doing it". He was stripped of all his achievements from 1998 onwards—including the Tour de France victories, and received a lifetime ban from all competitive sports. He was forced to repay the spoils from his prior legal cases against those who had accused him of doping, and to pay the US Dept of Justice $5 million to settle a civil case. He lost his sponsorship deals and saw a negative impact on the charitable institution he had founded. He was the subject of vilification, and numerous damaging media articles worldwide.

Some questions won't go away.
Save time, money, and stress by answering them earlier.

Accuracy

There are some endeavours, like planning the flight path of a rocket to Mars, where we need to gauge the strength of our answers with factors such as accuracy and precision. This is often an essential part of answering scientific questions, and can also be important in other arenas, such as social questions—if we are going to determine pension policy from the answers to your questions, for example. In strict terms, accuracy is the closeness of an answer to the true value, while precision is the ease with which a measurement can be reproduced to give the same answer. I measure my dog's height with a tape measure, and I note down a value of 100 centimetres from the floor to the top of the head. However, if the true height of my dog (measured by lasers) is 102 centimetres, then my measurement was inaccurate by 2cm. If I keep taking measurements, and write down results of 95, 103, 98, 96, 99, 102—because I can't hold the dog still—then the precision of my measurement has a spread of 8cm.

It's possible to be accurate but not precise: you could argue that the results above are accurate, but not very precise. It is also possible to be precise, but not accurate: let's say I use a photographic measurement where a picture of my dog is overlaid with a measurement grid. The answers might all be very (very precise) but the grid I used was the wrong type, showing my dog is 100 meters tall instead of 100cm (inaccurate).

Another classic example of accuracy and precision is a player throwing a basketball at a hoop. If they shoot the ball through the hoop, they are accurate. If they shoot the ball to the same place every time, on multiple shots, they are precise. To score a lot of points they need to be precise and accurate, reliably able to throw the ball to the same place each time (precise), which is the hoop (accurate).

Statisticians like to use the terms *bias* and *variability* to represent accuracy and precision. You may also come across the terms *sensitivity* and *specificity*, which again are terms from statistics, and often lurk in healthcare literature. Again, these terms are closely related to accuracy and precision. In some scenarios, such as a test for cancer, the accuracy and precision of the answer to our medical question: *Is this lump likely to be cancerous?* is incredibly important. In these tests, we talk about:

- **true positive:**
  the test is positive + the patient has the disease
- **false positive:**
  the test is positive, the patient *doesn't* have the disease
- **true negative:**
  the test is negative, the patient *doesn't* have the disease
- **False negative:**
  the test is negative + the patient has the disease
  [BAD!!]

Let's imagine that you were tested for a potentially cancerous tumour and were told that the sensitivity of the test was 99 percent. Sensitivity is really a measure of the accuracy of a test in picking out people that *do* have the disease (i.e. finding true positives). Specificity, on the other hand, is a better measure of how many people *don't* have the disease (i.e. finding true negatives). Imagine you were also told the specificity was 80 percent. The combination means:

- If your test was positive:
  there's a 99% chance you have the disease.
- If your test was negative:
  there's a 20% chance you have the disease.

Alternatively, if the sensitivity was 80 percent and the specificity was 99 percent. Now:

- If your test was positive:
  there's a 20% chance you don't have the disease.
- If your test was negative:
  there's a 99% chance you don't have the disease.

These are clearly very important results in a life-threatening scenario such as cancer. Yet most of us don't have a firm grasp of the meaning or maths behind these terms. Undergoing treatment for a disease you don't have will incur risks, costs and potentially severe emotional impact for no benefit—which is why healthcare professionals carefully watch for false positives. However, the threat of libel for false negatives, where a doctor missed a fatal disease, are so high that many healthcare professionals have erred on the side of caution, and begun treatments even when these have not, necessarily, been warranted. Increasingly, modern healthcare practice seeks to combine tests with high sensitivity/low specificity and low sensitivity/high specificity to balance out the potential risks; and correctly identify the patient's true status. If you ever find yourself facing test results on such an important topic, remember to ask good questions—including values for the specificity and sensitivity of the tests.

In many everyday scenarios, accuracy and precision are quite malleable:

"What time will you get back from work?"

"Probably just after 6."

Your partner may interpret this answer as meaning close to 7pm, based on their experience of the precision of previous answers. In the worst-case scenario, the dinner may be burnt. Not exactly life-threatening. In our healthcare example, or when measuring ingredients for a gluten-free product, or determining the optimum temperature for crude oil in a pipeline; we need to consider the level of accuracy and precision we need in our answers, which in turn may alter the way we ask the questions. If we don't have enough data to answer these questions to our satisfaction, we should collect more data. Not every question needs an incredibly accurate answer, but look out for those that do, and make sure the data has been sourced, gathered, and managed effectively.

No place for ambiguity

Pilots have a language all their own—'wilco, mayday, pan-pan,' never mind the whole alphabet thing where they spell out words using specific phonetics. A plane with a UK registration of G-OSFA would be announced over the radio as Golf Oscar Sierra Foxtrot Alpha. Each of the words in the radiotelephony alphabet was carefully chosen to avoid confusion, since radio transmissions can be interrupted and are often full of background noise, and so are hard to hear. English was set as the international language for aviation in 1951 by ICAO (the International Civil Aviation Authority), since English-speaking countries dominated the manufacture and operations of aircraft at the time. All pilots need to meet a certain standard of English language, and must memorise the radiotelephony alphabet before getting their licence to fly. Even with these regulations, and formalised language and standards that regulate how pilots communicate with each other and with air traffic controllers, there's still scope for ambiguity, which in a safety-critical industry can be lethal.

In 1977 the deadliest aviation accident in history took place, when two Boeing 747s crashed into each other on a runway at Tenerife, resulting in 583 fatalities. The incident occurred in fog, with one plane turning on to a taxiway, while another began its take-off run after mistakenly believing it had been given the clearance to take-off. In the detailed investigation into the accident, ambiguity in language and phrasing was considered to be a primary factor. A thorough review of the aviation and radiotelephony language was carried out, resulting in several changes being instituted. The word 'clear' can't be used in a taxi instruction, for example; only for take-off, route, approach and landing, for example: 'Foxtrot Alpha you are clear for take-off'. One of the other changes was to alter 'affirmative' to 'affirm', since a clipped radio message could previously be misinterpreted. Radio messages do frequently get cut-off or interrupted, as other pilots talk on the same channel. In the Tenerife disaster, a critical phrase by the Tower was lost as the pilot of the 747 on the taxiway simultaneously broadcast a message, which wasn't heard either. If I were to radio the Tower and request clearance for take-off and got a message back that said "zzzzzative" I could previously have interpreted that as 'affirmative,' when the Tower had said 'negative' and were telling me to stay put. By using affirm and negative, this confusion has theoretically been eradicated. Under ICAO regulations, 'affirmative' was replaced with 'affirm' in 1984. In the US, the FAA (Federal Aviation Authority) still lists 'affirmative' as the standard phrase, which is a little confusing. I've seen a few pilot bulletin boards with people arguing about why that is, whether ICAO applies before FAA rules, and so on. Ambiguity in questions and answers is almost inevitable, and even in a regulated industry it's not always clear where the truth lies.

7. ADVANCED TECHNIQUES

What is the answer? she asked, and when no answer came she laughed and said: Then, what is the question?

Gertrude Stein

Levelling

In our first chapter on Techniques, we looked at how you can drill into a person's knowledge by asking questions that go deep into a subject (even if you're not really an expert). There are also modified approaches that utilise this style of questioning for specific purposes. One is well known in the realm of quality management—often linked to approaches such as Six Sigma, Kaizen, and Lean Manufacturing—although the tool itself is independent— and called *Five Whys*. The aim of the approach is to identify the root cause of a problem, and often it seems to take five such questions (although it could be achieved in three, six, or any other number). Let's see an example:

Problem: Why can't our aircraft take off from the airport?

1. the starboard engine is not delivering enough power
2. the fuel line is not delivering the right quantity of fuel
3. there's a blockage in the fuel pipe
4. the fuel is not of the right quality and contains sediment
5. the aircraft was refuelled from the wrong tanker

We might ask more questions to find out whether the pilot was new to this airfield, or if a junior airfield operator had made a mistake and driven the wrong tanker to the aircraft. The point is that the problem is not that the starboard engine is not delivering enough power, but there's a root cause that we can identify by repeatedly asking *Why?*

The use of this technique is sometimes combined with Ishikawa diagrams (aka fishbone charts), named after Kaoru Ishikawa who was a Professor at the University of Tokyo, and an expert on 'organization theory'. He was a key thinker behind the quality management approaches that emerged in Japan in the 1950s and 1960s that allowed the Japanese to move from a perceived producer of low-quality tech products to a world leader in advanced manufacturing. Ishikawa diagrams are used to identify the root cause of problems, especially things such as product defects. In an Ishikawa diagram each rib bone linking to the spine of the problem is a category of potential causes to the effect that is displayed at the head (the problem). Smaller bones branch off the rib bones with more causes, and these keep branching off further until the root-cause is determined. Several template Ishikawa diagrams have been developed for specific functions, and show the major rib-bone categories. The Five Ms, related to Manufacturing, make up one example: Machine, Method, Material, Man, and Measurement. Some people have extended this to become the 8 Ms, by adding: Maintenance, Mission, and Money or Management.

You can also find Ishikawa for other areas, such as the Four Ss for Service industries: Suppliers, Systems, Skills, and Surroundings; or the Eight Ps of Product Marketing: Product, Process, Price, Performance, People, Physical Evidence, Promotion, and Place.

These are useful tools for experts, but practitioners have some warnings for those trying these techniques for the first time. One critical point is to inspect the process not the people, and to make sure that the root cause is not deposited on a person. In our aircraft example earlier, if we'd discovered that a junior employee had delivered the wrong fuel to the plane, we shouldn't have stopped our analysis there. We would need to continue asking questions to determine why there was no experienced manager with them, or why the employee had not received adequate training. Remember we want to fix the process, not find a scapegoat. It's hard to implement a Five Whys questioning process in your company to improve quality if the first few times you use the approach, somebody gets blamed for the problem and fired!

Another challenge with levelling is that people sometimes find the symptom rather than the cause, because they don't take the questioning far enough. Therefore, 'How do you know when you've reached the root cause?' might be a good question. I've not yet found a good answer to that, other than reaching the point where subsequent 'why' questions stop yielding any useful information or insights.

In some situations, there can be multiple causes for a single effect, e.g. *Why did company x fail?* Was it because of a single person's mistake, a poor product design, a key employee being poached; an unforeseen change in market conditions? Perhaps all these factors combined to deliver a perfect storm. The tendency to use the Five Whys to focus on identifying a single cause can prevent you from seeing beyond that.

Another aspect of the Five Whys that is often overlooked is knowing how to ask good questions! The technique says nothing about identifying the right questions to ask; that's something you can learn from experience, from industry (or functional) knowledge, or perhaps by reading this book. To get around these problems, practitioners recommend validating the results from each 'why' question before moving on to the next, and using a truth table to review necessity and sufficiency—which are logical tests to determine the relationships between statements. Here are a couple of examples:

To be classified as a dog, it's necessary to be a mammal, but that's not enough—certain other characteristics must be present too.

On the other hand (paw?) it is sufficient to be a dog, in order to prove that you're not a human, but it isn't necessary (you might be a cat, a giraffe, or a postage stamp).

This isn't a treatise on logic, so we won't descend into that discussion here. What we can say is that the Five Whys, with good, carefully chosen questions to which the answers are validated, is a great way of solving certain types of issues. This technique has proven its value, particularly in manufacturing, and can also be a highly effective approach in many other areas.

You look wonderful!

I was driving along in my car, listening to the British Prime Minister's question time when I heard the following exchange—I can't remember the exact words or which minister was asking the question, but this is the gist of it:

"Will the Prime Minister agree that our changes to the health service have meant that far more people have been cared for, and lives have been changed for the better, even though our opposition voted against every one of these changes?"

"I would like to thank the honourable gentleman for asking this question..."

This was followed by a fully rehearsed roll-call of all the benefits introduced under the government's direction. This was clearly a leading question, and fully rehearsed. It also paints both the Prime Minister and the government in a positive light, and the use of flattery makes both the asker and the receiver feel good. I'm sure that both the MP and the PM had smiles on their faces—hard to tell on the radio, but I'd put money on it.

This type of formal flattery is very common in politics. We're all familiar with the more usual flattery we hear from day-to-day, which has a slightly negative connotation in that people use it when they want to get something.

"Dad, that new shirt looks great!"
"What do you want, son?"
"Can I borrow the car tonight?"

People use flattery in this way because it works. I recall

seeing a cartoon many years ago about the difference between men and women. A lady was yelling at the man "You may be good-looking Jeff, but you're an arrogant, chauvinist pig, with no manners, you're rude, mean, cruel..." The thought bubble for the man said: "Wow, she thinks I'm good looking!" That tiny piece of flattery was the only thing that stuck in his mind. Flattery is powerful, and so are questions. Combine the two, and you have dynamite. Notice how the woman in the cartoon managed to deliver a tough and direct message using a small piece of flattery. Here are some flatter and question combinations:

> "I love that dress; did you get it on your trip to Paris?"
> "That sounded amazing, what strings do you use on your guitar?"
> "Your presentation was really good, Dave. Can we review the numbers you presented?"

The Oxford English Dictionary defines flattery as 'excessive and insincere praise, given especially to further one's own interests'. It has been the traditional way of addressing those in power: kings, queens, prime ministers—even today, as we saw above—and is generally considered as a way of using false compliments to ingratiate yourself with someone that has power or influence, or used in an attempt to woo a potential lover. The trick in the successful use of flattery is to make it sincere. If we do that, it's no long called flattery, instead we call it a compliment. Consider the following sentence:

"I love the way you've done your hair; it looks great."

First, we must decide if this is a true statement. A false compliment followed by a request for a favour, a promotion, or a date etc., is an obvious use of flattery. We can say that an insincere remark + request = flattery. However, if the statement is true, then we can classify the statement as a sincere, or true, compliment. True compliment + request = powerful questioning technique, but if it's done in a clumsy way, it can appear as flattery. Following a sincere compliment with a request also weakens the effect of the compliment though. It might be wiser to give the compliment then have a conversation, and ask your question or request later, but while the good feeling is still in place—without the compliment and request being too closely associated.

Don't immediately turn your nose up at this technique though—everybody likes compliments that are sincere. You should be aware that people will frequently understand what you're doing, although they may not care. Adding a compliment before a question is not a hidden technique, but a statement of intent. Even so, it can work wonders. I dare you to try it today!

What do you want to know?

When I was a new salesperson in Cheltenham, hitting my sales targets and generally doing well—beginner's luck!—it was natural that the junior salespeople in the office wanted to replicate my results. Enthusiastic and keen to learn, they concluded that my success was hidden in the questions I used in my prospect meetings. They wanted to know exactly what I did and said. They asked me to reveal the questions I used to unlock prospects, the questions that meant people would happily buy our product and not argue endlessly about discounts. Of course, they knew there were other important aspects to sales—the hard graft involved in phoning and emailing contacts to get meetings, schmoozing with marketing, writing proposals, and so on. They already did most of these things themselves, and so could easily compare my efforts to their own. The one thing they couldn't see though was what I did when I got into a room with a prospect.

My questions weren't a secret. I'd never really thought about it before, and as I had stock options with the company, I was keen to see it do well. I therefore decided to write down the questions I used, to share with my team and help the less experienced people become better sellers. I hoped other salespeople would also add their unique questions, so we could all learn from each other and improve. When I sat down to write my list, I was startled to discover that I didn't *have* any standard questions. I wasn't even sure if I ever asked the same question twice. All I did was to try my best to understand the customer's business. If I understood it well enough, then I could see where there might be problems, especially since I was talking to other customers in the same market with similar issues. Also, I gained credibility with the customers by listening and seeking to understand rather than trying to 'sell' to them. When people trust you, they open up, so I would soon grasp not only how the customer's business worked, but where their pain points were, and what value we could bring by fixing them. What's more, the customer had come on that journey with me, and we were able to work together to solve those issues.

What I discovered was that I had an underlying model of how a business works, and my research before the meeting helped me see how this prospect fitted into that model. My questions were aimed at discovering the missing elements and were really questions to myself—they certainly weren't how I would phrase the questions in a meeting. I wrote down the inner questions I had, which showed how I thought about a business. Here they are:

- What **scale** of business are they?
  Revenue, offices, employees, etc.

- What are their **revenue sources**?
  How many customers, who's the biggest, who's typical, which products are the biggest earners?

- What **do they do**?
  Products? services? pricing strategy? branding?

- Who **owns** the business, and what pressures do they apply?
  e.g. Nasdaq with Q targets? A family with succession issues?

- Where do they sit in their **market space**?
  Gorilla? Chimp? Who are the big names, and who do they encounter most frequently?

- How important are the **partners** and **suppliers** to them?
  Who are they? What level of integration? Risk of being eaten or will they do the eating?!

- What **challenges** do they face?
  What are the key issues, inhibitors to growth, legal changes, competitive pressures?

- How do they **measure** the business?
  What are the key metrics? Revenue? Profit? Customer satisfaction / longevity?

- How do they want to **grow** the business?
  Strategic 3-year plan? Tactical plan? M&A? IPO, new markets, new products?

I had a similar mental model for thinking about the *technology* used by the company—I was selling computer software —and another one for the *people* I met, which considered their responsibilities, opportunities, problems, background, and personality.

I wasn't aware of the questions I used. They came naturally from trying to construct my mental model. While this approach fits into the Advanced Techniques category, it also represents a simple lesson. You aren't a parrot learning questions by rote from a best-practices list. You should be questioning someone for a purpose. Whether that's to comprehend their business or to discover if they've committed a crime—if you don't know why you're asking questions, you won't get far. This technique is easy; understand why you're asking questions, and what you want to achieve. It may take some planning and thought in advance, but it pays off.

Silence

Silence is golden, they say. Silence is also powerful and can sometimes even be agony. Silence is a powerful weapon against questions, but also a telling answer. Everyone should learn to use silence—as it can be an incredibly useful device—but just like any other tool, it can be over-used or deployed incorrectly.

Lena had to perform a challenging performance review on Johnny, a member of her team, with her manager. Johnny was a tough individual to deal with; he didn't fit into the team particularly well, and he tended to go silent when asked difficult questions. Lena and her manager decided that at his Performance Review they would tackle several complaints about Johnny from other team members by sharing strong evidence regarding his under-performance. The plan was to follow the evidence with a question as to why this situation had occurred. They suspected Johnny might rely on silence as a defence. Lena and her manager elected, perhaps with poor judgement, to match his silence, and wait for an answer. Lena's manager instructed her to say nothing until Johnny had spoken, after she had asked the critical question. The meeting was tense as they laid out the evidence, and then Lena asked the prepared question. Johnny sealed his lips, folded his arms and said nothing, exactly as they'd predicted. Lena began to count in her head. One, two, three, four, five, six, seven…. she could feel her heart beating but, Johnny showed no signs of cracking. Lena continued counting. As she reached thirty seconds, she considered saying something, but waited. The tension was incredible. Heat was pouring off her, and there was a bead of sweat running down Johnny's forehead. Lena counted 45 seconds, 50, until she reached a minute.

Eventually, Lena's manager broke the silence, to the great relief of everyone. Johnny was not at the company for more than a few months after this event. His silence was interpreted as guilt, and/or insubordination, and he was moved down a disciplinary route to an eventual exit. Lena learnt a lesson or two about silence that she would never forget.

A minute can last a very, very long time subjectively. If you're not sure you agree, try this experiment; next time your wife/husband/partner/best friend/boss/ asks you a serious question, keep silent and slowly count to 60 in your head while you look at them. See how they react, just don't sue me over your lost job or divorce proceedings.

Of course, as already mentioned, the principle of remaining silent is permitted as a valid defence in many legal systems across the globe, even if it didn't work well in Johnny's case. It appears to have its origins in sixteenth century England, when people were tried for religious and political crimes, and were forced to swear a religious oath that they would answer questions truthfully before the court. If they lied, they were committing the mortal sin of perjury; if they remained silent; they were in contempt of court, and if they told the truth, they might incriminate themselves for a crime. Three poor options, which became known as 'the cruel trilemma'. The Latin phrase *nemo tenetur se ipsum accusare* ('no man is bound to accuse himself') began to be heard in court rooms. Then a remarkable man, a judge named Sir Edward Coke, began to instigate some changes. It was Coke, also Lawyer General and Speaker at the House of Commons, who restricted the use of the religious oath that created the trilemma. He also laid many of the foundations of the modern UK legal system, as well as leading prominent cases such as those against Sir Walter Raleigh, and the Gunpowder conspirators. This revision to the use of the oath was partly in response to the abuse of the religious and political courts, which were being used as tools of power and oppression, and during the seventeenth century the right to remain silent emerged as a general principle that was also adopted in the US Constitution and law, as well as throughout the British Empire. From there, it found its way into many other legal systems as well. During the English Restoration, the right to remain silent also migrated to witnesses.

Interestingly, silence is often seen as a sign of guilt. While the right to remain silent remains in English and Welsh, but not in Scottish law, a negative inference can nonetheless be made from silence, although you cannot be convicted based solely on your choice to say nothing. I find it fascinating to see how legal systems cope with the use of certain aspects of language; categories of questions, and silence, for example. The fact that legislation exists to defend or outlaw certain practices is a wonderful demonstration of the impact of such techniques.

Silence is very powerful if used with care and precision, as the following example shows. In a big manufacturing company situated in a small town, the Director occupied an office on the top floor. Most of the time he stayed in his office and enjoyed the view, while he was brought daily reports on progress. Once a month though, he liked to wander the lower floors and talk to the staff. There was a new employee called Dave, who hadn't yet met the Director. When Dave's colleagues asked him if he'd met 'Whistler', he asked his colleagues who that was, but they just laughed. Dave forgot all about this, until he was working at his desk a few weeks later. He suddenly became aware of a quiet, soft, whistling noise. Glancing over his shoulder, Dave discovered the Director had materialised next to him.

"What are you working on?" he asked Dave in a quiet

voice.

Caught by surprise, Dave blurted out a few lines about the task in hand.

"I'm working on a new process for Midas."

Dave's expectation was that the Director would ask a follow-up question, but he stood mute with his head tilted to one side, as though Dave had not finished answering his question. The combination of silence and authority was daunting, and Dave continued with more detail.

"...because the Midas process had a problem last night...."

More silence and the tilted head.

"...which meant we lost the entire overnight production run..."

Silence.

"...but I think I've found the problem...."

Silence.

"...which was something one of the night shift did incorrectly...."

Silence.

"Roger Smith."

After less than thirty seconds, with a careful use of silence and authority, the Director had seen Dave implicate a colleague in a disaster about which the Director may not have had any prior knowledge. Clearly, Dave could have handled it much better.

I'm not recommending the Whistler approach to management, although it may be effective in certain scenarios. What I do suggest, is adding a few more pauses—small silent breaks—into everyday questioning. Many people ask their follow-up questions way too fast. People often need time to contemplate their answer. Not everyone thinks at the same pace. Instead of lining-up your next question, try pausing to see if there's more information about to be given. You can often see if someone has finished talking by their body language. If their eyes are looking upwards, and they are making a noise like *umm...* then they're still thinking. Why not wait to hear what they say next?

Use silence as a prompt for information without having to ask another question. Use it as an answer to a question if that is appropriate. Fighting silence with silence can be unpleasant, as Lena discovered. Not everyone is comfortable with silence, so this is one technique that needs practice.

Bid-to-launch

You're in a meeting and you have a question, but the person speaking simply won't stop talking, or even worse, they're completely monopolising the airwaves; asking all their questions and leaving no gaps for you to interject with yours. What can you do?

- **Agree with team members in advance on who will take what role**. Sometimes, another person may not realise they're dominating the time slot allotted for questions. They may feel you're shy, or that as the manager they should ask the questions. They may have a hundred other reasons for taking the lead. A good approach is to agree in advance who will ask questions, in what domains, and possibly even to discuss a duration or time-split. For example, you may agree that you'll ask questions about the charitable donations programme, and that you'll need an uninterrupted 15 mins. Your colleague can then follow on with questions about the decision-making process and financial situation. Another benefit of this approach is that it can guide the way you answer questions, when the person being questioned reverses the process and asks you questions, agreed areas of expertise and authority make it clear who has responsibility for which topics in the meeting/relationship. If you're regularly working with the same people, then this is the best solution. You can monitor and improve the approach until it becomes natural for all involved.

- **Stand up.** That often draws attention, depending upon the context. When there's a gap in the conversation, you may get a chance to ask your question. You can, perhaps, make the action appear more natural by getting a drink, or walking to the person to look them in the eyes—much of how you handle this depends on context.

- **Put your hand up.** Yes, as you did at school. Again, this depends on context. It may seem strange to do this among a small group of friends in a bar, but it might be appropriate in a company presentation by your boss.

- **Pass a written note.** Many online conference facilities allow guests to type in their question while the presenter is talking or answering another question. There's no reason why you can't use the same tactic in a face-to-face scenario, especially if there are a lot of participants. Sliding a piece of paper across the table with your question written down may be the most effective way of getting it answered without interrupting the current flow.

- **Ensure the interaction happens in a group situation.** This works well where one person monopolises the conversation in a one-to-one scenario. Bringing together a larger group makes it harder for one person to achieve this—and so other people take their turn, and/or side conversations will spin off in smaller groups.

- **Let the individual know your concerns.** You can do this in a meeting, or in a friendly chat later over a cup of coffee: "You've got so much knowledge on [x], that sometimes when we talk it all rushes out too fast for me. Can you pause every so often, so I can ask you questions?"

- **Set expectations.** "We have only ten minutes left—do you mind if I ask a few rapid-fire questions?" If you can set expectations in advance, so much the better. Let the person know they have 20 mins to brief you on the state of the project, and you want to use the following 30 minutes for the others to ask questions. Make it clear you're keeping track of the time, and hold the person responsible for keeping within the timescale.

- **Alter your rhythm.** Nobody talks non-stop because at some point everyone must stop for breath. I've found the biggest challenge when there are two or more people asking questions is that the other person beats you to it with their question in the 'breathing gap'. Everybody has a pace at which they typically speak, and a set duration of pauses in between sentences (or breaths). If you find that every time your target pauses, someone else gets a question in first, they're probably running at a faster pace, mentally. Adjust your speed, and confidently ask your question a moment before you would normally.

My brother and his wife have a family phrase they call *bid-to-launch*, which describes the scenario when you are so keen to say something that you forget to listen to what's being said. It's hard to avoid doing this because we all want to contribute to a conversation in our unique way. When you're locked into a bid-to-launch though, you risk missing out on the interesting stuff being discussed. I once saw an excruciatingly embarrassing example of this at a company meeting. Our leader had called together an impromptu all-hands meeting, and a couple of hundred people were standing together listening to an important update on our business. After a few minutes, our leader stopped and asked for questions. There was a brief silence, as nobody wished to stand out from the crowd, but gradually, one or two folks began to engage. After the first few employees received encouraging replies, others began to raise their hands. One of the managers near me became very keen to have his question answered, and kept pushing his hand into the air, but as we were a fair distance from the leader, he didn't notice the raised hand. Eventually, he spotted my colleague's desire to engage, and prompted him to ask his question. The manager then asked a question that the leader had answered two minutes previously. Embarrassed, the leader explained that he had already answered that question but proceeded to repeat his prior answer. Meanwhile, the crowd edged back from the questioner, guffawing and laughing at the man's ignorance. He looked like an idiot in front of the entire company—all because he'd been too busy preparing his question rather than listening. His reputation never quite recovered.

Use the techniques listed here to ensure you get to ask your question, but never forget to listen while you wait your turn.

Dipping a toe

When you don't know the temperature of the swimming pool, you can in dip your toes and decide if you want to dive-in, wade, or stroll back to your lounger and soak up the sun instead. Likewise, there are questions you may want to ask, but aren't sure what the reaction will be—it could be very cold. There are ways to metaphorically dip your toe in the water with questions, too. Let's say you're at a party, or an after-work drink with a group of colleagues. You're attracted to a member of the group, and they seem to enjoy talking to you. Since they're friendly by nature, you can't be certain if your attraction is reciprocated. You could attempt to interpret their body language, or you could enlist someone else to help—tips on that in the next section—although that feels a bit like a school disco when you were ten. Alternatively, you could boldly ask them for a date. There are risks with that last approach. You can't be sure of a positive response, and a negative answer could have repercussions such as embarrassing meetings in the office or awkwardness in your social circle. There's less risk in scenarios where you may never see the person again, but egos can still get bruised. I have a few friends who don't care about their ego. They simply ask and move on if they don't receive the reply they hoped for. Interestingly, they're often good at noticing non-verbal signals, which reduces the number of negative reactions because they've learnt through trial and error which situations are likely to work for them. For many of us though—the introverts?—that's not an easy path. The alternative is to use trial questions. The term comes not from legal cases, but jargon used by salespeople, who use a

223

technique known as the *trial close*.

Here's how a trial close works. You're trying to persuade a prospective customer to sign a big deal. You've explored their problems, discussed the impact these have on their business, demonstrated how your product could solve their challenges, and even indicated how this solution would make them stars in their organisation. This process may have taken months. How do you now close the deal? There are several approaches, and a whole industry based around answering this apparently simple question.

A car salesman may use the *assumptive* close:
"Let me get the car cleaned while we sign the contract."
[Notice this one isn't even a question]

The double-glazing salesman might use the *alternatives* close:
"Should I place the order for the standard or security glass?"

Or we could use the straight talking, direct approach.
"Can you sign this before the holiday so we can get started?"

The trial close allows the salesperson to ask a question that indicates whether the prospect is ready to say 'yes' to a deal, without being too direct. It uncovers any hidden objections. e.g.:

Trial close #1. "Do you think your team would have time to handle this before the holiday?"
"No, we're overloaded, the team's not ready."
"Is there anything we could do to help—like have our consultants do the initial scoping now, ready for a kick-off in January?"
"We could do that, except the budget is fixed. I'd like to get a

head start, but I can't afford the consultants, this year."
[Clear buying signal here! Wants to start using in January... but we've uncovered that the team constraints and this year's budget are blockers.]
"Does the new budget year start in January?"
"Yes, but the budget was fixed in October."

Trial close #2. "How much did you set aside for consultancy on the project next year?"
[Trial close—the salesperson is asking if money has really been set aside to buy his solution.]
"About 200, 250k, I think."

Trial close #3. "Theoretically then, could we start the project now, and have the terms set so that the consultancy fees are paid from next year's budget?"
[Notice the softening of the question with 'Theoretically then', so that it's not a direct close.]
"Yes, I think that could work, it's a good idea."
[After trial 3 closes, we've had every indication that this deal can be closed, and that the customer wants to move forward. We've also uncovered a hidden objective and tackled it. Now it is time to ask for the actual close—you've got to do it eventually!]

Actual close "If I get the contracts amended so the consultants can start now and get paid in January, would you be able to get this signed off for a start in two weeks?"
"Sure, sounds good."

Okay, I know that's a simplified version, and it never runs that smoothly, except in my dreams, but the approach is solid.

Let's return to you talking to the attractive person from the start of this section. What does a trial close look like in that scenario? Well, it depends on what you've been talking about, but let's assume you've been discussing your collection of vintage vinyl, original manga artwork, or your shared love of Bruce Willis movies. You could create trial close questions that are non-threatening but that indicate the person's willingness to form a closer bond with you by asking something like this:

"Would you like to borrow the Bowie albums, and see what you think?"

"Yes, I'd like that."

[Result! they probably like you—now you can advance to trial close 2.]

Or they might say, "No, thanks. I'd be too scared I'd scratch them."

[Not interested—but you could try another trial close to be sure.]

That first trial was very easy, lending an item due to a shared interest. A second trial question might involve a date, but in a group, e.g.:

"They're showing that Bruce Willis gem, *Twelve Monkeys*, in the art house museum. Do you think we should get a group together to see it?"

[You may get a yes or no to this, or if they're keen, they may indicate they'd like to see it, but the group isn't required.]

A third level trial question might be the infamous 'come up and see my etchings', cliché, perhaps updated to manga.

"I've got a couple of original sketches in my apartment by

Chiho Saito from the *Revolutionary Girl* series if you'd like to see them."

I like trial questions because they let you understand a situation, save embarrassment all round, and are easy to ask. Each trial question should get closer to the 'actual' question you want to ask—you can't keep lending items and expect a relationship to develop, for example. If you get a rejection to your trial question, you may have more work to do before you can earn the right to ask again. You can use trial questions to good effect both in work and social situations, and I would class them as indispensable to anyone looking to master questions. I can't help think, after recent scandals, how much better the world would be if more people used trial questions effectively. Let's make fewer assumptions, and test our ideas with others before taking actions we might all regret.

Getting others to do your bidding

There are times where you don't want to be the person asking the question, but you still need an answer. There might be occasions when asking a question may cause a furious reaction from the person being questioned, and although you feel the question needs to be posed, you don't want to poke your head above the parapet. In situations like these, you can:

1. **Ask someone to ask the question for you.** They may not share your concerns, they may not even care, or they may be unaware of the consequences (see 3 below). There's no harm in this approach if you tell the person why you don't want to ask the question yourself and/or why you think it would be better coming from them. For example, you may not want to ask your girlfriend her ring size—it may spoil a big surprise you have planned—but you might get her friend to ask, casually, if she can be trusted not to spill the secret. Of course, you do run the risk of looking like a kid at elementary school: "My friend wants to know if you'll dance with him."

2. **Pay someone.** This seems extreme, but there may be a good reason to do this if it's not illegal. Members of Parliament may ask questions in the UK House of Commons that involve corporate interests in their region, such as: 'Would the Prime Minister agree with me that the High Speed Train service through Northamptonshire will bring a major financial benefit to the region and should be granted approval to move forward, since the environmental concerns have now been largely negated?' This is permitted, so long as the MP does not have a

financial interest in the project (MPs must declare any interests they have outside of parliament). It's a tricky area though, and there have been a variety of scandals linked to the process of 'lobbying' where advocates for a charity, corporate, or special interest group have provided campaign contributions or money directly to individuals who have raised questions on their behalf. The 'cash for questions' scandal in the mid-1990s was such a scenario, with accusations of MPs abusing their position to receive money from Mohamed Al-Fayed, the owner of Harrods. The result was that certain MPs were forced to step down, a full parliamentary report was compiled, and ultimately, legislative changes were enacted. However, since lobbying is an integral part of the political process, it continues to this day, although 'theoretically', it's not possible to pay cash for specific questions to be asked.

3. **Find a naive fool and trick them.** Don't think I'm recommending this—because I'm not. It is a valid approach, though. I'm including it because you don't want to be the fool they use. If someone approached you at the airport and told you they had to help their aged mother, and could you take this parcel through security for them? You would, hopefully, refuse and/or engage the local security teams. Yet if someone at work said he wanted to know why Product x had been delayed again, but had to dash for a client meeting—would you ask the Product Director at the all-hands meeting? That could also be a bomb, causing the Product Director to explode with anger!

4. **Find someone old who has nothing to lose.** I prefer this to option 3. Some people don't have the same concerns or fears as the rest of us. Perhaps they have a different

personality or are at a different stage of life—either young and fearless or about to retire and not concerned about how their peers view them. In any case, if you can find someone who has little to lose, they may be happy to ask your question.

5. **Use suggestion on a group.** This one is hard to pull off, and not guaranteed, but it lets you cover your tracks well. The idea is to get a group talking about a subject so you can raise the question you want asking in their heads and get them thinking about it. When the occasion arises for the question to be asked to the primary target—if you've seeded the idea in enough minds—someone who is bold/naive/has nothing to lose may ask the question on your behalf, unwittingly, thinking it was their idea. I've seen this approach skilfully deployed by at least one work colleague on a frequent basis, but I will warn you that it's hard to achieve. Definitely an advanced skill. This strategy also requires sufficient time and planning to put into action, so you need to be thinking a couple of steps ahead.

6. **Find a way to ask the question anonymously.** The use of online tools has made it increasingly easy to ask questions anonymously. Using a pseudonym email address or signing into a web conference without revealing your (true) identity are two ways of approaching this. Paper still works—the old 'suggestion box' that companies used to operate was an easy mechanism for encouraging anonymous questions, requests, and feedback. In the staff magazine of one famous UK retail company, anyone could anonymously ask a question of the senior management, and the magazine would publish the reply. I recall a great question about why the executives had all bought houses

in the vicinity of the new Head Office prior to the announcement of the chosen location—resulting in associated house prices in that region suddenly soaring when other employees tried to relocate. The entertaining reply/excuse fooled nobody.

7. **Pretend you're asking on behalf of another person/group.** This is a perfectly valid approach, but the trick is to not make it too transparent that the question is really your own. Here's the classic 'transparent' example: "One of my friends has a large boil on her buttock and was asking me whether she should see a doctor, or if I thought it would go away. I told her I had no idea—what do you think?" This may generate a response such as: "I think your *friend* would be very wise to get it checked by the doctor." Even when people see through this approach, it can help avoid embarrassment.

8. **Ask a large group to answer the question (in a form, survey, etc.)** You may need some technical skills to accomplish this, but setting up a survey online is much easier than you think. Otherwise, just type a sheet of questions and have friends with clipboards stop and ask people the questions, or send the sheet to the relevant target group. If you want to know the answer from one specific person, you'll need to make the survey named and not anonymous (unless you are happy to sail past ethics and secretly identify each participant). The benefit of this approach is that your target may not realise they're being singled out. It requires a fair amount of effort, and there's no guarantee that your primary target will agree to complete the survey.

9. **Choose the best time to ask.** The timing of your question could be key, and you could get your answer more easily by delaying it. Very early in my marriage, for

example, I learnt never to ask my wife to do anything just after she got back home from the office... she liked to take a few minutes to unwind first. This may not work for all scenarios, but it's worth keeping in mind as it can be a more effective approach in many situations.

10. **Don't ask. Find out another way.** There are many ways to gather information. If your direct question is too high-risk, find an alternative approach. Of course, that only works if the goal is to seek understanding. If you're using a question for other purposes—as a weapon, for example; then you may have no option. Where possible though, it may be best to avoid a difficult question and obtain the information using alternative methods.

Repetition

There was a cult TV series many years ago called *Babylon 5*, written by J. Michael Straczynski (JMS). It laid the foundation for subsequent programs such as *Lost*, *Battlestar Galactica*, *Breaking Bad*, and the directors of these acclaimed series have acknowledged this debt. One of the key innovations the writer deployed was to follow the arc, or psychological journey, of characters over several seasons. This came at a time when sci-fi fans were accustomed to *Star Trek* (the original version), where the lead characters survived every episode, and anyone else would undoubtedly get killed. You could watch the *Star Trek* series in any sequence since each episode was a standalone story. JMS changed this, and armed with a degree in psychology, he used his knowledge to incorporate interesting psychological elements into his writing. In one episode ('Signs and Portents', for the fans out there), he used *the repetition of a question* as a specific technique, and with far-reaching effects. The *Babylon 5* setting was a space station with aliens acting as ambassadors for their respective races and trying to maintain peace across the galaxy. There were tensions between alien groups and factions, as frequent skirmishes broke out—both political and military. In one episode a stranger arrived at the station and found a way to meet each ambassador. Without any real introduction—viewers didn't know who he was or who he represented either—the stranger asked each ambassador a simple question: "What do you want?" He got a variety of answers. Some ambassadors brushed him off rapidly: "To be left alone."

One critical character, however, began with a flippant reply but then began to reveal far more, following the repetition of the question:

"What do you want?"
"What do you mean? For supper?"
"What do you want?"
"This is pointless", the ambassador replies. "I want you to go away and leave me in peace."
"What do you want?"
"Wait. The Centauri stripped my world. I want justice."
"What do you want?"
"To suck the marrow from their bones, to grind their skulls to powder."
"What do you want?"
"To tear down their cities, blacken their sky, sow their ground with salt. To completely, utterly erase them. And then what? I don't know. As long as my Homeworld's safety is guaranteed, I don't know that it matters."

This is like the levelling we discussed earlier—with repeated use of the Why? question (and notice this also took five questions). In the previous case though, the question changed each time as we learned from the response. Straight repetition is very direct, and peels away layers to get to a truth or belief. Repeating an identical question multiple times is way of applying psychological pressure. In interviews, JMS mentioned how he'd learnt this technique when running encounter groups and group psychotherapy approaches such as the Synanon games (where you ask: "Who are you?" over and over, refusing to take the same answer twice).

Repetition is certainly a powerful approach, but it comes with a warning label. In our example, the Ambassador became angrier as he progressed through the conversation, until he was shaking with fury by the end—although this was the stranger's intention. It set the Ambassador off on a path that ultimately, proved destructive. Unless handled with great care, there's a high probability that repeating the same question will antagonise the one being questioned. That doesn't matter if you don't care about their reaction or if you're deliberately aiming to provoke an angry response. For an example of this technique taken to the extreme, see the sidebar below.

Jeremy Paxman vs Michael Howard

Shortly after the UK General Election of 1997, TV political presenter Jeremy Paxman interviewed Michael Howard, the former Home Secretary, in what has become an infamous encounter. During the interview, Paxman asked Mr Howard the same question 14 times in succession, and Mr Howard avoided giving a direct answer on each occasion. The actual question was "Did you threaten to overrule him?" and was referring to a meeting that had taken place between Michael Howard and Denis Lewis, head of Her Majesty's Prison Service, regarding the possible dismissal of John Marriott, a prison governor. For many viewers, the interview enhanced Mr Paxman's reputation as a ferocious political interrogator and made Michael Howard appear as a 'typical' politician, slippery, and incapable of answering a direct question. If you happen to be near a computer, I'd recommend you search for this clip online. It's worth watching, as Paxman gets increasingly infuriated with Howard's inability to answer a direct question, and Howard uses every trick in the book to avoid the question. It's an entertaining five minutes of video.

Jeremy Paxman did admit later that he had been asked to fill time by his producer as the next segment of the show was not ready and said this explained his repeated use of the same question. Several years later during another interview with Michael Howard (who at that point was leader of the Conservative party—perhaps showing that the interview hadn't damaged his career too badly—Jeremy Paxman repeated the original question and Mr Howard answered it directly, stating that he had not threatened to overrule Denis Lewis.

Other than being a marvellous example of the power and

ferocity of question repetition, there is a simple lesson to learn from this famous exchange, especially if you're a politician: always answer 'yes' or 'no' to a direct question if you can; and then give your explanation.

What if you don't know
what to ask?

If you don't know what question to ask, the obvious option is to say nothing. Unfortunately, that doesn't seem to be how the world operates. There are situations where you feel obliged to ask questions—perhaps you're even being paid to do so. What are the strategies, then, for when you don't know what to ask?

- **Keep listening.** Don't spend your time trying to think of a good question, but try to understand their message/point of view/position/explanation. Questions can then naturally flow from this knowledge.

- **Stay curious.** Take an interest in what the other person is saying, and the reasons for what they say. If you do this, you'll have no problem in thinking of questions.

- **Watch out for hooks.** The other person will indicate what they'd like you to question them about (see the Techniques chapter). That doesn't mean you have to swallow every hook, but if you're stuck on what to ask next, it's a good starting point.

- **Ask short, open questions.** Doing this for areas you don't understand or would like to know more about will lead you to a better understanding of what they're saying. It can also lead to follow-on questions.

- **Avoid controversial subjects.** If you run out of questions on a date, for example, that's no excuse for asking inappropriate questions about sex or race. Re-read step 3!

- **Do your research.** I often go into a meeting with a list of questions in my head, having already learnt as much as I could—given the limited time and resources available—both about the company and the person I'm meeting. I don't start the meeting with these questions because I hope that many will be answered during our conversation, but I can always fall back on any that are unanswered, later in the meeting.

- **Let someone else step in.** Never feel you need to be leading all the time. You may be dominating the conversation to the detriment of others. Let them ask questions too! That may also trigger more questions for you.

- **Pause.** Sometimes, if you leave a longer gap before asking your next question, the person may continue—they may not have finished. Remember 'Whistler' from the Silence section earlier this chapter!

One lesson I learnt the hard way was about using open and closed questions. I was on a sales training course, and faced a tough, experienced man called Pat, who was playing the customer role. I asked Pat several closed questions:

"Do you have x?"
"Can we talk about y?"
"Is there budget for x?"

He snapped out his answers without a pause. "Yes, No, No." It happened so fast, that I didn't have time to think of my next question, and I ran out of things to say. He laughed. "That will teach you not to ask a series of closed questions! You won't do that again, will you!". He was right about that. He was trying to help me, and I've certainly never forgotten his lesson.

Of all the techniques above, the one that buys you the most time to gather your thoughts is number 4—one good open question will give you space to think. Thankfully, most people want to help, and are happy to talk. Always keep a good open question ready in your back pocket though:

What did you do this weekend?
What's the latest news on the business?
How are your plans shaping up for _____?

8. NON-HUMAN QUESTIONS

Animals are such agreeable friends, they ask no questions,
they pass no criticisms.

George Eliot

Turing test

The Turing test has appeared in a multitude of books and movies, and has also found its way into popular culture. The test determines whether a computer can successfully imitate a human in conversation. At the time when Alan Turing came up with the idea, there was heated debate over whether computers could be truly intelligent. What Turing did was switch the argument from 'Can machines think?' to 'Can machines appear to be thinking?' If we can't tell the difference between a machine pretending to be a human, and the real thing, well that throws up some interesting philosophical puzzles! From our perspective, it's fascinating to note that Turing postulated his theory with questions.

The basic test involves participants A and B, who are in sealed rooms and can only communicate with the outside world by typing into a system to respond to questions proposed by a third participant, C, who is also the judge. C's job is to ask A and B questions and determine which one of them is human and which is a computer. Both A and B are attempting to prove they're human. If C can't tell them apart, then the computer—whether it is A or B—has passed the test because it has imitated human behaviour well enough to convince a human judge.

There are several fascinating aspects to this apparently simple test, and thousands of hours of academic study have been devoted to exploring the different facets of it. One common fallacy is that the test is designed to see if a computer can 'fool' a judge into believing it is human. This is certainly how several software developers have approached the problem—and with considerable success. Some of the more interesting algorithms built to play the game have included tricks such as deliberately mis-spelling words, to convince the human that another person was typing answers to their questions—clever, eh? Turing's intention, though, was for the test to help identify a machine with genuine cognitive capabilities. His work is one of the critical concepts underlying the modern field of Artificial Intelligence.

When you think about the test, you can see that Turing was showing how you should *ask questions* to determine if someone is human or a machine. I've often thought there were several humans I know that might fail the test. It also made me wonder: What questions should we ask to determine if someone is human? A few people have posted sample questions they would use on the Internet. Here are some examples:

- **How old are you?** Easy for a human, hard for a machine—it has to lie or divert you with an answer such as 'a lady never tells'.

- **What's the difference between a broken heart and a broken finger?** The computer needs to understand concepts for this one.

- **Tell me about the last dream you had?** Tough for a computer to get this right.

- **What would it feel like to walk on the moon?** Let's explore emotions—do you have any? Or will you just give a scientific reply?

- **Will you make up a story about a parrot and a pair of sunglasses?** Good test of creative imagination, and the understanding of concepts here.

- **How would you pretend to be x [celebrity name]?** Relies on knowledge of world and culture.

Of course, the human must be old enough to answer these questions. I hate to think of some dystopian future where this test is administered automatically, and a toddler is deemed non-human because it has not yet mastered enough language to answer the questions. There's also the Voight-Kampff approach from the movie Blade Runner that we looked at in the Scenarios chapter, where you ask a series of questions about emotional situations and gauge the reaction. The big question underneath these sci-fi movies and serious academic tests is: *'What happens to society when computers get better than humans at passing the test?'* That may sound crazy, at first, but it's only a matter of time before this becomes true. In many areas of Artificial Intelligence, computers have surpassed human capabilities. Kasparov, the Chess World champion lost a six-game match to IBM Deep Blue computer in 1997—and when was the last time you were able to beat a chess computer at a game? I can't even beat my phone. IBM followed up this success by using a computer program to win on the quiz show *Jeopardy* in 2011.

In 2016, Lee Sedol who was the 18-times World Champion at the ancient strategy game of Go, lost to a Google-funded algorithm called AlphaGo. For many years, Go was an exclusively human realm because it has far more potential game combinations than chess, and was therefore considered much harder to solve. The next year, another version of the algorithm, called AlphaGoZero, beat the previous version by a score of 100-games to zero, having learnt to play the game in just 3 days, with no human guidance or database of previous games. It taught itself how to win using the basic rules, and by playing against itself many billions of times.

Recently, we've seen computers surpassing humans in many other fields too... which brings us back to the question, what happens when computers get better than humans at passing the Turing test? I'm reminded of the slogan for the Tyrell corporation in the Blade Runner movies, 'more human than human'. This is the ultimate goal of many AI software developers. Of course, the answer is that they've already succeeded. You're dealing with computers masquerading as humans all the time. Right now, we think we can tell the difference, but I wonder if we really can?

Every year, the Loebner Prize is held to find the most human-like computer program. The first contests, back in the 1990s, were based on the Turing test, but the rules have changed over the years. In 2013 and over the three years from 2016 to 2018, the winner has been 'Mitsuku' by Steve Worswick, who is an AI developer at a company called Pandorabots. Mitsuku is a chatbot—just like Siri from Apple, Alexa from Amazon, the Google Assistant, and Bixby from Samsung. A chatbot communicates via text or audio to conduct a conversation with a human user—typically to answer questions and help perform tasks. Chatbots are designed to imitate humans, and while they're not completely convincing, they're becoming more capable each year. Essentially, they are designed to pass the Turing test, so they can interact with you to make it feel that you're conversing with a human. While almost everyone understands Siri or Alexa are just software programs, and not real people, that doesn't stop us interacting with them and finding them useful/irritating (delete as appropriate). These chatbots are simply the best-known examples in a much larger commercial market. You may not have heard of Avivo, ChattyPeople, Imperson, OctaneAI, LivePerson, Nuance, MoneyBrain, inbenta, and the list goes on... yet these platforms are delivering chatbots that underpin the conversations you may hold with your bank, a ticket booking website, a car dealer, a retail outlet, an online health clinic, or the customer support service at any major firm.

There are malicious chatbots too—these may be talking to your children right now; pretending to be their friends to capture data, or perhaps talking to you to influence your political beliefs or steal your bank details. While the Loebner Prize is not taken entirely seriously by academia, firms like Pandorabots are commercialising their success with Mitsuko to make chatbots for commerce and have created over 300,000 so far. These chatbots have processed more than 60 billion messages—a great way of learning and improving. Chatbots are cheaper than humans to operate, they can function 24x7x365, and provide services and feedback to the companies that deploy them. Sometimes, they're linked to visually appealing avatars, which—apart from their physical perfection—look more real all the time. Most of the time though the chatbots work via messages, live chat, or email, where it's harder for us to discern who we're talking to. While I can generally tell that I'm dealing with a chatbot, there are times, these days, when I'm not so sure. Sometimes, they mis-spell their answers. Sometimes, they pass me over to their 'supervisor', and I think *now I'm talking with a human,* but maybe I've just been passed to a more sophisticated chatbot that runs with more processing power? If the chatbot can solve my issue, do I even care if it's a real person or not? That's a profound question, and one we should consider in more detail, as a society. We can't wait for machines to pass the Turing test before we consider the implications. They already have.

The apes

We are primates, and our family includes chimpanzees, gorillas, and orangutans, along with a host of different monkeys and pro-simians such as the ring-tailed lemur. There are different classification methods, but most experts agree there are more than two hundred living species of primate, and possibly over four hundred. Primates are all mammals that share characteristics such as flat nails, a fissure in the brain that splits it into two halves, specialised touch in our fingers (known as Meissner's corpuscles), which is particularly useful when living in trees. Contrary to popular belief, not all primates have opposable thumbs, although this is a trait shared by apes, humans, several monkey species and some lemurs, but also by other tree-dwelling creatures like squirrels. We have forward facing, overlapping fields of vision from our eyes—common to many predators. Our teeth are a little different as well, with low, rounded molars.

Anyone who has spent some time watching our closest relatives in the wild, or in some of the stunning natural history documentaries produced in recent years, will recognise many human-like capabilities, emotions, and other characteristics in primate life, especially among our most frequently studied siblings, chimpanzees and gorillas—and that is not to anthropomorphise. There are well-recorded instances of tool-use, sophisticated social displays and rituals, hierarchies with roles and responsibilities, traits and patterns of deceit and manipulation, plus co-ordinated activities such as food gathering or hunting. These are also clear signs of high-cognitive capacity. Some people have gone further with research on primates and looked in detail at the use of language.

One of the earliest and most famous experiments was Project Nim, which set out to disprove Noam Chomsky's theory that language is a uniquely human construct. A chimpanzee was raised in a human family and taught sign language. The chimp was named Neam Chimpsky (a pun) but was known as Nim. He acquired 125 signs for words such as eat, drink, hug, apple, banana, grape, nut, and so on. Nim could combine these into sentences such as 'banana me eat'. Many visitors to the facility were impressed with Nim's skills and his ability to communicate with his human handlers. The results were strongly criticised on many levels, however. There were concerns around the ethical implications of the approach, while fellow scientists attacked both the methodology and the results—some claiming that Nim was simply imitating, and never demonstrated any clear use of grammar, or therefore of language. The results are still in dispute, but Project Nim was not the first or last project to study animal use of language. While it can be expensive and time-consuming to mount these experiments, there have been several significant attempts, with some fascinating results.

Kanzi is a bonobo that has featured in a variety of academic papers on the use of language in great apes. He lives in Iowa, at the Ape Cognition and Conservation Initiative, and as I write this in 2019, he is 38-years-old. As an 8-year old, Kanzi performed a series of tests that were also given to a 2-year old human girl called Alia. Both the bonobo and the human were given more than six hundred spoken instructions, related to objects they were familiar with, and asked to perform tasks. Kanzi outperformed the human girl by nearly 10 percent, performing the correct actions in 74 percent of cases. He was taught a lexigram—basically a set of symbols—that he could use to communicate with, and a basic grammar. His handlers claim that he has a vocabulary of more than 3000 words that he comprehends. He has starred in TV documentaries and National Geographic articles, and is an accomplished user of tools. There is a famous incident where he signed the symbols for marshmallow and fire, and then proceeded to cook his own! It also appears that he actually vocalises some of the words, but given the difference in the physical structure of the voice box in bonobos and humans, we cannot interpret the results so well, although there is plenty of evidence to show that he is 'speaking' too.

Other field tests on different animals have shown they have the ability to vocalise different sounds to signal meanings; the alarm calls of vervet monkeys can distinguish between eagles, python, leopards, baboons and humans, and the monkeys even know if the individual giving the alarm is a reliable indicator of that type of danger. If a specific monkey is known to be a poor judge of eagles, his alarm call may be ignored, but if he has a good track record on jaguars, then the troop will pay attention when he emits that alarm. The monkeys are believed to know more than 30 different alarms and can recognise the cry of their own baby compared to the babies of others in the group.

What is emerging from these research projects is the fact that many primates can communicate; either through 'acquired' language, such as American Sign Language, or using natural vocalisation. Other experiments have demonstrated their ability to solve puzzles and problems by thinking, not just by trial and error. There is one critical area, though, where they seem to differ from humans. In all the work that has been performed so far in animal language research, it has been the humans that have asked the questions of the apes. For some reason, the reverse is not true. If you think of a small human child, they will ferociously ask questions: *Where's Mom?*

When's Dad coming home? What are we having for dinner? Can I have another chocolate biscuit? Why are dogs not stripy like a zebra? Yet none of the primates in the studies listed above have asked questions of their handlers, even though they potentially had the required grammatical structures. There are those who believe the ability to ask questions represents the threshold between humans and other primates. In his book *Who asked the first question?* Joseph Jordania looks at the origins of choral singing, rhythm, intelligence, language, and speech. Having reviewed the scientific literature for language studies on apes, he noted that while they can recognise themselves in mirrors and show some aspects of the *theory of mind* they "understand complex requests and questions but fail to ask questions." It was his view that this lack of questioning ability is "something connected with the evolutionary distinction between the cognitive capacities of apes and humans".

The study of apes in the wild has shown that they use vocalisations with a rising tone to express curiosity or to request location calls from other tribe members. They are not questions in the way we would see them, though. These calls could be a statement, or a demand for information. Sometimes, these are referred to as proto-questions, and may be a precursor to additional cognitive capabilities that would result in full question-asking abilities. Given the training that apes in captivity have undergone, and the strong abilities they have demonstrated in answering questions: how many, what colour, what material, etc, it seems strange that they do not ask questions in a rapid cascade, like a curious human toddler. We might conclude that there is some missing gene, which means they do not think in questions. Jordania raised a marvellous point in his book, when he said that given the ability of apes to answer questions, and our similarities, when the first hominid asked the first question, there were probably lots of hominids able to answer. All it took was one smart hominid to ask that first question, and knowledge would have flowed.

It is quite profound to think that the core difference marking out humans from our fellow primates may be the ability to ask questions. Whether this is due to the sheer scale of our cognitive abilities, or perhaps a gene or two that we carry, we do not yet know. That is something of a chicken and egg question. We'll keep asking questions to discover the truth on this topic though. We'll do this because asking questions is what makes us human.

Theory of mind

How do you know what someone else is thinking? How do you even know they *are* thinking? The theory of mind is something humans possess and allows us to infer that others have minds like our own by the way they act, use language, and display emotions. Since we cannot make a direct connection to a mind, we have no provable way of knowing if they are truly a thinking animal like ourselves. We can only understand our own mind via introspection. If we're capable of using a theory of mind that presupposes we can understand and observe a variety of mental states in others, as well as predicting behaviour, such as how a person might react because they appear angry. While humans clearly have a theory of mind, work has been ongoing to demonstrate which other animals can also interpret the mental state of others and can identify themselves as unique individuals. There has been a fair amount of research on the development of the theory of mind in children, and how this affects them as adults; along with cultural differences, and those differences caused by certain mental conditions like autism and schizophrenia. As the research stands today, there is strong evidence to show that both primates and certain categories of birds (such as ravens), have a theory of mind. It may be that an increasing number of animals will be added to this category.

Dolphins & aliens

There's a thought-provoking website called SpeakDolphin that has a mission to expand communication between dolphins and humans, or dauphins and cumins, as my text auto-corrector insisted—now that would be a weird conversation! SpeakDolphin has a list of the 20 questions that researchers would most like to ask cetaceans (these generally include porpoises and whales), once we establish a true method of communication. SpeakDolphin invites readers to send in questions and continually revises their list as they receive new ideas. This seems a fabulous idea, although the scientific smidgen of my brain looked at the questions and wondered how many would make sense to a dolphin. It seemed the questions would require knowledge of a human world perspective, such as 'Are there environmental changes of concern to cetaceans?'. Perhaps these questions would need to be rephrased to a dolphin frame of reference: 'Have you experienced any bad changes taking place in your world?' But that sounds like I'm talking down to the dolphin. I suspect our first questions would be to understand the dolphin's world-view, society, culture, and so forth. My favourite questions include:

- What are the most important things we can do to help you?
- What are the oldest stories or traditions from your society?
- Can you communicate with any other species?
- Do you believe in an afterlife?

Personally, I'd like to know more about whale songs. Are they used for pragmatic purposes, or is there art and pleasure involved? We know that whale songs are similar by region amongst a group of whales, and that songs evolve over time—sometimes slowly, but at other times surprisingly quickly. It would be interesting to ask why and how they change the songs, and who changes them. There's evidence to show that blue whales have adjusted their tunes to compensate for noise pollution. Human-generated noise pollution, such as that from increased shipping traffic, may be having an adverse effect on the cetacean's ability to communicate. In particular, the human hubbub has reduced the range through which messages may be transmitted without interference. It would be great to ask the whales about this, although I suspect many commercial and governmental organisations would not be keen to hear the answers. It might also be interesting to gain insights on their view of us, and on whale-hunting. If we could talk to cows or sheep, I suspect we'd get a string of profanities thrown at us—given our exploitation of their species for food over thousands of years.

As I look at these questions, it leads me to wonder, what about aliens? After finding SpeakDolphin, I found similar lists to help us communicate with extra-terrestrial life. There are plenty of sites on this topic, many with reader-compiled questions and they make for frightening consumption. Here's a variety of typical questions contributed by random people, on what they would say when first encountering an alien:

- Why did you pick me?
- Will I remember this conversation tomorrow?
- Is the Bible true?
- Can I be your friend?
- Do you have any cool technology you could lend me?
- Can you grant me any superpowers?

- Do you have marriage on your planet?
- What took you so long to get here?
- Did you crash land in Roswell?
- Are there alien ghosts?

I hope that aliens landing on Planet Earth don't randomly talk to earthlings because they'd get a very weird idea of life here. I hope they meet a real-life equivalent of Amy Adams, who starred in the 2016 movie *Arrival*. She had empathy and knowledge of linguistics, and used these assets to great effect in this movie about first contact with aliens. I'd like to think the movie prompted the summer of 2018 workshop amongst academics to discuss how to communicate with aliens, hosted at the US National Space Society in Los Angeles, by METI (Messaging Extra-Terrestrial Intelligence, a privately funded group that is complimentary to the SETI group that searches for alien life). METI is less concerned with the actual questions to ask and looks instead at how to establish a framework for communication. Topics covered at the workshop were universal grammar, communal morality, and spirituality for non-human intelligence, interstellar misunderstandings, and the drake equation, used to estimate the number of active extra-terrestrial civilisations in the Milky Way. The generally perceived view is that for aliens to travel to Earth they must have a high level of technology, and therefore advanced maths and science—which is why it is believed that maths will be the first mode of communication.

Only so much can be accomplished with numbers, however; we'd need language for a deeper understanding of an alien species. The workshop explored some of the key debates about the nature of language, and the two main theories involved. There are those that follow Noam Chomsky's philosophy, and believe that language is an innate capability, and that two civilisations should be able to communicate. Just as 'eyes' have evolved in different animals, so language may have formed. While the language itself will not be the same, the constructs should be familiar enough that we could, over time, learn to communicate. There's another group, though, that believe language is formed by characteristics such as body shape and environment. An alien life-form not made from carbon, accustomed to extreme temperatures and perhaps more like a gas in nature, may have a very different 'language'—perhaps more akin to the flashing colours and symbols that an octopus might make. The perceived wisdom is that an extra-terrestrial that was different in form would be much harder to communicate with. It could be like speaking to a dolphin or an ant.

The workshop also reviewed the messages we send to aliens. Right now, amateurs are sending messages into space, and nobody is logging or managing that communication. If anyone answers, we won't necessarily know what people have told them, and the answer itself may be kept private by whoever receives it. In 2008, the tortilla chips maker Doritos, sent a 30-second advert into space. You'd think this would be very puzzling for any alien recipients, but perhaps no worse than the 100,000 classified ads sent into space by Craigslist. According to one view, sending messages into space is both foolhardy and dangerous. Any civilisation advanced enough to pick up the messages and visit us will be significantly more advanced than us and could take advantage of our planet and of us. Humanity's record of colonisation does not make for pleasant reading. Slavery? Mass genocide from disease or advanced technology? Extraction of goods to export back to the homeland? Devastation of local culture, of religious, and historical sites? Our record is not impressive. There are other groups, though, with a more optimistic view. METI has published a series of goals in its strategic plan, and one of its key objectives is to establish METI as the world leader in interstellar message design. The design would involve the formation of a common language and incorporate many items, including, intriguingly, the goal to 'Introduce Humanity'— which begs the question: *What would an extra-terrestrial want to know about us?*

I'll leave you to ponder that, and we'll return to aliens after reviewing the cognitive capabilities of another smart species: birds.

Singers, talkers & expert tool-users

We've determined that humans seem to be unique amongst primates in asking questions. That statement makes me nervous, as we've been very good at placing ourselves in the centre of the universe many times before, only to learn that we're not quite as special as we thought. What about other creatures, like birds? Great vocalisers and singers, birds can be incredibly social—rookeries exist with thousands of birds; and seabirds like penguins and puffins also live in large communal groups. Birds can cooperate in breeding, hunting, and in avoiding predators. Let's look at ducks, which don't have a common reputation for being the smartest of birds. Ducks will sometimes sit in a circle with young birds in the middle. Each duck in the defensive ring will open a single eye—the one facing out —while the other half of its brain 'sleeps'. Dolphins also possess the capability for this uni-hemispherical type of brain sleep, which allows them to rest while still moving through the ocean with the rest of their pod. Could you sleep with one eye open and half of your brain resting? That's not the only visual trick that ducks have. Their 340-degree field of (colour) vision enables them to see both near and far simultaneously. Good thing they have three eyelids, to protect those precious eyes. Ducks live on every continent apart from Antarctica, and they're born with their eyes open. They usually learn to fly within two months of hatching. Pretty impressive stuff.

We also know that some birds use tools to crack open seashells, clean social display areas, build nests or catch larvae, and have shown advanced cognitive capabilities. The talents of corvids such as crows, ravens, and magpies have been the subject of a decent amount of research, and corvids have shown remarkable feats of intelligence that demonstrate beyond doubt that they possess a theory of mind. Tests where crows have had a selection of items to drop into a tube of water to get a treat to float to the top have shown their understanding of the displacement of water, and which sized rocks will work, as well as which will jam the tubes. Other tests have shown how crows can reason cause and effect, and how they may even hold grudges against certain people. What's even more remarkable is that they can inform other crows about the grudge. Researchers that tag crows or ravens have learnt to wear masks; otherwise they get hassled by the birds wherever they go, and the number of birds that recognise them increases over time—showing a remarkable act of communication. There are also known cases of birds holding funeral-like gatherings, or even court-like trials. Nobody has been able to fully interpret this behaviour. Additionally, corvids are known to hide food, but if they realise they've been spotted, they continue with the process and return later when they're not being observed, and move the food to a different cache—amazing, right?

For anyone still not convinced about the remarkable intelligence of these birds, I would recommend they read the incredible *Corvus* by Esther Woolfson. Part memoir and part natural history study, the book is about living with a rook named Chicken, alongside various other birds, and eruditely reveals many of the birds' abilities. One anecdote is about a magpie that Esther rescued when it fell out of the nest. She and her daughter named the bird Spike. He ran, jumped, and rolled about her house, before eventually learning to fly. Even after this he would still hop up the stairs, before gliding back down. He was amiable, bright, vigorous and enquiring. The goal was to keep him only long enough to allow his full flight feathers to grow. Any longer, and he would become too adapted to life with humans and wouldn't survive in the wild. One evening, Esther and her daughter were in the kitchen discussing when to take Spike to their friend Kevin, who had a place that acted as a halfway house between domestic and wild, where Spike could learn what he needed before being released. Spike stood on the ears of a wooden rabbit on the mantelpiece; apparently listening to the conversation. Then, as Esther reports it:

"Hello", he said very suddenly, loudly, and with astonishing clarity. Esther and her daughter stared and gasped. Then, even louder: "Spike!" He was pleased with his effort. "Spike, Spikey. Hello! Spikey? SPIKE!" His voice was a voice so human as to be shocking.

It was too late to send him to the wild. He would remain with the family. Esther's book is full of amazing examples of the intelligence of birds, with speech (or mimicry) being just one example. I notice that in her text above, one of the repetitions of his name includes a question mark. While he probably wasn't asking a question, he was certainly repeating a sound he had heard, using a rising tone.

We haven't even got started on the astonishing feats of navigation and migration that many birds perform. *Jurassic Park* fans will also be aware that birds are the direct descendent of dinosaurs. This is all very impressive, but to return to our core topic—given their clear intelligence, theory of mind, and ability to vocalise human words, can birds ask questions?

In the early 1970s, Irene Pepperberg bought a one-year-old grey parrot she named Alex (for the Avian Learning Experiment). She had recently completed a doctoral thesis in theoretical chemistry at Harvard University, and had seen a TV program about the use of language by chimps (Project

Nim). Pepperberg also knew of similar studies on dolphins, as well as research on why birds sing. Intrigued, she switched fields and over the course of the following thirty years, she worked with Alex to accomplish many remarkable results in animal communication and learning. To briefly summarise, by the time of his death in 2007, Alex could identify more than 50 objects, 7 colours, 5 shapes, and quantities from 0–6, along with the concepts of bigger and smaller, similarity/difference, categories, and the absence of something. He could use phrases like 'I want x' and 'Wanna go y', adding the object or place he desired. When given the object or taken to the place he'd specified, Alex would show pleasure or frustration, depending on whether or not his demands had been met. He demonstrated other emotions, showing surprise when he received an object different from the one he was expecting, for example. Alex was able to identify an object's colour, shape, and material, as well as its name. All these achievements are remarkable, especially given that parrots in particular were considered to be only mimics. In previous animal/human tests, such as Project Nim, the handlers were sometimes accused of producing a modern variant of the Clever Hans trick of the early twentieth century. Clever Hans was a German horse that appeared to be able to tap out the answers to arithmetic puzzles, but it was proven that the horse picked up on involuntary body language clues from his handler, who solved the simple puzzles himself and inadvertently signalled to the horse when to cease tapping his hoof. The handler was not aware this was the case, and the accusation in Project Nim and other such projects was that the handlers' examples, were also somehow indicating to the animal the answer they required. In the case of Alex, the test results were reproduced using a variety of handlers, and even strangers. While the conditions did not entirely satisfy those who believe that Alex was following operational conditioning (which is what academics label the Clever Hans phenomenon), it did satisfy most people. The results have been filmed and recorded for numerous TV programs and magazines, with Alex becoming something of a celebrity, appearing on the BBC, PBS, Discovery Channel, and in *USA Today, the Wall Street Journal,* and the *New York Times.*

Alex's biggest achievement, however, was to be the first recorded non-human *to ask a question.* He was looking at a reflection of himself in a mirror and asked, "What colour?". He was told "grey". We may assume he was looking at himself (a grey parrot), but it's possible he was referring to the mirror itself. This was not the only question Alex asked. For the first time, we have evidence of another creature asking questions. Interestingly, Irene Pepperberg never classified Alex as having the ability to use language, she described his talent as interspecies communication. African grey parrots can live to 80-years-old in the wild, but very sadly, Alex died unexpectedly at the age of 31. His last words to Irene were the same that he said to her every night as she left the lab: "I love you". Irene continues to work on avian intelligence, and in 2018 published some studies on her African Grey parrot called Griffin, who can draw conclusions based on repeated experiences, and understand probabilities. Given that the latest research has shown how many birds have the same number of neurons as primates, an interesting picture of avian intelligence is beginning to emerge. Perhaps we shouldn't be surprised if they're the first creature to ask more questions of us, and possibly of each other.

Take me to your leader

Earlier in this chapter we raised the question 'What would an extra-terrestrial want to know about us?' First, we should determine who they have come to speak to, so that when they make the infamous 'Take me to your leader' proclamation, we know what to do. I'm not asking whether they should meet the king or queen, the president of the USA, of China, or the Russian president, perhaps—who actually is the world leader? My question is more fundamental. If our planet were measured with super-advanced alien sensors, a bit like the scanning devices that Dr Spock would peer into during Star Trek, then aliens would not necessarily conclude that humans were the dominant species. Of course, there are different ways of counting, and with our poor-quality systems, we're not always very good at adding up the numbers. We tend to over-estimate our species' importance to the planet. Thanks to the kind people at Wikipedia who put together a few tables, I can tell you that:

**Most numerous creatures,
in descending order:**
- Prokaryotes (bacteria) 1×10^{31}
- Ants 1×10^{16}
- Antarctic Krill 7.8×10^{14}
- Chickens 2.4×10^{10}
- Humans 7.7×10^{9}

That's not to say we're the fifth most numerous creatures, as the numbers were shown for comparison. We're outnumbered by fish, many insects, rats, spiders, probably crabs, and many more. There was a well-publicised, rather gruesome academic paper produced in 2017 by Martin Nyffeler and Klaus Birkhofer that estimated the biomass of prey killed by spiders on an annual basis. It concluded that if they switched their diet to humans, they could eat the entire human race in one year and still be hungry! To be fair on the scientists, what they actually reported was that the total biomass (the combined weight of all creatures) consumed by spiders per year was estimated to be between 395–805 million tonnes, while the total human biomass was 290–350 million tonnes, although there was no indication of a sudden switch in diet for the arachnid predators—so there's no need to have nightmares about the coming spider apocalypse.

Instead of counting the number of individual entities, let's look at a different measure. Perhaps exploring biomass would be more in our favour, since we're bigger than ants. We'll cheat a little, by removing the plant statistics—since on land they outnumber all the animals, including us, by a factor of 1,000. Fungi alone are estimated to make up a quarter of the entire biomass of the planet, but we don't want our extra-terrestrial visitors talking to mushrooms, so let's focus on animal species—surely we come out on top here, right? Oh, we'd better exclude bacteria too, since they have a biomass nearly equal to the plants.

Largest animal species biomass on earth, in descending order:

• Plankton	1–2 billion tonnes
• Earthworms	7,000 million tonnes
• Fish	1,500 million tonnes
• Antarctic krill	379 million tonnes
• Domesticated cattle	520 million tonnes
• Termites	445 million tonnes

- Humans   350 million tonnes
- Sheep & goats   105 million tonnes
- Chickens   48 million tonnes

We come a long way down this list too, beaten by the humble earthworm and our own domesticated cattle. Of course, these numbers are estimates, but to an extra-terrestrial, it may not be as obvious as it seems to us that we're the primary 'owners' of this blue and green rock. How about intelligence, I hear you say. What if we ranked the creatures by intelligence, surely any alien would want to talk with *intelligent* life? Well, intelligence has always been rather hard to measure—is the IQ test really an accurate method? Anyone who has performed an IQ test in a different country will have noticed the cultural bias. Plus, we can't ask other primates, or even smart corvids or parrots to complete a human designed intelligence test. Let's focus on numbers—since maths is the universal language of the galaxy—and compare brain sizes, instead.

**Largest brains by mass,
in descending order:**
- Sperm whale   8kg
- Killer whale   6kg
- Elephant   5kg
- Bottlenose dolphin   1.6kg
- Human   1.3kg

This isn't looking good, for humans. What's more, there are some animals with multiple brains; an octopus has a central brain and then additional ganglia in each of its eight legs—essentially nine brains! The leech has 32. I've heard though, that it's the ratio of brain to body weight that's critical for intelligence. Let's see where humans rate on this list:

**Brain to body weight ratio,
in descending order:**
- Ants   1:7
- Shrew   1: 10
- Small birds: 1:12
- Humans   1:40
- Dolphin: 1:50
- Elephants   1:560

Yet again, humans don't score well. A cursory glance shows that the brain-to-body ratio may not be a useful metric since some heavy animals, such as elephants, clearly demonstrate intelligence, while a shrew is not necessarily the smartest creature but happens to be small and light. In practice, a more frequent measure used is the Encephalization Quotient (or EQ, but not to be confused with Emotional Quotient). This considers other factors in addition to the body-to-weight ratio. On this list, humans come out on top, ahead of dolphins, chimps, elephants, and dogs (who beat cats and squirrels, but narrowly lose out to chinchillas). I can't help but feel this is an artificial list skewed in our favour, though. Finally, let's look at neurons:

**Neuron count,
in descending order**
- African elephants   257 billion
- Humans   86 billion
- Gorillas   33.4 billion

Some work has been done on measuring the cerebral cortex—or the pallium, which performs a similar function in reptiles and birds—as a critical area for intelligence. Even here, with 16 billion neurons, we lose out to the long-finned pilot whale, which has more than double our number. However you look at it, humans may not be the group that an extra-terrestrial visitor approaches first to inquire about life on our planet. We may take solace in being the only species that could potentially ask them a question in return—except perhaps for a clever grey parrot! If there is one other area where we may stand out to an alien species, it would be our use of technology. Perhaps more than any other denizen of our planet, we've mastered advanced tools to help us survive and thrive.

Machines

We've looked at machines asking questions while pretending to be humans, but what type of questions do machines ask other machines? This question may not be as daft as it sounds. We're already in the age of IoT (the Internet of Things). This technology term—that has now become mainstream —refers to the billions of devices connected to the internet, and to each other. People naturally think of smartphones, but there are a plethora of devices and sensors that form IoT, such as drill bits, shipping containers, forklift trucks, cars, wind turbines, submersible pumps, jet engines, tractors, trains, and almost every piece of industrial equipment you can imagine. The benefits of machines talking to other machines can be huge. They could for example, predict and diagnose faults between themselves—if a jet engine has a peculiar vibration, it could ask other engines if they've experienced the same issue. A group of engines might link the problem with flights from Abu Dhabi when there was a significant quantity of sand in the air. Alternatively, a group of wind turbines across a large wind farm can let each other know about the quality of wind, so those further back can adjust their speed or rotor angle. With the advent of new technologies like blockchain—made famous by Bitcoin—machines can perform secure transactions between each other, using smart contracts. A shipping container might request to be moved from a port terminal yard to a waiting train as a priority, for example; and could pay a premium to the autonomous forklift truck that takes it. These, and many other actions in different scenarios, are already being deployed. The age of machine-to-machine communication has been with us for some time and continues to grow.

The earliest commercial success stories of machine-to-machine systems (M2M) were in telecommunications. In the 1940s, AT&T was using Automatic Number Identification to work out the origin of a telephone call, so it could calculate the correct charges without involving a call operator. M2M technology then took a huge step forward with the advent of cellular communications, which allowed machines to begin connecting to telecom networks, and each other. In recent years, M2M has been deployed to show commuters the arrival time of the next bus (via a sign at the bus shelter, or on a mobile phone app), to automatically read the electricity meter in your house, or to display adverts relevant to a passenger in a car passing a billboard. The applications are everywhere, ubiquitous. For machines to be able to communicate though, they need:

- A standard **communication protocol** such as Wi-Fi, TCP/IP, HTTP, and so on. In fact, most systems use a suite of protocols that are layered on top of each other.

- The ability to **trust** each other. That sounds very 'touchy-feely', more human than something you expect calculating hardware to need. It is critically important, though, as we'll see in a moment.

- Finally, machines need standard ways of **asking questions**. There are several specific computer languages and tools that have been built to serve this purpose.

Before we consider M2M questions, we need to look at that matter of trust. In 2009, the Natanz uranium enrichment facility in Iran was hacked with a software virus called Stuxnet. The virus hijacked the nuclear plant's control system, instructing the centrifuges to spin so fast that they broke, while at the same time sending false signals back to suggest that everything was working normally. The damage was so severe that the plant was temporarily closed, and many of the centrifuges had to be replaced. One interesting aspect of the attack was that the plant was not connected to the Internet. It was defended by what industry insiders call an 'air-gap'. That means the systems are physically isolated, so they're not connected to the outside world. Unfortunately, that doesn't stop people gaining access, or plugging in USB drives, etc. Sometimes, the air-gap breeds a complacency about security that can be dangerous. In the Natanz case, the virus was introduced to other computers in Iran, and gradually passed from system to system, but only activated when it found the exact configuration of systems present in the power station. This probably means it was deliberately built to target Natanz. Who built it? Nobody knows, although the intelligence services of several countries have been suggested.

Since the Stuxnet attack on Iran, the number of industrial attacks has continued to grow. In 2014, a German steel mill suffered severe physical damage from a cyber-attack, and a similar software virus has been found in Japan's Monju nuclear power plant, in a South Korean Hydro and Nuclear Power station, and in a German power plant. America has not been immune to such attacks either. The Davis-Besse nuclear power plant in Ohio was infected with the Slammer virus within 10 minutes of its release in 2003. Incidentally, a cybersecurity expert at a global oil and gas company told me they'd discovered how an exploratory rig had been drilling at the wrong location for several months because the GPS data had been hacked, and they were told it was at a different location.

Trust is clearly a big issue in M2M communication and collaboration, especially as machines become more intricately involved in our lives. What if the machine in question was a pacemaker that was infected with a virus that caused it to stop? Or if the braking system on your car was told not to activate? I hate to say this, but both situations have already been demonstrated. So far as we know, nobody has been targeted or suffered from such a hack, but the ability to successfully accomplish these feats has been proven.

When it comes to questions, providing there's a network and appropriate levels of trust, devices can send each other messages, asking for specific data. At the moment, machines have the same limitations that we saw in animals. They're great at answering questions or providing insights that help us to answer questions, but they don't ask questions of each other or us that haven't been programmed into the system. When you call someone's smartphone, the M2M communication between your two cellular devices will show you the name of the person (unless they have a privacy option switched on), but your phone will not spontaneously ask the other phone how much battery life it has left. Perhaps it should, so you can be notified if this call needs to be short because the other person's phone is about to die. It can be programmed to ask this question, but no machine will spontaneously come up with this idea. There are, however, people working on ways to help computers achieve this. Not to fool humans in Turing-based tests, but to add value by doing tasks like generating English comprehension questions based on a passage of a novel for a school exam, or more advanced work such as finding causal factors for a specific disease. The goal is to have machines ask questions so they can learn independently and share their discoveries with us.

I read a well-written, if unnerving book, called *Superintelligence* by Nick Hostrum. His thesis is that as machines gain further intelligence, they won't stop at

'Humanville' but will swoosh right past to become far more intelligent. When we think in terms of 'smart' or 'stupid,' our frame of reference is other humans. The author suggests that an Artificial Intelligence machine would have significantly greater cognitive capabilities and be "smart in the sense that an average human is smart compared to a beetle or a worm". He points out that a genuinely intelligent computer has several advantages over a human brain: much higher (almost unlimited) storage capacity, and the ability to operate at a speed at least ten thousand times faster than a biological equivalent, allowing it to read a book in a few seconds. If the system were running a million times faster than a biological brain, it could accomplish 1000 years of intellectual work in one working day. It would never forget anything it learnt and potentially, could have access to billions of data feeds showing everything from weather to the locations of certain people, health records, stock values, crop data, and much more. An artificial mind of this type would not have the same values as ourselves, unless we programmed them in, and even then, as a learning system it could change its values. Nick looked at how a system like this could emerge. He points out there are multiple ways such a system could be built, such as by a brain emulation or a community of software agents, and that researchers are currently pursuing all avenues. Whichever route is successful, if learning is present, the system will ultimately enter a period of strong recursive growth. Superintelligence could gradually evolve over a period of years or materialise almost instantly—from our perspective. As Nick says, "if and when a take-off occurs, it will likely be explosive". He reviews the various strategies that humans could take to restrict or control this take-off, and then debunks each of them. In simple terms, when a computer system arrives that is superintelligent, it will out-think or socially engineer us to remove any obstacles we have placed in its way to restrict its growth.

Interestingly, Nick does not predict a terminator-style armageddon where the machines try to eradicate us. As he says, we haven't tried to eliminate ants. More likely, we'd suffer as the system changes the environment to support itself. It might, for example, decide to replace millions of wheat field acres with solar panels, to give itself more energy. There are some fabulous questions in the book about what we want from superintelligence—how do we avoid catastrophe, and should we hand over the reins to a paternalistic supercomputer? As Nick says, "The point of superintelligence is not to pander to human preconceptions but to make mincemeat out of our ignorance and folly."

Dogs & bees

When I talk to strangers about animals and questions, most dog owners smile and tell me their pet asks questions all the time. Things like:

Where's my dinner?
Are we going for a walk now?
What was that noise?

As a dog owner, I completely understand this. This is clearly a form of communication, a demand for action, but it's very different from a dog asking which route you might go on for a walk tomorrow. It may, however, be the first step in questioning, the proto-question as it has been called.

There's a wonderful story in *The Lucifer Principle* by Howard Bloom, which looks at the behaviour of a colony of bees (from original research by Thomas D. Seeley in his 1985 book *Honeybee Ecology*):

"In one experiment, scientists began by placing a dish of sugar water at the edge of a hive. Over the course of time, they moved the water, first a few inches from the hive, then a few feet, then a few feet more—always increasing the distance by a precise increment. The researchers expected that the bees would follow the dish and cluster around it. To their surprise, after a few days, the insects were doing far more than merely tagging along after the moving sugar water. The bees would fly from a hive and cluster on a spot where the dish had *not* been placed—the site where the insects *anticipated* the dish would be put next—and their calculations were right on target."

The bees were solving a mathematical puzzle to make successful predictions on where to find the food the next day. I think we could argue that the bees were asking the question: 'Where is the best place to search for food tomorrow?' Some may argue with that interpretation, and say that we're being too anthropomorphic, giving the bees too much in the way of human identity and human thought processes. That may be true, because it was the colony as a whole, and not the individual bees, that were 'asking' the question. Nevertheless, in whatever terms we phrase it, a decision was made on where the bees would go to explore in the morning, and it suggests the colony—if not a specific insect—is considering how to best use its resources, which is undoubtedly the answer to a form of question.

In the award-winning novel *Children of Time* by Adrian Tchaikovsky, a colony of ants—admittedly with a few genetic tweaks—begin to solve a series of mathematical problems transmitted to their planet, even though the ants don't really understand the problems. Essentially, they act as a neural net, capable of solving problems in the way that a modern computer might, but without necessarily having any sense of self-awareness. The spiders on the same planet, with similar genetic advantages, are more thoughtful and question what the messages from space mean, why they're being sent, and by whom. When we consider the approach of the ants and the spiders in this novel, there's a clear difference in the levels of cognition and consciousness, and the type and quality of questions the insects ask about the world.

There has been academic research into human levels of consciousness, and into the theory of mind for other animals. In medical training, human consciousness is related to the ability for a person to respond to stimuli, and they might record multiple LOC (levels of consciousness—medical

275

practitioners love acronyms) that fit between the basic 'conscious' and 'unconscious':

- confused
- delirious
- lethargic
- obtundation (I had to look that up: according to Wikipedia it means "less than full alertness, typically as a result of a medical condition or trauma. It can appear in hypercalcaemic crisis. The root word, obtund, means 'dulled or less sharp' cf. obtuse angle.")
- stuporous
- comatose

Even then, there are sub-classifications. The Grady Coma Scale breaks the coma down into five levels:

Grade	State of awareness	Calling name	Light pain	Deep pain
I	Confused, drowsy, lethargic, indifferent and/or uncooperative; does not lapse into sleep when left undisturbed	Yes	Yes	Yes
II	Stuporous; may be disoriented to time, place, and person; will lapse into sleep when not disturbed; or belligerent and uncooperative	No	Yes	Yes
III	Deep stupor; requires strong pain to evoke movement	No	No	Yes
IV	Exhibits decorticate or decerebrate posturing to a deep pain stimulus	No	No	No
V	Does not respond to any stimuli; flaccid	No	No	No

Incidentally, sleep is considered a conscious state, in case you were wondering.

Similar work has been done to classify states in animals. It's generally accepted amongst the scientific community that animals possess consciousness, although it may not be the same as ours. In 2012, a group of neuroscientists at a conference held at the University of Cambridge put forward a Declaration on Consciousness:

"Convergent evidence indicates that non-human animals have the neuroanatomical, neurochemical, and neurophysiological substrates of conscious states along with the capacity to exhibit intentional behaviors. Consequently, the weight of evidence indicates that humans are not unique in possessing the neurological substrates that generate consciousness. Non-human animals, including all mammals and birds, and many other creatures, including octopuses, also possess these neurological substrates."

As work on animal cognitive behaviour continues, and the research deepens, it seems likely that we'll discover multiple states and levels of consciousness for many creatures—and the ability to ask questions could be mapped on a similar scale, with 'proto-questions' asked by dogs, and examples of the bee hive communal calculations, placed on a sliding scale as our understanding of questions becomes more nuanced. Our primary obstacle in determining animals' ability to communicate may often be our own blinkered views, in fact. For example, one of the standard tests of self-awareness is a 'mirror test' where a creature sees itself reflected, and then has some mark secretly put on it overnight. If the animal inspects or grooms the mark after looking at the reflection, this is taken as a sign of self-awareness—and several animals, such as apes, have passed this test. Some animals such as dogs are less visual though, and rely on other senses, such as smell.

Given how much stronger their abilities are in this area compared to humans shows that we may sometimes be using the wrong tests to identify self-awareness. Just because an animal can't ask a question in the same way as us, may not imply they are not capable of questioning.

I spoke to a schoolteacher who told me that in the youngest years, the children in her class rarely asked questions. If they had a fireman talk to them, and the teacher asked for questions, the kids would make statements:

"My Dad's a fireman."
"We have a fire station near our house."

Yet within another year they start to ask:

"Are those boots heavy?"
or "Have you rescued anybody?"

In the chapter on Professions we'll look at the age at which children begin to ask questions, and how that capability develops over time. As a species, we have developed the capacity to ask questions. As other animal species evolve, we may see them start to ask questions, especially if we can find better ways to communicate with them in their own paradigm.

9. TECHNOLOGY

The real question is not whether machines think,
but whether men do.

B.F. Skinner

Computers are better at answering some questions

Here's a question for you—a little mental maths (no calculators allowed):

What's 97,406,784 divided by 123,456?

The answer, as any computer could tell you, is 789. That was an easy problem, using only integers. If you managed to calculate the answer by hand, my estimate is that it took you a minimum of 10 seconds (it took me a lot longer). My computer made the calculation in one or two cycles at most, and since it has a 3.1 Gigahertz CPU, it performed the calculation in 1 or 2 / 3,100,000,000 of a second. If I needed to recruit someone to do maths calculations for me, one of you, made from silicon, would be doing much better at the interview than the other. You might argue that humans aren't very good at these types of questions, and that I was biased towards the machine (is human discrimination a thing yet in job interviews?). You might have a point. There are tasks where computers and robots have proven to be superior to humans. A list of these might include maths calculations, the next move to make in a game of chess, or repetitive jobs like attaching a bolt, spray-painting a car, or planting seed plugs in pots.

There are other tasks where you might believe that humans are better than computers—like visual recognition, working out whether a photo is of a Chihuahua or a muffin, or seeing the difference between a mop and an Old English sheepdog. However, in the past couple of years AI algorithms have proven to be more accurate than humans at these visual recognition tasks. Here's what Ophir Tanz wrote, summarising the latest scenario in *Entrepreneur* magazine in 2017:

"At the 2014 ImageNet Large Scale Visual Recognition Challenge (ILSVRC) in 2014, Google came in first place with a convolutional neural network approach that resulted in just a 6.6 percent error rate, almost half the previous year's rate of 11.7 percent. The accomplishment was not simply correctly identifying images containing dogs, but correctly identifying around 200 different dog breeds in images, something that only the most computer-savvy canine experts might be able to accomplish in a speedy fashion. Once again, Karpathy, a dedicated human labeler who trained on 500 images and identified 1,500 images, beat the computer with a 5.1 percent error rate.

This record lasted until February 2015, when Microsoft announced it had beaten the human record with a 4.94 percent error rate. And then just a few months later, in December, Microsoft beat its own record with a 3.5 percent classification error rate at the most recent ImageNet challenge."

Similar results are appearing repeatedly for a range of visual tasks: identifying and classifying images from YouTube videos or hand-drawn sketches, for example. Computers are rapidly getting better than humans at answering these types of questions. There are still some problem areas, such as partial images—a tiger's paw, for example—or where context needs to be understood, such as someone wearing a goat or devil mask, where humans can better identify the image, but this category is shrinking. The same is true for audio recognition. Do you think you can tell the difference between the calls of 50 different male sperm whales communicating across the Atlantic? A trained computer can. In fact, it turns out that humans aren't very good at audio tasks. A study by Carolyn McGettigan and Nadine Lavane, published in the *Journal of Experimental Psychology*, showed how challenging it can be for listeners—even those familiar with the target—to identify a specific person, because of the variability of the sounds we make, including laughter, serious tones, whispers, talking in fake accents, and so on. Listeners were given a pair of sounds, such as two vowels, or two recordings of laughter, and asked if they were made by the same person, but didn't need to identify the actual individual. The results for this first phase of the test had a high success rate, but when the sounds were mixed—so a listener might have to identify if a laugh and a vowel came from the same person—then the results were a lot less impressive. Writing about their work in *The Conversation*, the authors noted that other studies had identified how difficult it was to identify a bilingual speaker across their two languages. Although human voices are unique, we're not very skilled at identifying them. Ear-witness evidence in a court of law must be treated with great care, as the reliability is variable. Computers, though, are becoming uncannily accurate in this sphere.

Next on the list is olfactory powers. Yes, we all know that dogs are much better at this than humans. A human has about 6 million olfactory receptors in the nose, compared to 300 million for the average dog; and the area of the brain that processes smell is about 40 times larger in a dog, too. This explains why trained dogs can detect faint traces of explosives at airports or locate a disease like prostate cancer from urine samples. Did you know that trained dogs can also detect skin, breast, lung, colorectal, and ovarian cancer? They can tell the time of day by smell and predict diabetic episodes several hours in advance. The quest for computer scientists then, is not to beat humans at smell, but to surpass the dogs' capabilities. Deep in the research labs of many AI centres, teams are trying to crack the secrets of olfaction—about which we know far less than light or sound. Late in 2019 Google announced a research project using a specialised form of AI called a Graph Neural Network (or GNN) that is being used to predict what something may smell like based on the molecules that make up its chemical structure. They're trying to produce a 'colour-wheel for smells'. There are still plenty of challenges—and the dogs will stay ahead for a while yet because we're late to the smelling-party—but it's probably only a matter of time before working dogs are phased out of their sniffing-roles.

What *are* humans better at? Certain tasks are still more easily performed by people—highly dextrous work or large-scale creative items like writing a novel or composing music, although computers have been trying their hand at both of those endeavours. There's a scene in the movie version of Isaac Asimov's book *I, Robot* that expresses the conflict we have over the differences between men and machines. The policeman (played by Will Smith) is interrogating a robot that's believed to have committed a murder, even though robots are theoretically incapable of harming a human. Trying to get a reaction from the robot, the policeman notes the machine's lack of human abilities:

"Can a robot write a symphony? Can a robot turn a canvas into a beautiful masterpiece?"

"Can you?" the robot asks him.

The policeman doesn't answer the question. Later, the robot is asked to describe a scene. Instead, he makes a drawing at lightning speed, using both hands simultaneously, producing a fantastic picture. We realise that the robot has better skills and potentially more talents than the human.

As the range of tasks that computers can achieve grows,

the number of people with 'special' abilities that computers struggle to replicate will shrink. Some worrying reports have been published by governments on which jobs computers will replace, and by which time. The AI experts agree this is coming but liken it to the transformation that took place during the industrial revolution. Many traditional jobs (largely agricultural) were eliminated, but new roles appeared that we hadn't anticipated before. The hope is that the same will apply to the AI revolution.

Today, while computers get better at answering questions, we should remember that we do have something that's unique—the ability to ask good questions. This is something we seem uniquely adapted to do well, and that may keep us employed for a time, perhaps even longer than our dogs!

Search engines:
what do we ask?

In the past, many of us would have gone to friends, family, or colleagues for information, and to help us answer questions. These days, we turn to technology. Despite competition from Bing, Baidu, Yahoo, and others, Google remains the predominant search platform on the Internet, with more than 74 percent of the market (according to Net Market Share statistics). Just under half of the global population has access to the Internet, and this figure continues to grow. More than 3.5 billion searches are performed on Google every day, which results in a staggering 1.2 trillion searches per year. By the time you read this, these numbers will probably have increased significantly. You can find the latest statistics by searching the internet yourself. Most of the searches are performed on mobile devices (compared to just 0.7 percent a decade ago). This makes Google the biggest global centre that people go to for finding answers to their questions. At the same time, Google is a machine that produces a huge revenue that's based on advertising. Each year, Google publishes a summary of the major searches performed on their site. Here's a sample:

2018 Global Searches
1. World Cup
2. Avicii
3. Mac Miller
4. Stan Lee
5. Black Panther

2017 Global Searches
1. Hurricane Irma
2. iPhone 8
3. iPhone X
4. Matt Lauer
5. Meghan Markle

Google also break down the results into subcategories, so you can see the most searches for People, Songs, Movies, TV Shows, Memes, News, Actors, and so on. They also allow you to view the results by country. In 2017, they included a question specific category: 'How to...' that showed the most popular searches starting with those words. Here are the global results:

2017 Global 'How to...'
1. How to make slime
2. How to make solar eclipse glasses
3. How to buy Bitcoin
4. How to watch Mayweather vs McGregor
5. How to make a fidget spinner

When you compare this to local results, you'll see that in Australia, 'How to make fluffy slime' appeared in place of the solar eclipse glasses. The other results were the same, although the order was subtly different. In the UK, we were less interested in the eclipse, and weren't interested in making our own fidget spinners, but we did want to watch the Joshua vs Klitschko fight, and perhaps most intriguingly, the third most popular question for the UK was 'How to stay young'. It's harder to check results from countries where English is not the main language, but I did check Canada. People there clearly follow some global issues but also have their own unique questions. Without comment, here is their list:

2017 Canada 'How...'
1. How do they name hurricanes
2. How many teaspoons are in a tablespoon
3. How soon should you take a pregnancy test
4. How to make solar eclipse glasses
5. How to buy bitcoin in Canada

For some countries, additional questions are listed. The United States trends in 2018 include categories for Who...? (Who won mega millions), What is...? (What is Good Friday?), and, Where is...? which has the following top 5 results:

2018 United States 'Where is...?'
1. Where is Villanova University?
2. Where is Croatia?
3. Where is Parkland Florida?
4. Where is Hurricane Florence?
5. Where is Hurricane Michael?

In case you are puzzling over those questions, Villanova's University Basketball team won the NCAA Championship (for the second time in three years), and Croatia made it to the finals of the World Cup. In February of 2018, a High School in Parkland, Florida was the scene of a mass shooting where seventeen students and staff were tragically killed.

The overall list of United States questions is perhaps the most revealing—possibly due to the sheer number of searches and the deep penetration of modern technology into society. The top celebrity search was not for an actor or sports personality (although Sylvester Stallone and Michael Jordan both made the top 5), but for Logan Paul—the YouTuber who caused a stir by posting pictures of a suicide victim on his channel. While fashionistas were concerned with how to apply magnetic lashes, removing individual lashes, or getting a lash lift, there was also interest in the background stories of the deaths of Mac Miller, Kate Spade, and Anthony Bourdain. The top food search was Unicorn Cake, followed by romaine lettuce (which had caused a large outbreak of food poisoning). I was quite surprised to see that Trump did not feature in the searches, but it was fascinating to see the top two US questions in the 'How to…' category were: 'How to vote' and 'How to register to vote'.

If you want to review the results for yourself, go to the Internet site trends.google.com or simply search for Google Search Year in Review 2019, or 2020, etc. We can learn a lot about ourselves from the questions we ask.

Search engines:
how do they work?

The world now relies on search engines to determine what to buy and where to eat; for news and for discovering obscure facts. Have you ever considered how search engines work though? The underlying techniques are understood within the technology industry, but the finer details that represent 'the secret sauce' are hidden. These details frequently change in the bid for one search engine to stay ahead of another. You'll occasionally, see a news item about how a change in a search algorithm (usually Google's, given their size) has decimated someone's business—where they used to appear first in searches, they're suddenly listed on the dreaded second page, and given that Forbes reported (in 2017) that 92 percent of users will click on a search result on the first page rather than move to a second page, a change in ranking can have a devastating effect. Here's a primer, then, on how the engines work—and guess what, they're driven by questions!

First, the engines employ pieces of software known as spiders, or web crawlers. These visit a web page, take a copy of that page, and add the web page's unique identifier (the URL) to an index. The web crawler then examines the (copy of) the page for further links and repeats the process. You can check to see how frequently a site like Google has 'crawled' your website. Google provides tools to help website owners make it easier for the spiders to find information about their sites. One thing they won't do is accept payments to crawl a website more frequently, although you can request a re-crawl. Anyway, these spiders also track which server computers are connected to the internet, how many websites each one is hosting, and what format the data they store is held in, as well as many other pieces of data.

The indexing is a critical part of the process. When you consider how much data exists on the Internet (current count is in the trillions of pages), it's no small feat to keep up with this data, with how it is related, and with its changing nature. When you search 'the web', you're searching the index, not the web itself. So how do they organise the index? In a Google video, one of their engineers, Matt Cutts, states that when indexing, they "Ask questions, more than 200 of them..." They look for words appearing in the URL, in the page title and adjacent to it, check for any synonyms of the keywords, whether the site is 'quality', when it was last refreshed, and so on. Many of the search engines add other types of data to the system too—such as the text from non-copyright protected books, for example, or public transport or weather data.

After indexing the data, the search vendors then run the 'secret sauce' algorithms to decide which pages will be served, and in what order, for the search query that you asked. PageRank is a software algorithm that was invented by the founders of Google, and rates a site according to the number of other sites linked to it, and their relative 'importance'. A search engine will use many algorithms to rank a page, and it may look at how many pictures the site contains, if these relate to the keywords in the title, the language used in the page, and so on.

When you type a query into a search engine, it will look up the best matches in the index. It will also consider context, e.g. where and who you are. Searching for football results in America will display NFL results, such as the last score of a Patriots vs Chiefs game. In England though, you would be served soccer results from the English Premier League. Interestingly, as an Englishman living in America, Google knows enough about my habits to show me Premier League scores. It knows what I've clicked on in the past.

In recent times there's been talk about bias in social media and search, especially related to tampering with political events. The search vendors claim impartiality and will not accept payments to improve a site's search ranking. However, a whole industry is built around optimising websites to get better results on search engines, called Search Engine Optimisation (SEO). There's an ongoing battle between SEO and Search vendors, as each try to outwit the other—SEO vendors charge to improve rankings for their clients, and search engines battle to stay impartial and non-biased. Given the critical importance of search engines in our everyday lives, it's easy to see how a search engine could be manipulated for nefarious ends. Imagine if you were interested in a certain person—it could be a political candidate, someone you're interviewing, or a potential date—and every time you searched on that person you saw negative stories and images. While these stories may not be true, your perception would certainly be influenced. Equally, imagine a person that had performed despicable acts, but none of this appeared in the first few pages of search results. There are good reasons why search engine companies and the media frequently discuss bias—the platforms are powerful tools to be manipulated. As has been the case in other industries, the threat of draconian legislation is forcing major vendors to alter their behaviour.

One final point is that search engines only document what they can find, that is; the sites available for the spiders to index. You may have heard of the dark web—this includes the sites that use technical tricks to ensure you can find them only if you know the address, and not via a Google or Bing search. Not surprisingly, much of the dark web is used for illegal activity—selling credit card data, drugs, guns, spam sites, and more. There are some legitimate locations, and even specialised browsers to access the dark web. In countries where free speech is not encouraged, the dark web can be a critical lifeline. There are whistle-blower sites, and several corporate organisations even have a presence. I wouldn't recommend the dark web as a safe place to hang out, but it's important to know that the search engines that answer our questions don't have a monopoly on information.

The Google suggest game

This is great fun to play on your own, but even better with a partner—preferably someone from a different demographic, so you can compare results. All you need to do is visit Google.com, type in the first few words of a search and see what phrases are suggested to complete the search. There are some very odd ones, and you quickly see how your searches are altered by your profile and previous searches. To give you an idea of how it works, my daughter and I tried typing in a few key words, such as: *How do, Why did, I am, How to*, and then compared results.

For *Why did*, my daughter was offered a series of celebrity searches, e.g. "Why did celebrity x shoot celebrity y?" or "Why did YouTube star x do y?" My top search result was "Why did I get married?" which I hoped was related to my age and not my search profile! My wife was interested to know why that result popped up, but since we also tested it for our friends of a similar age, I got off the hook. The search engine is changing all the time—I hesitate to say evolving or improving—and you can go online and find some hilarious and/or odd examples posted by other people, like these examples (search terms in bold):

what became the symbol of the industrial revolution
why would you leave us
why can't I own a canadian
sometimes when I'm alone I use comic sans
how would I look with bangs
I like to tape my thumbs to my hands to see what it would be like to be a dinosaur
sometimes I like to pretend I'm a carrot

don't you hate it when a llama named carl
why isn't 11 pronounced onety-one

Give it a go!

Search engines:
how should we ask?

Google often seems to think it knows what we want better than we do, and let's face it—most of the time it does. I've lost track of the times I've entered a search phrase with a misspelt word, and Google shows my search with the spelling mistake corrected. It gives me the option to change, but I rarely do. One interesting aspect of internet searches is that people don't use the question mark and often omit linking words as well. A natural human question like, 'How can I avoid getting Alzheimer's when I'm older?' might become 'avoid Alzheimer's'. There are good reasons to do this, and essentially the software itself has trained us how to use it. Here's a quick guide on how to make *better* use of Google (or any other search engine):

- **Don't type a full question.** A search engine will ignore the linking words and focus on the key search terms. Rather than typing 'Is there a pizza hut near to my hotel?' you would be better served by entering 'nearest pizza' or perhaps 'nearest pizza delivery'.

- **Focus on keywords.** You don't need to ask for documents, articles, or whitepapers. Simply use keywords. Instead of 'Articles related to xyz drug for heart conditions', simply type 'xyz drug heart conditions'.

- **Word order is important.** Words at the beginning of your search term normally carry more weight than those at the end. In the example above, 'conditions heart drug xyz' is not likely to be as successful as the reversed 'xyz drug heart conditions'.

- **Be specific where necessary**. Sometimes a search throws up too many results. Searching for 'grey coats' will result in male and female options. If you were looking to buy a man's coat, you need to say, 'grey coats mens'. If you were looking for a book on grey coats, you might need to add another search term, and so on. You can start simple and keep adding words to the search. This is especially true if you're searching for a person, and there may be many people with the same name. You may need to add a tag that specifies their career, like 'Tim Cahill soccer'.

- **Learn to use quotes**. If you have a sentence that you want searched for exactly as you typed it, such as a quotation and you want to find out who said or wrote it, then put the phrase in quotation marks; otherwise it'll be cut down to its key terms. Type in "to be or not to be" using double or single quotation marks.

- **OR**. Let's say you want to search for holidays in Cornwall or in French cottages. You can do both at the same time by using the OR operator. Your search would be: holiday cornwall OR "french cottages". Notice that I put French cottages in quotes, because otherwise I would be searching for cottages in Cornwall too, because the keywords would have been holiday, cottage, cornwall, french. By the way, you don't have to use the word OR. You can use the vertical bar character | if you can find it on your keyboard! You may be wondering if Google has the AND operator too. The answer is that AND is the default— if you search for holiday cornwall cottage, you are searching for holiday AND cornwall AND cottage.

- **Use wildcards (aka*)**. This is useful if you want a certain phrase or thing but can't remember the details. Imagine you partially remember a lyric from a song "We were blahblah in Paris", but can't remember what blahblah was—could it have been staying, or living, or sleeping? You can search with the wildcard "We were * in Paris", and up pops the lyric "We were staying in Paris" by the Chainsmokers. Incidentally, in many computer systems, if you look for a file that starts with certain letters, e.g. 'Cha', you can search by using a wildcard "Cha*' (searching just for 'Cha' will try to find a file with exactly that name). However, you don't need to do this with single words in Google, as the search engine will automatically look for words that begin with Cha as well as the whole word Cha. You only need the wildcard if you have a gap in a phrase, or some similar search.

- **Minus away search results**. Sometimes you'll want to find something specific, such as an Australian shop where they sold great nuts. You recall the shop was called Trumps, but when you search, all you get is a mountain of political news about President Trump. What you can do is remove search results that contain certain words, by simply putting a minus sign in front of a word. When you search for trumps -president -donald -politics, you'll suddenly have a smaller, more manageable list.

- **Find synonyms with the tilde (~).** Let's say you're looking for a cheap villa in Cannes. You can search for synonyms of cheap (low-cost, inexpensive, affordable, etc.) by putting the tilde character before the word you want to find synonyms for: ~cheap villa Cannes. Easy, eh?

- **Set a range.** If you want to buy a car within a certain price range, or look for events between two dates, you'll need to search using a range of numbers. You do that by putting two dots between the numbers. Let's say you want to know about wars between 1850 and 1899. You'll need to type war 1850..1899 (note there are no spaces between the numbers and dots).

Knowing these tricks should help give you better search results. If you want to get further into the nitty gritty, type a phrase into Google, and you'll see a toolbar that shows a row of options, including 'Tools' and 'Settings'. I frequently use Tools, it lets me restrict my searches by time—I often refine the data to show results from the last day or month. You can find the Advanced Search option from the Settings tab, for access to the features mentioned above and several more. You don't have to be an expert to use it, so don't be put off by the word 'Advanced'.

Silicon & crystal balls

There's a branch of technology that specialises in using data to answer questions about the future. Like a modern crystal ball, we use this technology to discover things like:

- Will this turbine fail in the next month?
- If we increase pipeline pressure, will we get better flow or an explosion?
- Which 5 percent of my customers are most likely to buy my new product?

Analytics is a fancy word for looking at data and learning something from it; for finding patterns and insights to inform our decisions. Some of these analytics approaches review the past to see what happened, and others predict the future—or even change it. There's a framework of four commonly recognised approaches:

- **Descriptive analytics:** *What happened?* How many ice creams did we sell in our Oxford store? This relies on historical data, and typically does some maths to aggregate and consolidate the information to provide the answer.
- **Diagnostic analytics:** *Why did this event happen?* Typically, this involves comparing historical data and looking for patterns—why did we sell so many ice creams today? Because the temperature was around 100 degrees Fahrenheit! It often involves the ability to 'drill down' into further levels of detail to understand the issue

at a finer grain.

- **Predictive analytics:** *What's going to happen?* Uses the historical data, statistical models and patterns to make predictions about future events, perhaps telling you that the temperature will be over 100 degrees Fahrenheit for three days this coming weekend.

- **Prescriptive analytics:** *What's the best action to take now?* This approach may rely on machine-learning algorithms and/or information on past behaviour. For example, given the forecast of hot weather, it may recommend ordering more ice cream for our stores— specifying types and flavours of ice cream for each location, as regional shoppers may have different preferences.

Prescriptive analytics is the level that organisations aspire to, although many have not reached the capability maturity necessary for this. Of course, answering questions about the future has been a popular theme throughout human history, and we've been practicing the art long before we had modern technology. Whether it's been reading the entrails of a sacrificial animal, flipping Tarot cards, or observing the flight of an eagle, certain professions have been built to answer questions about the shape of things to come. Underneath this hotchpotch of experts and charlatans, the techniques have involved:

1. **Guessing:** "The [atomic] bomb will never go off, and I speak as an expert in explosives." Admiral William D. Leahy, first ever 5-star military officer in the US, speaking in 1945, with a clear lack of knowledge on nuclear physics.

2. **Extrapolating** from current trends. In the 1950s, with

world population expected to grow to 8 billion by the end of the century, many experts believed there would be famine, malnutrition, and food wars because the volume of grain production was not growing fast enough to feed the world. However, the green revolution saw the introduction of new seed-hybrids, pesticides, fertilisers, increasing mechanisation, and new irrigation techniques, which resulted in yields going from 1.4 tons per hectare in the 1960s to 3.2 tons today. The extrapolations were a useful warning, but ultimately wrong because they did not predict the use of new technology.

3. **Lying**: "The coronavirus will not affect us here in country x because of reason y" There could be various motives here, such as avoiding panic while the country prepares for a pandemic—but ultimately this prediction is a lie.

4. **Believing** what you need to believe. When Steve Ballmer, Microsoft CEO was asked his opinion of the Apple iPhone in 2007, he said "There's no chance that the iPhone is going to get any significant market share." You might consider this to be a category 3 prediction, but I think Ballmer believed this statement because he had so much faith in his own company's ability to succeed.

5. **Obfuscation**: Giving a fuzzy answer, open to interpretation: "you'll meet a tall, dark stranger."

This last technique has proven the most successful. As the saying goes, it's very easy to predict the future; the hard part is getting it right. The obfuscation approach was the one taken by Nostradamus, the Oracle at Delphi, and many others. It doesn't actually predict the future—it makes broad statements that leave the final interpretation to the audience. The reason Nostradamus is still quoted is because his predictions can appear to come true again and again, like a good horoscope:

"In the city that the wolf enters, enemies will be close by. An alien force will sack a great country. Allies will cross the mountains and borders."

"That which neither weapon nor flame could accomplish will be achieved by a sweet tongue in council."

"From the depths of the West of Europe, a young child will be born of poor people, he who by his tongue will seduce a great troop; his fame will increase towards the realm of the East."

Many people believe this last quote predicts the rise of Adolph Hitler, which would be an astonishing piece of soothsaying, given that Nostradamus died nearly four hundred years before the rise of Nazi Germany. These predictions are ambiguous enough that they can fit many events—especially when you consider that Nostradamus made more than a thousand predictions, published in ten volumes. He was certainly prolific, if not accurate—and with enough vague forecasts in his back catalogue, it's easy to see how at least one could be twisted to fit a current event.

The Oracle at Delphi is a more interesting situation from our perspective of questions, since travellers—often wealthy individuals or their emissaries—came to the temple of Apollo at Delphi in Greece to ask specific questions of the god. The visitors were received by the keepers of the temple, and the answer was given by the Pythia, the high priestess. Given that many of these questions were asked by powerful kings or warriors, it was a delicate balancing act to answer the direct questions without causing offence, while protecting the reputation of the temple as a successful predictor of the future. We don't know all the questions and answers provided by the Oracle, but several hundred have survived in the writings of classical authors. They make for interesting reading, and show how the questioners could be very specific, and how the Pythia were skilled at providing answers their patrons wanted to hear, which were ambiguous enough to appear true whatever kind of future events occurred. Over the few hundred years the Oracle was in operation, there were many Pythia, young and old, educated and wealthy. Several met untimely deaths—one was burnt alive by the Emperor Nero for her pronouncement on his future. The Pythia told him, "Your presence here outrages the god you seek. Go back matricide! The number 73 marks the hour of your downfall." Given Nero's fearsome reputation, you would think the Pythia might have chosen her words with more care. The next year, Nero committed suicide after revolts began in Gaul, Africa and Spain, and the 73-year old Governor Galba declared himself legate of the Senate and the Roman People.

When Philip II of Macedon met the Oracle, he was told: "With silver spears you may conquer the world." I love the word *may* in that sentence. You may conquer the world, but then again, you may not... No doubt he bought large quantities of silver, and I wouldn't be surprised if the Oracle purchased a silver mine shortly before this pronouncement.

I also like this ambiguous statement by the Oracle to the Spartan Lycurgus: "Love of money and nothing else will ruin Sparta." Does that mean the Spartan's sole focus on money will be their imminent downfall, or does it mean that they have nothing to worry about, except being overly focused on money? Classic ambiguity.

A close reading of historical prophesies and predictions indicates that the best Delphi predictions were nearly always an extrapolation with a clever dose of obfuscation thrown in for good measure. On numerous occasions the Oracle was consulted over the potential success of Greek forces against the numerically superior Persian forces, and the answers were clear warnings without specifying the result: "The strength of bulls or lions cannot stop the foe. No, he will not leave off, I say, until he tears the city or the king limb from limb."

We can laugh at these prophecies now or be shocked by the accuracy of the few that were correct, ignoring the hundreds of the other forgotten ones because they proved false. Our modern systems, with machine learning algorithms and big data provide far more accurate methods for asking questions about the future and receiving solid answers, don't they? On 8 November 2016, the actual day of the US presidential election, the New York Times presented poll results that showed Hilary Clinton had an 84 percent chance of winning. She lost. We can't feel smug about that in the UK, since our poll results have historically been worse than those in America. To quote Nate Silver, a journalist with FiveThirtyEight: "...the final polling average has missed the actual Conservative-Labour margin by about 4 percentage points" (this is *twice* the average error rate in the US presidential elections).

As Nate points out, there's good news for the British Conservative party in that the results tend to be biased towards Labour, which means the Conservatives do better in the actual election than predicted. In the US, the bias has moved between the Democrats and Republicans, making it harder to read the polls. Every year, the pollsters tell us that the latest technology has erased the errors of the past, but I sometimes wonder if they'd be better off reading tea-leaves. Of course, one reason that the results are inaccurate is that the questions they ask are flawed. As we have seen, devising unbiased questionnaires is no easy task.

Attempting to see the future reflects a powerful, human desire, and we will undoubtedly continue to do it. We should view the answers as informative, but not definite —not matter how persuasive the seer.

Consultants should ask the questions

As a little side note, I'd like to mention that the people who took the arduous journey to the Oracle at Delphi to ask a question were known as consultants—they went to 'consult' the Pythia and seek knowledge. It's interesting how in today's language, a consultant is one who dispenses wisdom. In the past, a consultant was the one seeking wisdom, through asking questions. The best management consultants understand the etymology of this professional name, and recall that the consultant's goal is less to provide knowledge than to seek it and share their findings.

Big data

In the last few years we've seen an unprecedented growth in the volume, variety, and velocity at which new data is produced (see sidebar). There are various reasons for this explosion of information, but the ubiquitous use of smartphones, the rise of sensor technology in machines, the growing use of email and social media, and the increasing number of devices connected to the Internet, have all contributed. The more traditional methods of managing data, such as spreadsheets, databases, or data warehouses; along with the tools we use to visualise this information, have struggled to cope with this rapid growth. New approaches have been created to support this paradigm, and *big data* is the term given to this new world of rapidly growing information, as well as the techniques and tools used to take advantage of the opportunities.

Think of a farm of wind turbines—those giant white windmills you see as you drive around the country. Not that many years ago, they had sensors on board that would capture ten pieces of data every minute—things like the wind speed and direction, the current angle of the blades, and so on. Over an hour, each turbine might capture 600 individual items of data. These days, a modern turbine may record tens of thousands of data points *every second.* This is an order of magnitude change in the volume (and velocity) of data. What happens when an engineer goes to performs maintenance work on a turbine? They might file a report electronically on a tablet computer. There may be digitised copies of the engineers' reports from five years ago, when the field engineers didn't have tablets but filled in a paper form. The data will almost certainly include related weather forecasts and local power usage. Some of this data is structured—the information that is captured directly in an application, for example, and stored in a database, like the date and time of an engineer's visit. Other data, such as the handwritten notes, is unstructured. There may also be time-series data—which is continuous, and changes over time. The fluctuations of wind speed recorded at a micro-level is one example. If we want to answer key questions about the performance of wind turbines, we may need to combine both the structured and unstructured data with the time-series and discrete data. As this data is normally held in disparate systems and formats, it's hard to combine it. This is what big data is designed to help with.

A wind farm may process data locally and use it to control the turbines. Sometimes though, we may need to move data to another place for processing, which can be a difficult and costly process. Whether or not this is necessary depends on the questions you want to ask. If, for example, in a city with 10,000 streetlights, each one has a camera recording a rolling 6 hours of video, do you need to send all that data to a central location, or are you only interested in keeping the video if there's an incident—like an accident or a murder—in the vicinity of a camera? You may argue that you want to keep the data, but who's going to pay for it? Some 240,000 hours of video per day will consume a lot of storage.

So why is big data such a big deal? The answer is that once you start to integrate these different types of data, at scale, you suddenly have the power to ask questions that were not feasible before. One of my favourite questions for business decision makers is: "If you had a magic device that could answer any one question about your business or competitor, what would you ask?" The first response is laughs and guffaws—the typical person running a business isn't given to flights of fancy—but if you force people to really consider their answer, the results can be revealing. I had this conversation once with a man who headed the marketing department of a major telecom provider. First, he wanted to know:

"Which customers will churn this month?" (by churn, he meant leave them for a competitor, i.e. switching from T-Mobile to Vodafone, for example). His current team's focus was to prevent churn—that was a primary metric he was being measured on. After a little more thought, he added:

"Which 20 people have the most influence on the customers most likely to churn?"

I asked him how they measured influencers. He told me they tracked data on social media sites. It emerged that he had tickets for Centre Court at the Wimbledon tennis championship that month and was considering a gift to key influencers. With a bit of prodding, his magic question became:

"Which twenty people who are interested in tennis, have influence over the largest number of customers that are most likely to churn in the next two months?"

Notice how the question has become much more specific. With big data, it's now feasible to answer this type of question. We can see who's posting images or news about tennis players, we can see their connections; and predictive analytics can determine which people are most at risk of churn. It might be someone of a certain age or gender, for instance; someone using a specific brand of phone, or someone who has not upgraded their phone in over 15 months. By combining data, and asking good (and specific) questions, we can answer such 'magic' questions that were simply not feasible before. That is the promise of big data. It can answer questions we couldn't even consider asking with previous generations of technology.

There's a dark side to this which has been demonstrated by the scandal around Cambridge Analytica and their role in the Leave.EU campaign for Brexit and in Donald Trump's presidential election campaign. These are two high-profile cases of the two-hundred elections that Cambridge Analytica was involved in, worldwide. The company closed operations in 2018, and there are ongoing legal cases around its behaviour. The basic thrust of the operation was that Cambridge Analytica collected (big) data on voters from a variety of sources—standard demographics, internet activity on social media platforms, consumer behaviour, and so on— then derived psychological profiles from online surveys to provide a detailed portrait of each person. Their CEO stated in 2016 that they had "close to four or five thousand data points on every individual across the United States". They used this information to micro-target individuals with political messages. Some political scientists have argued there's nothing wrong with this approach, and that it's hard to change a person's political views if they already have a strong partisan position; so all that can be done is to encourage the person to become more active and engaged. The focus of the legal cases has highlighted some interesting points, however. It is alleged that Cambridge Analytica was capturing certain data without the participants' consent and without due regard for their privacy. This is how Facebook and others have been dragged into the legal and moral ethics of the case. At the same time, it is alleged that Cambridge Analytica used tactics like honey traps, stings, bribery, and prostitution to capture compromising footage of political targets, and manipulated videos to create material for micro-targeted voters. Whatever the ultimate outcomes of the Cambridge Analytica legal cases, we are now undoubtedly in an era where big data can potentially be used to manipulate people—whether it's to vote a certain way or to buy particular product. While additional safeguards have been placed around certain classes of data, the power and money at stake will ensure that this is an ongoing technical battle, with certain companies and individuals always looking to gain an advantage, legitimately or otherwise. We can see nation-state involvement in some of these big-data cases, and this will continue to grow as data and Artificial Intelligence become integral parts of economic warfare.

The four Vs

Originally, data was measured by volume, variety, and velocity; but many technology marketing teams have now added a fourth v to the mix, to differentiate themselves

VOLUME: *the amount of data*
Historically, large amounts of data have been collected, cleaned, partitioned, indexed, aggregated, and made available either within the walled garden of an organisation, or externally via secure links.

VARIETY: *the type of data and its structure (or lack of)*
Most organisations have traditionally focused on structured data (like that in a database). Certain types of firms, like insurance or healthcare companies, have data in an unstructured format—typically handwritten documents such as insurance claims or doctors' notes. We can now add sensor data, clickstream (the information that comes from a website), social media feeds, and much more to the list—all of which increases the variety of forms and structures that must be understood and managed.

VELOCITY: *the speed at which the data collects or changes*
Many new types of data have immediate value when analysed at the point of birth, or soon after. If a jet engine is indicating that it has a problem with icing, the pilot will need to know immediately—not get a notification a week later. The increasing real-time nature of business means it's no longer acceptable to clean and aggregate data overnight for review in the morning. Faster insight can result in more informed, rapid decisions that can have a significant impact.

THE FOURTH V: *veracity, validity, volatility, value*
How much do we trust the data? How quickly does it change? How much is it worth? There are several additional aspects of the data that we may consider critical.

It's a challenge to an organisation's Information Technology team if any of the Vs rapidly change. For example, a sudden increase in the volume of data means buying additional storage facilities—either more disks on site, or in a cloud infrastructure. The real challenge of big data has been that these aspects are altering at once: we have more data, of different types, arriving faster and changing more frequently, and that we need to use this data to make faster decisions in an increasingly competitive world.

Single version of the truth

Technology trends come in cycles—old ideas become new again, and then fade back into obscurity. Not that long ago, and not for the first time, there was a drive towards data centralisation, and one of the mantras was to achieve a *single version of the truth.* If you want to know the sales figures for a particular region, and you have three different computer systems that track the numbers, such as a finance application, the sales management system, and the manufacturing system, then you don't want three different values, because which one is correct? You need to check the numbers, integrate them if necessary, and present one, correct answer - the single version of the truth. But things aren't always so simple, unfortunately. According to an old saying, if you own one clock, you'll always know the time, but if you have two, you'll never be quite sure what the real time is, as the clocks will be out of sync. A single version of the truth seems like a great idea, until you try to achieve it. Early practitioners discovered there are many scenarios where it seems impossible to deliver, because as we discovered in our chapter on answers, the truth is a slippery concept, and there can be multiple perceptions.

In the Cotswolds countryside in England, there's a stone circle not as famous as Stonehenge, but beautiful in its own right. Very often the site is deserted, and you can explore it on your own. According to a legend about the site—known to the locals as the Rollright Stones—the stones are the soldiers of a king that were petrified (literally, not metaphorically) by a witch. The legend says that if you go around the circle three times and count the number of stones and measure the same value each time, then you will be turned to stone yourself! Kids love to run around the ring, chanting numbers as they count. It's surprisingly difficult—even for adults—to arrive at the same number each time though. The reason is that some of the stones are broken into pieces, and so you need to decide what counts as a separate stone. Is one stone broken into three pieces to be counted once or thrice? Is the grass-covered lump next to it the stump of another stone, or a fourth fragment of the last stone? Also, you must remember where you started, when many stones look similar. Much depends on the way you classify a stone. The same is true in any single version of the truth initiative. You need to decide on the ground rules, and ensure people count the numbers in the same way. When something is sold, for example, is the sale complete when the order is signed, when the purchase order is scanned into the sales management system, when the customer has paid for the product, or when the product has been delivered to the customer? In many organisations, each department may have a different definition.

There are murkier areas where truth gets even harder to quantify and define, such as with human feelings. Can we truthfully say that a flu injection is painless? For some people, the answer may be yes. I suspect a large slice of the population would disagree though, and getting children under the age of ten to agree on this point might be exceptionally hard. Patients are often asked to rate pain on a scale of 1–10, but we must accept that this is subjective. You might be told, as a woman, that 1 is equivalent to a pricked finger, and 10 is childbirth—but how can you measure your fractured arm on that scale if you've never given birth? There's no objective measurement of pain that says a flu injection rates 2.3 on the scale or a fractured arm scores 4.7—and how could there be, when we all feel pain differently?

The same is true with regards to death. It may seem obvious to the layperson when someone is dead, but medically, the term is harder to define. A person's brain can survive without oxygen for a period of minutes, even when the body may have been decimated. Certain animals can function without key body parts for a period. A male praying mantis that has its head bitten off by a female during the reproductive act can continue to copulate—so when exactly is it dead? In the past, death was defined as the separation of the soul from the body. These days it's usually understood as the irreversible cessation of cerebral function, alongside cessation of the respiratory and circulatory systems (i.e. when the brain, heart, and lungs cease to function). Even that definition has me wondering—if we put someone into a suspended state that preserved the body, might it not be possible to reverse some or all the critical functions using advanced technology at some point in the future? If so, would it mean you were dead and then came to life again, or that you were never actually dead, but in some transitory state? Again, the point is that it's not always clear when something is true.

Many organisations have abandoned the hunt for the mythical single version of the truth, embracing multiple versions, instead. Alternatively, they operate with estimated values or clearer definitions. As individuals, we often operate with false values that are 'good enough'. Our understanding of the world goes through revisions that change our beliefs, both at a macro and a personal level. First, we thought the centre of the world was the axis mundi—that is a central pole/tree/cord in the middle of a two-dimensional model of the Earth. Then we moved to a geocentric model, with Earth at the centre of the Universe. Next, Copernicus changed our position by showing that the Earth, and other planets in our solar system, revolved around the sun. Of course, our belief system has moved on further from this heliocentric model. As a little game here, take a moment to consider where the centre of space and time is now. Do you know? (Answer at the foot of this page.) All these models contained a fact that was believed to be true for hundreds of years at a time, but which we subsequently understood to be false. However, the 'truth' was good enough to allow science to progress and make new discoveries that have ultimately changed our version of the truth. Sometimes, it is more important to have a consistent view of the world than one that is entirely accurate.

If you still want to attempt to achieve a single truth, you're going to have to do two important things. First, you clearly must define your rules and terms. If you're measuring a business, for example, looking at the Revenue alone is not enough. You also need to define the Gross Revenue, Net Revenue, the difference between the two, the point in time (or trigger event) where Revenue is officially recognised, and so on. Second, and most importantly, you need to ask the 'right' questions by using the phrases and definitions you've defined. 'What is the net revenue for Q3?' is a much better question than: 'How much revenue did we raise last quarter?'

*Current scientific theory states that there is no centre to space and time. You might argue that the location of the big bang was the centre, but the cosmological principle argues that space and time is homogeneous and isotropic, which in plain English means that space and time is the same no matter where you look, or from which direction. There is no centre...at least, that is our current 'true' model!

Ask the crowd

One of the most interesting ways the Internet has been used is to change the way we ask and answer questions, through sites that connect people with questions and answers. Places like Quora, or WikiAnswers as well as the search goliaths. You can pose a question, and someone in the community will probably know the answer, or you may find your question has already been answered. It's not uncommon to see many different answers offering alternative perspectives or approaches. As a random sample, I looked at Quora and found the following questions:

What's it like to be a priest hearing confessions?
Fr. Larry Rice
In my experience, it can be both very humbling, and an amazing movement of God's grace. That said, it's not usually as interesting as people think it must be. Read More»

What's it like to be close friends with a genius?
Jessica Su, to be brief:
My sister is a genius. She has a >150 IQ and went to MIT when she was 16.
By all accounts she's like my other friends, except that she has a quick sense of humor. Read More»

What happens if an astronaut gets unlinked during a space walk?
Robert Frost, trained NASA, ESA, JAXA, CSA, and RSA...
If they are lost, they die. US EMU suits have a device called SAFER attached. It provides propulsion by firing small gas

jets. If the crewmember somehow loses...Read More»

Why is there no 4th Ave in Manhattan?
Matt Falber, Aspiring Hero
In 1831, the New York Central and Harlem Railroad built the
first rail into New York City. It ran down Fourth Avenue from
the north and ended at their depot on 27th St. Read More»

**Can alcohol-based hand sanitizers create resistance in
bacteria?**
Zachary Conley, M.S. in Molecular and Cellular Biolog...
No. This is a common misconception. Ethyl alcohol, the main
active ingredient in hand sanitizers, kills bacteria by
dissolving their lipid membranes and denaturing their...Read
More»

You'll have to dig into the site to find the full answers to those
questions, and sometimes people will come to a consensus
answer (often voted for by readers as 'the most helpful') but
on other occasions there will be different perspectives and
you'll have to make your own decision on the truth.

The WikiAnswers site has a different style. Let's say you
wanted to play the card game *Magic: The gathering*, and had a
couple of card sets, but no idea of the rules. WikiAnswers
could give you a simple, beautifully illustrated idiot's guide on
how to start. WikiAnswers does this type of illustrated guide
especially well. When I did a quick check of the site, it stated
there were 7,196,614 edits on 1,162,132 questions.
(WikiAnswers has now been replaced by Answers.com—
things move fast in the digital world!)
    Of course, as well as these dedicated sites, there's nothing
to stop you posting a question to your networks—on

whichever social media platforms you prefer. Whether you choose to do so may depend on the question and on finding the right community to ask. I'd be quite happy posting a comment to my local community site asking about recommendations for a dentist, or someone to refurbish furniture. I may not ask the same people, living nearby, to recommend a doctor that specialises in fatal tropical diseases. Generally, you want to match your question to the community most likely to provide a good answer. With a community of friends, you have a level of trust, but for certain questions you may have to address a broader group—either geographically, educationally, or culturally.

Following James Surowiecki's very successful book *The Wisdom of Crowds,* there was a surge of technology platforms to help groups give more accurate answers to certain question categories. The core idea of his book was that a diverse group of individuals can often give a better answer than an expert for tasks such as guessing how many jellybeans are in a large jar. An average of all the responses may very well give a more accurate answer than that from one individual. Surowiecki indicated that a good community is smarter than the brightest individual in the group. There are some provisos though. The group has to include a diverse set of opinions, for example; so you can't get a council of right-wing experts to judge an election result, say. Another key criterion is that the group should be independent from the enquirer—so they can make their own decision without any influences from popular, charismatic people in the group, and essentially succumbing to peer pressure. You also need a mechanism to pool ideas and aggregate the results—whether that's counting paper slips in a box, or something more sophisticated like an e-voting system. If these criteria aren't met, you'll get the reverse of crowd wisdom—which is like the crazed buying of tulip bulbs in 1636 or the dotcom bubble in the late 1990s, where the crowd suffers from delusional behaviour.

Only a handful of books become memes, but *The Wisdom of Crowds* has achieved this. Published in 2004, it has spawned a niche industry of software, new opinion poll strategies, forecasting and planning approaches within organisations, and has been subject to a variety of criticisms and refinements. Often, the approach is regarded as being especially good for optimisation problems. However, it has been pointed out by Jaron Lanier, amongst others, that the crowd are not always great at *defining the right question*. The framing of a question is the key!

Ask the swarm

We've looked at a few alternatives for answering a question; either by asking a person, a computer, or a crowd. But there's still another choice—*ask a crowd of computers*. This type of system, known as a multi-agent system (or MAS), has been around for a few decades and shown success in certain niches. Several telecom companies have used MAS to calculate the most efficient routes for sending packets of data across their networks; for instance; Intel have used one to work out the best pattern for drawing circuits on their silicon chips. More recently though, advances in other areas of technology—especially the growth in Artificial Intelligence, and better sensors for capturing environmental data—have brought a lot of attention to MAS systems as they become more applicable to a wide range of problems. One of the main advantages of these systems is the ability to solve highly complex optimisation questions in a situation that is changing rapidly. The systems are also highly reliable and resilient.

Think about trying to manage the traffic in a city. We can use a variety of sophisticated techniques to control the flow, and rate each city based on the maturity of its approach. A level-one city might have timed intersections that vary with the time of day—altering patterns around schools in the afternoon, for example—but a level-four city would be able to receive sensor data to dynamically alter the lights and traffic corridors according to the traffic conditions, events, weather, and so on. At this most mature layer (which I haven't experienced yet), the system can cope effectively with traffic and unexpected incidents, providing it's fully integrated and remains connected. This system is expensive and complex to install and manage.

Instead, what would happen if we gave the vehicles more autonomy, with each acting as an independent agent instead of having a controlled and centralised plan? What if your autonomous car could communicate with other elements in the vicinity, and as you approached an intersection, it knew the speed and location of each nearby vehicle, along with its destination and route? The cars could time their crossing to slip between each other like synchronised dancers—or aeroplanes, which use a slot-based system, since there are no traffic lights in the sky. When cars don't stop, we not only reduce congestion, we also lower emissions and reduce fuel consumption. Who needs traffic lights? [Answer: bikes and pedestrians, although we might find/build alternative routes for them]. When a major sporting event takes place and the streets around the stadium are busy, or when the first major snowfall of the winter comes, the MAS style of traffic management copes beautifully; taking all the disruptions in its stride. Even without disruptions, the traffic throughput is typically 3–5 times higher (based on simulations). There's a wonderful YouTube video of this approach by Peter Stone at the University of Texas. Many people watching the simulation find the idea of being inside one of the cars terrifying, while others say: "It's like the Arc de Triomphe in Paris!" which has 12 roads that come together at one central roundabout, and is famous for its heavy traffic. Traffic around the Arc is not always as smooth as we might like, but perhaps it could be if we let the cars do the driving.

While traffic management may need to wait for a critical mass of safe autonomous vehicles, there are other areas where MAS is being adopted. Systems are being used to optimise logistics for supply-chain companies, to manage the flow of containers through ports, or set the best price point for perishable goods. There are opportunities to use MAS to balance electricity loads across micro-grids, and make the movement of water or waste products more efficient. The fascinating thing is that these computer-based MAS are inspired by nature; the same approach is demonstrated in ant colonies, in bees exploring and exploiting sources of nectar, the interaction of bacteria, or the power of neurons firing in your brain to solve a murder mystery—these are all examples of MAS in action. The ability of these systems to answer complex questions is proven, and the wisdom of the swarm can be delivered at high speed, at the location where decisions are needed. Even so, the crowd doesn't always ask the right question in the first place. So how can we do that better?

It seems that we should leave the task of defining questions to the human, and let the software agents provide the answer. Humans appear to be uniquely built to ask questions. We're not perfect at forming the right question in the right way, especially not at the first attempt, but we are also learning-machines. Therefore, we need to let people easily change the question as they learn, redirecting the behaviour of the software agents. If we can find better ways of allowing humans to define questions that can be automatically answered by MAS, then we're looking at a step forward in how we tackle difficult issues. With advances in machine-learning approaches—the branch of Artificial Intelligence where computers teach themselves, these MAS can continue to improve, especially if we are guiding them.

I believe the synthesis of unique human capabilities and advancing technology will provide us the greatest benefit in the future. We shouldn't rely on machines to do our work for us; we should partner with them, educating and directing them with the most effective questions.

10. PROFESSIONS

Everywhere in life, the true question is not what we gain,
but what we do.

Thomas Carlyle

Experience counts

Database specialists spend much of their time asking questions of their corporation's data. They're skilled in defining the layout of information and writing questions in a structured format. I spoke to a database specialist who'd recently been training teams of people in his firm's latest technology, but he said he'd found the experience frustrating. "These were smart, highly educated individuals, but they were asking all the wrong questions", he explained. I've heard this sentiment expressed time and again by experts—amazement that people don't ask the right questions. Why such surprise? You might say it's because everything seems obvious when you understand it. Often, the experts comprehend a subject at a deeper level. They know not just *how* but *why* something works as it does. Therefore, a question that shows ignorance of that deeper knowledge appears stupid to them. You don't need any knowledge of engine mechanics to drive a car. You could cruise through the neighbourhood, and when your car rolled to a stop one day, you might ask a whole series of questions to an expert about what has gone wrong: has the alternator failed, the battery died, did the engine overheat? You might produce many questions with a mere smattering of knowledge. An expert might start with "When did you last fill it with fuel?" If the car has run out of gas, the expert will think you're ignorant or foolish, and he may well be right! Yet if you don't know how a car works, this is not an obvious question.

For many years, I played badminton for a local club with my doubles partner, Dave. Every Sunday, we met to play against each other, instead of in our normal doubles partnership. They were great games, hotly contested, and afterwards we would drink gallons of watered-down orange juice in the sports centre cafe. One Christmas, for fun, we decided to play left-handed (we were both right-handed). Being badminton 'experts' we knew exactly how to hold the racket between the finger and thumb, we knew the footwork required, and so on. All we had to do was to follow the same methods from our years of practice, but in reverse, by using the opposite hand and foot. Of course, being two teenage boys, doing it as a joke didn't make the game any less competitive. For the first few minutes, we could barely hit the shuttlecock. Knowing how to do something in theory and having the co-ordination and muscle memory to do it are very different things. We began to play badminton rapidly, but clumsily, just like the beginners we coached. Our grip slipped around the racket, so we were holding it 'frying-pan' style, and we punched the shuttle using muscle rather than technique, to get the thing over the net. Anyone watching would have said we were absolute beginners. I don't remember who won the game—which suggests I lost—but I was chastened by the fact that I could not apply my detailed knowledge about a subject. I knew which questions to ask, and I also knew the answers; but it was so hard to do, and importantly, the bad methods gave better short-term results.

I suspect that many of us take shortcuts, especially in areas where we don't have expertise, and don't know the best question approaches. I don't know how to interrogate people like a trial lawyer, so I'd use my normal interviewing technique if called upon to perform that role. Maybe I'm never going to solve a murder case, but those legal techniques might be useful in getting to the truth about why that project at work failed! Legal experts have trained for cross-examination. In writing this book, I discovered that each industry has a unique approach to using questions. A teacher, a policeman, and a salesperson all have different goals when they question you. Not surprisingly, there are specialist firms to train people how to ask questions in each field of expertise. In this chapter, we'll look at some of the tools and tricks used by a handful of professions. I'm not aiming to make you an expert, but it can be helpful to understand what they're trying to achieve.

Teachers

Teachers have a unique approach to questions because their goals are substantially different from other professions. A teacher does not usually try to get information from a person or establish credibility with a question—but focuses instead on helping students learn. This means they use questions to:

- test knowledge: 'What's 9x9?'
- build confidence: 'Fiona, can you name an invertebrate? Well done!'
- open a discussion: 'What were the primary causal factors for WW2?'
- channel a discussion: 'Why do you think they responded like that?'
- challenge ways of thinking: 'Is it always wrong to steal?'
- focus attention: 'Can you write a pronoun on the whiteboard?'
- spark interest: 'What if I told you this device can turn lead into gold?'
- involve everyone: 'What do you think, Erin?'

The best teachers strive to enable students *to learn how to ask good questions themselves, and to develop productive thinking approaches.* This was certainly how Socrates approached his students—and gave rise to the Socratic Method. The very word 'educate' comes from the Latin *educo*, 'to draw out'. Bloom's Taxonomy (see sidebar) is the standard approach to questions that has been taught at teacher training colleges for many years now. While there have been various modifications to this research, the core principles still stand and are used in teacher training and therefore student learning, to the present day.

An interesting study in 2009 by Tienken, Goldberg and Dirocco focused on the number of questions asked, as previous research reported that teachers may ask 300–400 questions per day. That means an average teacher might ask 18,000 questions per year—or to put it another way, a student may be on the receiving end of a quarter of a million questions during their school career. These researchers set out to analyse how many 'productive' questions were asked, and to gauge the influence of teacher experience on these statistics. Taking their question categorisation system from a study by Anderson and Krathwohl, they labelled questions according to one of the following criteria:

Productive: Frequently open-ended, these questions allow students the opportunity to create, analyse, or evaluate. Here's an example from Grade 10 United States history is: "Based on your study of the United States Constitution, how does the new Iraqi constitution compare in terms of comprehensiveness, and what recommendations would you make for its improvement and why?"

Reproductive: These questions prompt students to imitate, recall, or apply knowledge and information taught by the teacher, through a mimicked process. e.g. "What right does the First Amendment of the United States Constitution protect?"

The results showed that only 15 percent of the questions asked by novice teachers—defined as those with less than 4-years' experience—were in the productive category. On the other hand, 32 percent of the questions asked by experienced teachers were productive-category questions. Why does it matter? Let me quote Tienken, Goldberg and Dirocco:

"Several studies and meta-analyses conducted in the 1980s and 1990s reported positive influences of productive, higher-order questions on student achievement (Redfield and Rousseau 1981; Wise and Okey 1983; Bloom 1984; Hamaker 1986; Walberg 1999). The influences on **achievement ranged from 12 to 27 percentile points** gained on commercially prepared, norm-referenced, standardized tests by students whose teachers consistently used productive questions compared to students whose teachers did not regularly use such questions."

That's a HUGE difference. When you recall the average grade spread is perhaps 10 percent, a better teacher using more productive questioning could raise a C-grade student to B or A grade! It also links to the theme of this book—the right questions make a massive, quantitative difference. Everyone benefits; the student, the parent, society, and the teacher—no doubt lifting a class from C to A is a hugely rewarding experience. The academic paper encouraged teachers and teacher training colleges to step up their game, and make a more concerted effort to help plan out questioning strategies in advance for classes, just as a lawyer would do for a case, and to make greater use of productive questioning (is 32 percent high enough, even for experienced teachers?)

We all teach at some point in our lives; it might be for our work colleagues, friends, children, or even our parents. There are lessons to be gleaned here for everyone. Open-ended questions that let people think for themselves are incredibly useful for learning, especially when compared to questions that ask people to parrot what they've been told. Seems obvious but then, Dale Carnegie wrote one of the most famous self-help books ever with *How to Win Friends and Influence*

People which is filled with seemingly obvious advice. I have a 1980s version on my bookshelf that lists 15 million sales to date, and it continues to sell. The book is filled with 'obvious' guidance that we seem to forget along the way: smile, use people's names, begin in a friendly way, let the other person do most of the talking, be sympathetic to the other person's ideas, and so on. The book can be read on its own or used with a series of training courses run by the Dale Carnegie organization. Part Four of the book is 'Be a Leader: how to change people without giving offense or arousing resentment.' Principle 4 of 9, says "Ask questions instead of giving direct orders." Amen.

Something else that teachers do, which differs from many other questioners, is to engage every member of a class; or at least they try to. Teachers aren't focusing on an economic buyer or power sponsor as a salesperson might; neither are they interrogating an individual in a court of law. Teachers must use their questions to engage and educate potentially 30 people at once (hopefully less, if the teacher/pupil ratio is better). They've developed special techniques to achieve this aim:

Collective vs direct
The simplest choice a teacher makes is whether to address a question to the entire group (a collective question) or to an individual (a direct question). Collective questions tend to be used earlier in a session, to start a discussion. Direct questions are used as the session develops to bring people into the debate and keep a high level of engagement.

Here are a few other approaches that teachers use, which should be familiar:

- **Talk to your neighbour:** a teacher will ask a question and then suggest you talk to your neighbour for a given time period to discuss your thoughts/answer. Typically, the roles in the pairs are reversed at some point. This technique isn't limited to pairings, but can work for small groups as well.

- **Sampling/sharing:** this is often used in conjunction with (1) above. After the pairs have had a chance to discuss their answers together, the teacher may ask a member of the pair, or a randomly selected person, to share their key findings. This sampling is a good way of learning what other groups or teams thought, and helps to keep teams honest as there is an expectation they may have to 'report back' on progress. If the number of teams is small, then every team will contribute. Otherwise, the teacher will choose a sample.

- **Random selection:** when a teacher does ask a direct question, they may randomly choose a person to answer. The expectation of such questions ensures that everyone answers the question in their mind, as they may be the one who is chosen to answer. Of course, as we all remember from school, if you know the answer, they never ask you!

- **Action-based questions:** these have been demonstrated to be highly effective for students learning new material. It means the teacher involves physical movement in the answer, e.g. 'Will everyone who believes the earth is round stand on the right-side of the room; everyone who thinks the earth is flat please stand on the left.'

- **Raise your hand:** 'Who knows the answer to…?' Several excited children rush to put up their hands, indicating that they know the answer. This is an interesting approach, which we don't often see as we get older but is a useful tool for a teacher. They can see who knows the answers, who is reluctant to answer, which students are fully engaged in the lesson, and much more. Of course, raising your hand does not mean that your answer is right.

Many of the techniques above are also frequently used in conferences: 'Raise your hand if you're running an xxx project right now?', and in corporate sessions facilitated by consultants. Of course, this shouldn't surprise us, since we should be continuing to learn throughout our lives. Questions are a great way to encourage this, and what good teachers know is that the best questions for learning are the ones that make us think, act, and engage.

Bloom's taxonomy

Benjamin Bloom was a US educational psychologist from Pennsylvania who chaired a group of experts that produced the 1956 standard text: *Taxonomy of Educational Objectives: The Classification of Educational Goals,* for which Bloom was also the editor. Bloom was especially interested in the thought processes of gifted students, and the Taxonomy was a hierarchical categorisation of cognitive skills, from a low order—such as the ability to remember previously learned information like place names on a map—to high order skills, like the capacity to create novel solutions to problems by bringing together several component ideas into a whole.

Bloom's Taxonomy has been hugely influential in education. Teachers have used it to plan lessons, evaluate task complexity, plan the curriculum, design valuable assessments, and many other things. There have been various minor revisions over the years since its publication, and a more substantial revision in 2001, but the generic nature of the six hierarchical levels mean that it can be applied to almost any form of teaching, making it malleable and adaptive. The 2001 revised edition lists the six cognitive levels as: Remember, Understand, Apply, Analyse, Evaluate, and Create (replacing Synthesize from the original version). As you might expect from such a wildly successful system, there have been critics, including those who dislike the idea that students have to work their way up through the various levels to achieve the 'nirvana' of Create. Overall, though, the Taxonomy has proved flexible enough to accommodate different teaching styles and subjects and has coped admirably with the introduction of new digital techniques and aids. Bloom's Taxonomy is as influential today in the education of students as it was in the 50s and 60s.

Lawyers

When we see lawyers (or attorneys, in US parlance) in a movie, it is normally in an exciting cross-examination, where they use a cunning question to expose the criminal. Sometimes a sequence of questions provokes the suspect into a furious response, inadvertently revealing a fact or emotion that proves their culpability. Think of Tom Cruise and Jack Nicholson in the movie *A Few Good Men*, during the scene 'you can't handle the truth'. Cruise is a military lawyer provoking the senior officer played by Nicholson, repeatedly asking him "Did you order the code red?" until eventually Nicholson spits back "You're damn right I did"; thus proving his culpability. This dialogue is so popular it's been turned into a series of YouTube memes, with, for example, Cruise challenging Nicholson about his use of the company expense account on behalf of the sales department, with the question "Did you expense the lap dances?" In *A Few Good Men*, and in many other courtroom dramas, tension builds as questions are asked, and the plaintiff and defence lawyer take turns to ask patterns of questions, or leap from their bench to object to the opposing side's questions. In the real world, most cases are built—not on dramatic cross-examination—but on direct examination, where the lawyer is on the same side as the person being questioned. A lot of important work also takes place outside the courtroom, such as in depositions, where each side will interview witnesses as well as reviewing documentation and research, to build their case.

The first rule for lawyers is never to ask a question in court to which you don't already know the answer. The reason is, that by the time the trial begins, they're not trying to understand the truth, but are telling a story; and the person in the dock is filling in the blanks, as the lawyer already knows what the witness or accused will say. Legal professionals are highly skilled at questioning, and use standard techniques quite effortlessly, alongside a broad range of more advanced techniques, such as:

- **Errors of omission:** 'Is it true that you kicked a dog to death outside Mrs Smith's house?' [The fact that it was attacking your toddler, who suffered permanent facial scars, isn't mentioned.]
- **Pressuring you into an answer:** 'You committed the murder, didn't you? Yes? Yes? Yes?'
- **Loaded polar questions:** These cannot be answered without incrimination, such as the infamous: 'Have you stopped beating your wife yet? Yes or No answer please.'
- **Funnel questioning:** where a series of closed questions build a narrative:
  - Do you have a degree in Maths, or in any scientific domain?'
  - Do you have an MBA?
  - Do you have any formal qualification in accountancy?
  - Did you review all the invoices before they were sent to the customers?

  Note how the lawyer is using several techniques here. First, they use a pattern of No questions to fool the witness into answering 'No'. In parallel, they are trying to discredit the witness by showing the lack of expertise/qualifications. Although the person may have 20+ years' experience in a different field, this fact was conveniently omitted from the funnel sequence.
- **False leading statements:** Some scrupulous lawyers

have been known to lie in the lead up: 'Since you were aware your manager has never invested a penny in this business, would you think that...'

Although leading questions are not generally permitted in direct examination either in US or UK courts, there are certain exceptions. These include for eliciting basic information like name, occupation, and so on, and in cross-examination or with a hostile witness. Leading questions are also permitted in depositions. In practice, they're used whenever someone can get away with it, and while the opposing advocate can object, and ask for the question to be removed or rephrased, the judge may overrule. It's interesting to think that a specific form of questioning is so dangerous that it's banned in a court of law. I wonder if other forms of questioning should also be eliminated, and perhaps not just from legal trials?

A key point here is that lawyers are not necessarily attempting to discover the truth; instead they're usually building evidence to support a constructed narrative. The early stages of a case may entail gathering information; collecting statements which they can take out of context later (yes, that's harsh). In sessions before a judge and/or jury, they're telling a story for the benefit of their audience, with the witness or defendant as their mouthpiece. The questions and answers are part of that process. One of the most interesting techniques is where a lawyer doesn't ask any question. They may read aloud a damaging statement, for all the room to hear, and then move to the next part of their story, giving the defendant no option to reply. There are strict rules on who can speak, and when; so it's critical in any fair legal system to provide the time and opportunity for both sides to put their questions, and to challenge the evidence given.

For the legal system to function correctly, we need

lawyers who will do their utmost to defend the guilty and make the innocent look criminal or complicit, to the best of their ability. That doesn't make lawyers bad people—they're playing a role in a legal system, but it doesn't help their public image. If they're highly ambitious, or have a strong desire to serve the public, a lawyer may choose to switch from the legal profession to politics. According to an article in the Law Society Gazette, nearly 20 percent of politicians in the UK House of Commons in 2015 came from a legal background, and this percentage has been growing. The British Cabinet that year contained 18 percent of people with legal training, compared to 4 percent in 2010. Many other countries show the same pattern. In America, the Bloomberg Law reported in 2019 that 40 percent of the 535 members in the 116th US Congress were comprised of law school graduates. Among the senators, the score was even higher, with 54 percent having attended law schools. To quote the article directly, in relation to presidents: "Obama studied law at Harvard, Bill Clinton at Yale (alongside Hillary). Nixon learned his way around the law at Duke, while FDR did the same at Columbia. A legal education has long served as a springboard to a political career."

In the UK, our last Prime Minister with a legal education was Tony Blair (along with his wife Cherie, who was a barrister). UK Prime Ministers have a somewhat varied background, including Chemistry (Margaret Thatcher), History (Gordon Brown), Geography (Theresa May), Classics (Boris Johnson), Philosophy/Politics/Economics (Edward Heath and David Cameron). Don't get too excited about that apparent diversity though, since out of the 15 Prime Ministers who have served post-World War II—some on more than one occasion—eleven were educated at Oxford University. I have one simple question to ask about that. Why?

Politicians

Politicians—everyone's favourite people, right? One of the reasons we love them so much is the way they handle questions. Politicians of all parties are renowned for their habit of not answering questions (remember Michael Howard in the Advanced Techniques chapter, avoiding a direct answer to the same question 14 times in succession). Historically, and right up to the present day, there has also been a tendency for politicians to answer questions directly, but with a lie. These days we have 'fact checkers' that track statements by our politicians and show the veracity of our leaders' comments. Not that everyone is interested in the truth. Something I have frequently seen in sales is becoming true in politics too: facts matter less than emotions.

The UK sitcom *Yes Minister* gives some wonderful examples of the way politicians and their administrative teams think about questions. At one point, a minister was given the following advice on how to answer political questions: *"go for the man, or the ball, and always pick the weakest element."* See the sidebar for more examples.

Of course, most politicians are adept at handling questions because they've had formal training in this. As we saw in the previous section, many politicians have a legal background, which gives them skills in asking questions and in managing answers. In fact, questions are so powerful that the UK parliament has special rules about how to use them. The government has two chambers: the House of Commons (elected MPs—Members of Parliament) and the House of Lords (also known as the second chamber; filled with appointed and hereditary peers). In both chambers Questions are the first order of business from Monday to Thursday, following prayers. In the House of Commons, there's a weekly schedule that shows the specific time and date that each governmental department, as well as key ministers, will be answering questions; and it limits the number permitted.

Also, questions must be submitted several days in advance, giving the department plenty of time to prepare a response. Despite the fact that questions are submitted in writing, these are known in parliamentary speak as 'oral questions'. The questions are printed in a book, using a deliberately random sequence, and the Speaker (Chair) of the house asks the relevant MP to raise his question so the government minister can provide an answer. At this point the MP, or other MPs, may be called on to ask a supplementary question related to the same topic.

The last few minutes of each Question Time are reserved for topical questions, allowing MPs to ask general questions related to the department's responsibilities, or for any non-related questions that are urgent. After the event, the questions must also be answered in written form. MPs can request a specific date by which they need to see the written answer. They must declare any relevant interest, e.g. asking a question regarding a dispute with a company when they act as an important advisor to that company.

The second UK government chamber—the House of Lords—has a similar system, with questions presented between a day and a month in advance (or two days for topical questions). The major difference being that questions are addressed to Her Majesty's Government in general, rather than to a specific department or minister.

Theoretically, Prime Minister's Question Time follows the same format. However, there's a twist. The session traditionally starts with a general question from an MP about the prime minister's (PM's) engagements. This is termed an open question and allows the MP to then ask a supplementary question on any subject. Many MPs will put forward the standard question on the PM's engagements in advance, resulting in their names appearing in the Commons Questions book against the open engagements question. This allows them to be called by the speaker to ask supplementary questions, and results in the PM having to handle questions on the hop that have not been submitted in writing. Undoubtedly, the PM will have been briefed on likely topics and should be able to handle the questions, but it has resulted in some entertaining exchanges over the years. The Leader of the Opposition also gets to play a special part in the game, being permitted to ask up to six questions during PM's Question Time, and is the only MP allowed to question the answers given with further questions.

The government's structure of these sessions is fascinating, as it demonstrates the effectiveness of questions. The fact that the sequence of questions is randomised demonstrates that patterns of questions can be highly effective. There is also a time limit for questions (introduced in 1881), which has varied in duration, but is presently 30-minutes for the PM. Most commonwealth countries including Canada and Australia have similar systems, with set times for asking questions. Even Japan has adopted a system loosely based on the UK model, with the very first question ever asked being "Prime Minister, what did you have for breakfast today?".

America seems determined to hold out from this model, although a few presidents and candidates have dabbled with the concept. In America, there's no direct system for formal Q&As inside the government. Instead, the system allows for unlimited debate, with senators able to ask as many questions as they like. This has resulted in the use of so-called filibusters, where senators block legislation by prolonging debates to prevent action on a Bill. Interestingly, the word filibuster is Dutch in origin and means 'pirate'. Senators can speak on any topic they choose, and the longest filibuster on record is by Strom Thurmond who spoke for 24 hours and 18 minutes in August 1957, on topics that included his grandmother's biscuit recipe. Various tweaks have been made at the Senate to prevent filibusters, and three-fifths of senators (usually 60 from 100) can vote to close a debate. For some types of legislation only, a majority is now required. Even so, the practice is still used, especially where there's some form of political advantage to be gained, such as delaying a vote before a potential government shutdown, or recess.

Except for America, most countries have adopted some form of formal questioning, with policies in place to avoid misuse. Many of those involved in the process are professionally trained at asking or answering questions. These are the people who govern our nations.

Yes Minister

Yes, Minister and its sequel, *Yes, Prime Minister,* were a series of political satire programmes broadcast by the BBC in the 1980s. The two main characters were Jim Hacker as a cabinet minister (and subsequently Prime Minister), and Sir Humphrey Appleby, his Permanent Secretary (i.e. the civil service department head). Each episode finished with a question posed by Jim, the answer to which was the title of the programme. The series won multiple awards, and had some wonderful exchanges on the nature of questions in politics:

Jim: Opposition's about asking awkward questions.
Sir Humphrey: And government is about not answering them.

Sir Humphrey: Well Minister, if you asked me for a straight answer then I shall say that, as far as we can see, looking at it by and large, taking one time with another, in terms of the average of departments, then in the final analysis it is probably true to say that, at the end of the day, in general terms, you would find, that, not to put too fine a point on it, there probably wasn't very much in it one way or the other, as far as one can see, at this stage.
Jim: Is that yes or no?
Sir Humphrey: Yes and no.
Jim: Suppose you weren't asked for a straight answer.
Sir Humphrey: Oh, then I should play for time, Minister.

Sir Humphrey: There's always some questions unanswered.
Jim: Such as?
Sir Humphrey: Well the ones that weren't asked.

Sir Humphrey: I strongly advise you not to ask a direct question.
Jim: Why?
Sir Humphrey: It might provoke a direct answer.
Jim: It never has yet.

Children

I guess we can't really classify this as a profession, but children are adept at questioning. They are known to start asking verbal questions at an age of approximately two-and-a-half to three years' old, simple questions like 'Dat?' (see table). Any parent knows that long before verbal questions, the child can still pose questions by pointing, or by using a puzzled facial expression or vocalisation. Babies experiment with intonation, making noises that rise or fall, at between 4 and 8 months.

Age Range	Questions Asked
21-24 months	"What's that?" (Or simply, "Dat?")
25-28 months	Questions are asked with rising intonation
26-32 months	Asks *where* questions
36-40 months	Asks *who* questions
37-42 months	Asks "Is...?" and "Do...?" questions
42-49 months	Asks *when, why,* and *how* questions

Source: Zero to Three website; developed using information from pages 269–272 of: Linder, T. (2008). Transdisciplinary play-based assessment, 2nd edition. Baltimore, MD: Paul H. Brookes Publishing.

Looking at the table, it's fascinating how the questions progress—from what, to where, and who; then eventually on to when, why, and how. Of course, there's a lot of change prior to this table's starting point. In the first year, the child communicates via crying, but also smiling and laughing, and with the first words—mama, dada. There's also a fair amount of babbling towards the latter part of the first year, and imitation of tone. In the child's second year, a huge amount of growth in language occurs, so that by the age of two a typical child might have a vocabulary of 50 words, be able to link several together to make commands like 'more milk', have a rough grasp over a few pronouns, and ask the first verbal questions.

A survey reported by *The Independent* newspaper in 2017 showed that the average 4-year-old asked 73 questions per day, half of which the parents struggled to answer. Parents reported that children tended to ask more questions when they overheard adult conversations. Some of the questions that parents found hardest to answer included:

- Why do people die?
- Where did I come from?
- What is God?
- Why can't I stay up as late as you?

Children are clearly proliferate askers of questions. The fascinating question these statistics provoke is when and why does this change? Why don't adults ask as many questions? Perhaps there's an answer in this wonderful quote from Richard Saul, founder of the TED organization:

"In school, we're rewarded for having the answer, not for asking a good question."

The author Richard Berger, who wrote *The Beautiful Question*, quotes a Newsweek story which shows that children rapidly reduce the number of questions they ask from the age of 5 and that by Middle School the number has plummeted and continues a strong downward trend through to adulthood. There are probably multiple reasons for this. One is surely the point highlighted by Richard Saul—too often we don't reward people (at school or at work) for asking questions. In fact, many organisations persist in doing the reverse, and punish people who ask questions. There may be a whole book, or at least a dissertation, waiting to be written to explore that topic. There's also an element of self-discovery that surfaces as children's reading skills improve. Technology has made it easier to answer questions for yourself, especially in these days of amazing resources like the Internet and Wikipedia, or through good access to books, either in electronic or paper format. On some levels, we might argue that technology has made the barriers for discovery too low—'Need to know how to build a pipe bomb?', 'Or perform nuclear fusion?', just search online. I might also venture to suggest that we stop asking questions of people who don't know the answers, or if we don't trust them to give us any valuable answers. There's no point in asking my colleagues for information when they claim not to know the answer, so I need to search for someone who can help, or find a different way to learn.

It may also be the case that we're failing our children by not preparing them on the best ways to *ask* questions. One key message I hope you take from this book is that there are a multitude of different ways to approach questioning, and each has advantages in certain circumstances. By educating children in effective techniques, we can help them get the optimal results from questioning. What better time to instil and encourage their curiosity, and give them the tools to pursue it into life-long learning, than in childhood?

Sales

There is a whole industry for sales training, much of which is based on questioning techniques. I'm not sure whether sales is unique in having so many specific questioning methodologies, or if I'm simply more aware of them because the industry is familiar to me. If you're a salesperson, then there's a high probability you've been trained in at least one of the following: SPIN, Solution Selling, Target Selling, Miller-Heiman, Precision Q+A. Each approach covers a range of tools and techniques, but the right way to ask questions is central to each.

Over the years, I've been lucky enough to attend training courses on most of the sales skills listed above. Perhaps because I did SPIN first, or because it set some of the gold standards, it seemed to me that many of the other approaches owed a lot to the work done by the founders of SPIN, the Huthwaite Research Group. This methodology stands out from the crowd because the approach is based on science—they sat in on many sales meetings, and correlated their observations in the form of the questions, habits, and techniques used by the salespeople, together with the results of each. The research produced some fascinating insights that have been used to produce a guide for the rest of us. It's a proprietary system, so I can't reveal the secrets here—you'll need to attend a training course—and you'll also need practice and guidance to use the SPIN approach effectively.

SPIN is an acronym for Situation, Problem, Implication, and Need-Payoff. Each of these is both a phase in the conversation and a type of question. The general idea is that you ask questions about the situation first, then explore the problem, the implications of that problem, and finally offer a solution, showing how it could deliver benefits.

Shortly after receiving my first SPIN training, I went as a technical specialist to a sales meeting, along with an experienced sales guy called Brian. The prospect was a catalogue-based retailer. We were selling a tool that could visualise slow-moving stock in a warehouse. Brian asked a series of questions that explored the situation: How many warehouses did they have? How many products? How quickly did the stock turn over? What type of revenue were they generating? and so on. Then he started exploring the problem: Did they have any issues with slow-moving stock?

After half-an-hour, Brian had revealed that the slow-moving stock was costing the company several thousand pounds a month. I was itching to demonstrate my carefully constructed visual mock-up. Brian, though, kept going. He began to ask about the implications of slow-moving stock. Did they have this problem in every warehouse? What capacity did the warehouses run at during peak times of the year? What happened if they ran out of space? Before I knew it, Brian had got the customer to admit they were considering the purchase of an old mill to convert into a warehouse because they were struggling with capacity. The cost of the purchase and refurbishment was in the millions. When I finally got to show the demo, our sale was practically complete. Instead of having to argue why our product was of value, the customer was more interested in how quickly it could be implemented... that's what they call a *buying signal!* After the meeting, I told the salesperson what a great demonstration of SPIN he'd given. Brian smiled. "Our job," he said, "is to make a mountain out of a mole-hill." And he did that, repeatedly, with questions.

Unfortunately, when many of us think of sales people we conjure up negative images: persistent telesales callers, door-to-door guys with a boot wedged in the hallway forcing an old woman to buy overpriced double-glazed windows, or a used-car salesperson asking if you'd like the vehicle in red or blue, when you haven't even decided if you want it. These stereotypes certainly do exist. We've all experienced negative sales approaches, but this does a disservice to the professionals in the sales industry. Good salespeople can help us solve problems, find creative solutions to our challenges, and identify potential issues before we're fully aware of them. A true sales professional is looking for a long-term relationship, and while they're championing the products or services from their company, they are also representing themselves, and their credibility.

Each of the sales methodologies includes an aspect that is unique, with real value to sales practitioners, or to you and me—since we're all selling something, even if it's just ourselves. What adds most value during the training though, is the practice and roleplay with other people. While the courses involve tasks like writing sales-accounts plans, analysing market data, and other desk-bound tasks, the core element of most such training involves sitting down in meetings and asking questions. In some courses, observers will record the type and number of questions you ask, to review with you afterwards. The sessions effectively change our behaviour in sales situations. They can also be fun—especially for the observers. Many of the sessions I attended years ago are still fresh in my mind and have continued to guide my own sales activities. If you want to improve your questioning techniques, there's nothing like practising in front of a knowledgeable audience.

One of the classic sales-training techniques is to ask people to form pairs and take turns at selling the other a pen. When I first did this task, we were all carrying pencils supplied by the hotel. The inexperienced salespeople pulled pens out of bags or jackets and started listing the features and functions of their amazing pen—the ink is permanent, it feels so good in your hand, look at how stylish it is, etc. The more experienced salespeople asked questions. Do you prefer writing in ink or pencil? Do you ever write documents that need to be permanent, like a signature on a cheque? Is the look and feel of the writing device important to you? They tried to tease out requirements which only that pen could deliver. The exercise helps people learn to sell by asking questions, and not by listing all the product features. My paired colleague was a big guy with a personality to match, from New Zealand.

"Can I take a look at your pencil?" he asked.

"Sure", I told him, and passed over the hotel pencil.

He studied it carefully for a moment or two, then snapped it in half. "I believe you need something to write with?" he said.

I wasn't too pleased at the time, although I could see the funny side. He understood that sales happen when there's a compelling event, sometimes called a burning platform— when the person buying *must* make a change. It's much easier to persuade someone to buy a pen when they have no writing implement but need to take notes. My colleague's approach taught me the important lesson that while salespeople want to build a relationship with you, they don't need to be your best friend. A lot of salespeople spend too long trying to be everyone's mate. An effective salesperson must challenge people a little, asking questions which may make people uncomfortable. That makes the ability to ask difficult questions, in an easy and acceptable way, a key sales skill.

Historians' favourite game

Writers and historians love to play the *What if* game. They wonder how the world might have turned out if one small change had occurred. Historians call this counterfactual history, and writers refer to it as alternative or speculative history. When Apple launched their inaugural TV service, one of the initial programs was a *What if* concept called *For All Mankind*, based on the Russians winning the 1960s space race. A year or two earlier, Amazon had a hit series based on the Philip K. Dick novel *The Man in the High Castle*, which explored the idea that the Nazis had won WWII and split the US with Japan. Nazi Germany is a popular subject for such games. There have been Hitler-thought experiments that looked at *What if* Germany had won the war, and a journalist uncovered the holocaust (Fatherland by Robert Harris), *What if* Hitler was cloned (The Boys from Brazil), and *What if* the Nazis escaped to the moon (Iron Sky—which wasn't meant to be taken seriously). Here are a few more examples:

1. **323BC—Alexander the Great dies earlier:** before creating the empire that spans Greece, through Africa and Asia, spreading and sharing culture.
2. **1914—Archduke Ferdinand is not assassinated:** potentially averting World War I and II. His assassination involved such a strange set of coincidences, it almost seems impossible that it actually happened at all. What if he'd never been killed?
3. **1812—Napoleon does not invade Russia:** instead, he dominates Europe and forges a dynasty that changes the shape of Europe for centuries.
4. **1944—D-Day invasion of Europe fails:** would we have

then used a nuclear bomb in Germany? There are plenty of WWII *What ifs*, even three different scenarios for: *What if* the Wehrmacht had not invaded Russia?

5. **1963—John F Kennedy is not assassinated:** This is one of several intriguing counterfactuals on US history. *What if* the Japanese hadn't invaded Pearl Harbor? *What if* the British had been more lenient on the Thirteen Colonies War Debts?

Psychiatrists

We've all watched movies where a patient lies on a psychiatrist's couch talking to the psychiatrist, perched on a comfy leather armchair. It's a cliché: the psychiatrist asks clever, open questions while the patient reveals their past, and either has amazing insights into their motivation or becomes enraged, and storms out of the room. As the two most famous psychoanalysts of all time, Sigmund Freud and Carl Jung, were both German speakers (although Austrian and Swiss nationalities, respectively), the questions in our stereotype are voiced in a softly spoken German accent. The impact of these two fellows on popular culture has been immense. From Freud we gained the model of the id, the ego, and the superego; along with the perspective that sex underpinned everything—hence the 'Freudian slip' when you ask someone to show you their lust instead of the list. Freud developed free association as a therapeutic technique, which encourages speaking or writing without censorship from the conscious mind, to access the underlying thoughts and feelings.

Freud saw dreams as unconscious acts of wish-fulfilment, but it was Jung who further developed the view of the collective unconscious, and believed that the symbols in dreams came from a set of archetypes, by which he meant certain universal images and themes that we all share. Jung gave us the concept of the introvert and extrovert, of synchronicity, and even wrote a book explaining why people saw UFOs in the sky.

While modern psychology and psychoanalysis have moved on from these two titans of thought, it was nonetheless Freud and Jung who established many of the foundations. The famous Rorschach 'inkblot' tests, or the lesser known but still widely used TAT (Thematic Apperception Test), which uses a set of pictures from which participants are asked to make up a story, are both developments of the free-association concept.

At this point, we should define the difference between a psychiatrist, a psychologist, and a therapist. Lazily, I use the terms interchangeably. Let's be clear then: a **psychiatrist** is a trained medical doctor who subsequently spent several years' residency training in psychiatry. As a medical doctor, they can prescribe medicine. A **psychologist** has a PhD or PsyD qualification (which takes 4–6 years) and is trained in mental and emotional disorders; their diagnosis and treatment. A psychologist typically undertakes an internship and spends 1–2 years in supervised practical work before they're granted a licence to practise. A **therapist** is a catch-all phrase, which could include a psychologist or psychiatrist, a marriage counsellor, social worker or life coach. Many therapists are licenced, depending upon their field. This is a broader term though, and does not imply the same training as the more precise psychologist or psychiatrist titles, although many therapists have a qualification in psychology or psychiatry. Confused? They all share the goal of trying to help people; the difference is their level and type of education.

If you walked into a psychiatrist's office today and lay on the couch (or more likely, sat on the chair), what questions would they ask? What special techniques have they developed? In a revealing online discussion, Dr Elinor Greenberg PhD, a psychotherapist in private practice in New York, listed her most common questions with a new patient as:

- Why now? What prompted you to seek help at this point in your life?

- What are your goals for this therapy?

- If you had a magic red button in front of you, that if you pressed it would make your problem disappear, would you press it? (The answer seems obvious, but not everyone likes change and sometimes humans are more complex than we imagine.)
- If you woke up tomorrow and you no longer had your problem, what would your life be like? How would you know your problem was gone?

The magic red button question is particularly interesting. It creates a visual and tactile scene, before the actual question is asked. Interesting approach. One of the other questioning techniques common in psychotherapy sessions is for the expert to respond to a question with a question. They want you to talk and discover the answers yourself—they're not necessarily there to provide answers. For example, if a patient asks:

"Why do I keep self-harming?"

They might respond with: "Good question, what do you think might be the reason?"

"It's probably related to my childhood", you might say.

"Why do you say that?" they would prompt.

Why? is a great question if you want somebody to think about a situation more deeply. Why do you feel that way? Why did you say that? One of the other common techniques used by therapists is the follow-on question, or prompt, to keep the patient talking. The prompt can be a guttural noise 'uh-hu', 'mmmh', or a gesture—a head nod, for example. If required, it can be turned into a question to force the continuation, or to nudge the conversation in a certain direction. 'What happened next?' or a nudge: 'What did your wife do then?'

One of the most revealing comments I saw from

therapists discussing their approach was by Sharyn Wolf, a New York State licenced psychotherapist with 28 years of clinical practice and six books to her name, plus a host of TV and radio appearances (including nine times on Oprah). She was curious about how people constructed their inner and outer worlds and wanted patients to tell her their story and then she would ask for details. I think this is a fascinating insight, and it ties in with my own personal experience. If you recall the chapter on Advanced Techniques, when asked "What are the best sales questions?" my response was that you should understand what makes the company tick by looking at their internal and external connections to the world. I explained how the underlying theme to all my questions was curiosity, and it's no coincidence—unless you believe in synchronicity—that Sharyn starts by saying she is curious about how you construct your mental map. Curiosity is fundamental to good questions, as is letting the other person do the talking by using prompts and questions that are well-framed.

As a final thought, there's been a belief in certain psychological circles, originating from Freudian approaches, of 'repressed memories', which are unpleasant experiences the mind has hidden away to protect itself. Through appropriate questioning and/or hypnosis, some therapists have sought to uncover these repressed memories and hold them accountable for a patient's behaviours. This practice involves the risk that inappropriate questioning can cause the therapist to *suggest* repressed memories, however; causing the patient to believe that certain events occurred, even when they have no actual memory of them. For example, a patient could come to believe they were abused as a child, even when no such activity had taken place. Earlier in this book we saw that questions can affect our memories. It is therefore feasible for a person with an agenda to suggest, enhance, or provoke memories of a certain type. For professional therapists, this is not an issue, however. They use careful language to ensure they're hearing the patient's genuine thoughts and memories, without influence. The goal of a therapist is to help, and questions are one of their most valuable tools.

Cautionary Tales #4

Doctor, how long have I got?

The medical profession has some tough questions and answers to tackle. Healthcare is an interesting combination of hard science—where practitioners gather data, run tests, and check a hypothesis about your condition—and the softer, social aspects of delivering the results to you and your family. In fact, the term health + care combines these two elements. Within the multitude of roles in a typical medical institution are the people who specialise in delivering bad news, handling the questions and answers required, and providing access to social support in order to help people through difficult times. My wife and I know a lady who works in a children's hospital, helping patients and their parents through issues like childhood cancer. I can't think of many jobs that are psychologically harder to perform on a day-to-day basis. At some point in our lives, we may all be faced with asking difficult questions, for which where there is no simple or good answer. In that case, even though you may be emotionally distressed in the extreme, remember that the other person is suffering too.

Some questions are just as hard to answer as they are to ask. Spare a thought for the other side.

Journalists

Nasir, a new product marketing manager, was sent on a brief training session on 'How to handle the press'. His company sold a specialist computer system and he understood the product well. On the train journey to the session in London, Nasir read the newspaper, which was filled the latest news of a financial collapse due to a trader that had gone rogue at a major investment bank—let's call the trader Bandare. When Nasir reached the training location, he was expecting a classroom with a group of students and someone running through a presentation. Instead, he was led into a room that looked like an interrogation cell from a cop show. There was a table, two chairs, and a plastic cup of water. A few minutes later a friendly looking journalist in her mid-30s came into the room. She introduced herself as Jenny, and they exchanged a few pleasantries. Jenny explained she would spend 20 minutes doing a 'real' interview, as though she were a journalist for a national newspaper, and then they could talk about it afterwards. It all sounded harmless.

"Ready?" asked Jenny.

"Sure."

"Your company's software was used to prevent fraud at Bandare. What went wrong?"

Nasir sat, dumbfounded. He had no idea if his company's software had been used at Bandare. To deny it seemed very risky though. It would mark him and his company as liars if it turned out to be true. Then again, if Nasir said he didn't know, it would look as though he were covering up. If he said 'yes' but couldn't explain how the fraud had been achieved despite their software, then it condemned his company again. He stumbled around some sort of reply, and was incredibly relieved that this was a training course and so his answer would not appear on the front page of the papers. Jenny went on to finish the interview and give him some feedback.

"I have no idea whether your firm has Bandare as a customer", she said. "I wanted to see how you'd react. Do you know if they are a customer?"

"I don't", Nasir answered. "We have lots of customers in finance, like Barclays, Zurich Insurance, and American Express. Never heard Bandare mentioned, but they could be."

At this point, Jenny taught Nasir the second lesson—there's no such thing as *off the record,* for a journalist. She explained how saying 'the interview is over' was a standard trick to put you off your guard. The headline the next day, Jenny said, might have read "Barclays, Zurich, and American Express at risk of fraud, according to Nasir, spokesperson for the software supplier to Bandare"... Gulp.

Jenny explained that the correct response was to twist your answers on to what you can do; the positive aspects. The aim was to make the points you wanted to make, not be forced into a blind alley by a dangerous pen-wielding journalist. For example, Nasir could have answered the initial question by saying: "This is exactly the scenario our software is designed to prevent, it does a great job of preventing fraud by doing x and y, as our customer z has shown by..."

Journalists have a set of skills, and one of them is asking good questions. They'll often start with a series of open questions to explore the subject, and then use closed questions to seek clarification on the specific areas they came prepared to discuss. They'll also want to explore any points you red-flagged for them in your meandering or cagey answers to their first questions. Journalists know all about the 'hooks' mentioned in the Techniques chapter. Given the deadline-driven nature of their work, coupled with the need to cover a lot of different topics, a journalist's knowledge about the subject of a piece can vary widely. This means they must know how to use questions to gather information. The usual journalistic goal is to write an informative piece on a given subject within a tight timeframe. They want drama and entertaining quotes, not boring platitudes. Part of their trick then, is to put you at ease, and ask questions that provoke interesting responses—once you've dropped your guard.

Journalists are not the spawn of the devil; they're paid to find and write newsworthy stories. Marketing people use the same techniques, and for the same reasons—nobody wants to listen to a boring case study. I was involved in producing a series of video interviews once, and one of the tips from our marketing manager was to keep the camera rolling and ask a few more questions after you've officially finished the interview. Remember, nothing is off the record... It sounds underhand, and ethically wrong, but here's what we discovered: after people were told the camera had stopped, they relaxed. They laughed; they gave better answers, and stopped trying to be someone else or to answer as they thought they should. When we edited the videos later and showed them the pieces from the 'off the record' section, people were surprised it had been recorded, but without exception, they were happy for it to be used because it was better quality material. Using the footage without their say-so would have been unethical, and we wouldn't have done that— but after getting their approval afterwards, it gave a much better result for them as well as for us.

Time for the disclaimer and warnings: journalists have certainly been known to step over the line. Whatever your own political leanings though, you'll be aware that news channels and papers have their own bias. Although some strive for independent and accurate reporting, others have a blatant slant towards an ideological viewpoint. Watching journalists ask questions of interviewees and panellists can be fascinating and/or infuriating. The common tactics appear to be:

- **Errors of omission:** they simply won't ask certain questions
- **Lack of airplay:** they ask fewer questions, or they cut off the answers, of people whose views oppose their own
- **Loaded/polar questions:** journalists use closed questions of the 'have you stopped beating your wife?' type when interrogating those with a different ideological stance
- **Directing the conversation:** a careful choice of question can move the debate off (or on to) a particular theme. I saw some classic examples of this during a school shooting tragedy in the USA. On one channel, the questions went along the lines of 'When will the President do something about this problem?' while the alternate news programs on their rival station with a different political slant delivered questions such as 'Why don't we arm school teachers?'

You may spot some similarities in this list to the favourite tactics of lawyers. Journalistic questioning, just as we see in legal proceedings, is a critical part of a democratic society. There are times and places when journalism has proven to be a dangerous profession. I have nothing but admiration for the men and women who risk their careers or lives to reveal the truth. President Nixon and his administration were famously brought down by the Watergate scandal; a conspiracy centred on the abuse of power. Nixon was ultimately uncovered by the work of a handful of journalists at papers such as *The Washington Post* and *The New York Times*. Two of the journalists, Carl Bernstein and Bob Woodward wrote a non-fiction book called *All the President's Men* that was subsequently turned into a film, and it was a blockbuster. Applications to journalism schools rose to a record high in America following Watergate, and important journalistic work continues today, with people questioning manufacturers' safety policies, head injuries in sports, the fate of people who have 'disappeared' in various countries around the world, police bias, human rights policies, corporate environmental policies, and other vital topics. At its core, journalism asks important questions, in a public forum, to those we have entrusted with some authority in our society. If any group should be equipped with excellent questioning skills and deep curiosity, and given free rein to use these skills, then journalists are the obvious choice. This is not always a popular perspective, and care needs to be taken so journalists do not wield too much power, especially over individuals who may not be able to defend themselves. This delicate balance between freedom of the press and the protection of an individual's right to privacy is a continually evolving situation. At its heart, it is a question of how much we want to allow questions to be publicly asked and answered.

Philosophers

We finish this chapter with philosophy, as the profession dedicated to the study of critical questions—on the meaning of life, physics, the universe, happiness, values, and such like. The word 'philosophy' has a Greek root that means 'to seek wisdom'; and some of the Greek philosophers are well-known names, including Aristotle, Plato, Pythagoras, and Socrates. They defined many of the fundamental techniques that have driven critical thinking in the centuries that followed, such as approaches to questioning, rational thinking, logic, and the creation of hypotheses. Here's a brief list of philosophical questions, some old, some new. None of them have a perfect answer. In philosophy, the value is in the debate.

- What is time?
- What happens when we die?
- Are humans simply machines made from flesh and blood?
- Are we living in a simulator?
- Who am I?
- Is free will an illusion?
- Why do we dream?
- What does it mean to live a good life?
- How do I know if you're the same as me?
- Should Artificial Intelligence creations have rights like humans?
- What rights should animals have?
- How can we be happier?

As a broad subject that encompasses all knowledge, philosophy has historically been broken into distinct branches: ethics, political philosophy—with Machiavelli an early practitioner—metaphysics, religion, maths, and so on. Several early branches of science were simply known as philosophy before they took on their own character and name. One of the major trade journals for physics has long been called *Philosophy,* and Isaac Newton's classic text on physics was named *Mathematical Principles of Natural Philosophy.* Of course, many of those we think of as the great philosophical thinkers are from the West, and therefore take a Western perspective. These include Descartes ("I think, therefore I am"), Hobbes, Kant, Hume, St. Augustine, Bacon, Thomas Aquinas, Nietzsche, and even Karl Marx. There are also large swathes of alternative philosophy in different cultures: Indian, Middle Eastern, and African for example, with many sub-groups. That's apart from the array of philosophical schools that have vanished with their race and culture—the Mayans perhaps, or the Egyptians. Occasionally, teachings and views have been able to cross cultural boundaries—with writers like Confucius or Sun Tzu, for example.

In the modern day, there are popular philosophical writers such as Alain de Boton and Paulo Coelho, who became a global sensation with his book *The Alchemist*—written in only two weeks. The story follows a young shepherd called Santiago, who journeys to Egypt in search of treasure; a fable about finding and following your destiny. Rather quirkily, the book was published in Brazil to moderate success, but after a year the publisher told Coelho the book wasn't going to sell very well elsewhere. Paulo found another publisher and campaigned for his book. It has sold over 35 million copies and has sold more translated copies than any other book by a living author. Paulo Coelho has written many more books that espouse his personal philosophy. Other modern writers have toyed with alternate ways of living—such as the narrator in Luke Reinhart's *Dice Man* series, who makes life decisions based on the roll of a dice. Philosophy, and the deep questions it seeks to answer, weaves itself into fiction and non-fiction alike.

What can we learn about questions from philosophy? The answer is, almost anything. For those who want to delve deeper into specific subjects, such as politics, ethics, how to age gracefully, or live a happier life, there are philosophical tracts—both academic and in popular fiction—that will help you explore these questions. For those who want to learn more about the art and science of questioning itself; then a study of logic, along with deductive and inductive thinking is a great way to start; or a course in philosophy is another option. It's no accident that many graduates hold the qualification of a PhD—making them a Doctor of Philosophy. This credential emerged in Germany in the mid-seventeenth century. In the USA, the last figures I could find showed that approximately 42 percent of college graduates will go on to gain a Master's Degree, and 3 percent will obtain a PhD. The study of philosophy, which is the study of questions, is the pinnacle in the education system. Since we're talking numbers, I can tell you that the US is believed to have at least twice as many PhD graduates as Germany, followed by the UK. Those are raw numbers though, not drawn up in a ratio to the population, which might be an interesting question to explore. There ought to be some economic benefits to having experts in questioning, although some questions may be focused on how to be happy rather than making money; who knows?

11. PUTTING IT ALL TOGETHER

The first question which you will ask and which I must try to answer is this, What is the use of climbing Mount Everest? and my answer must at once be, It is no use.... What we get from this adventure is just sheer joy. And joy is, after all, the end of life. We do not live to eat and make money. We eat and make money to be able to enjoy life.

George Mallory

What questions reveal about you

In an earlier chapter, I described how I used to present the same six slides to different groups every few days and became so familiar with the responses that I could predict who would ask which question. When I adapted the slides to make the narrative clearer, it resulted in nobody being able to think of any good questions, which meant for flat presentations with zero audience engagement. I reverted to using the original presentation, with its gaps and flaws, since that gave people the space to ask questions and participate. I had discovered that a person's questions can be incredibly revealing about their inner state.

I'm not the only one who holds this belief. My friend Julia was learning Italian at an evening class. Each week her teacher would ask the students to read a short story from Racconti Romani by Moravia. The class would then debate the tale (in Italian), and ask questions of each other about the morality, motives, and ethics of the story. One day, the teacher stated that she had studied these stories with her classes for over ten years. Julia asked the teacher if she ever learnt anything new about the stories from the classroom debates.

"No", she said. "But I learn so much about my students from the questions they ask."

People learn about who we are by the questions we choose to ask or avoid asking. Let's say you're walking on stage to talk to a big audience. It could be a conference, a wedding, or a school assembly. There's a loose cable trailing across the floor, and you trip and pull over a large electric fan, which hits you on the head. You fall sprawling on the stage. Someone dashes over to help you up. Here are some questions they could ask, and what these might reveal:

Are you hurt?
You're important to me (or, I hope we're not going to get sued)

How do you feel?
I care. The injury is one thing, but there's embarrassment too.

Didn't you see the cable?
I think you're an idiot. It was your own fault.

Who set this stage up?
Let's find someone to blame.

Can you still go on?
I really hope so, because I don't want to have to do this myself.

Why do you always have to make such a big entrance?
I hate the way you try to be centre of attention.

What is the cable attached to?
Who cares about you; is the equipment broken?

Do you want me to carry on for you?
I'd love to grab the limelight and look like a hero.

Incidentally, I saw the situation above happen in real life. It was at a big event, and the audience all went "oohh" when the guy got hit on the head by the electric fan. Nobody rushed to help him, and we should have done, but he was on stage and we were scared or shocked. He stood up, staggered to the microphone, which he grasped like a drunk to a lamppost, then dabbed at the cut on his head with a handkerchief. There was silence in the audience. He lifted his head, and said:

"That must be the first time ever that the fan has hit the shit."

The audience roared with laughter, and he had their full attention.

The questions we ask, along with our actions, not only determine how we're perceived, but reveal who we are.

Big life-questions

These are questions you may ask frequently, or perhaps just once or twice in your life. Some of them will be relevant now; others may never apply to you. They all require careful thought before asking or answering.

Questions to ask yourself:

What makes me happy?

How do I live a good life?

What's the meaning of life?*

How do other people see me?

Is there a better way to do this? (the entrepreneur's question)

What do I believe to be true that nobody else seems to?

How can I best spend my time?

What would I do if I wasn't scared?

What should I do next?

Questions to ask others:

How can I help you?

Can you help me?

Will you marry me?

Which way should I go?

Luckily, Douglas Adams has already answered this for us: 42.

How to ask a killer question

What is a killer question? I would define it as a question that silences someone, or a room of people—and makes everybody stop and think. A killer question has the potential to change someone's perspective or understanding. It could result in the closure of a building project, prove the guilt of a murder suspect to a jury, or simply change the opinion of someone you love. That is, of course, looking at a killer question from the perspective of the asker. For the receiver, a killer question is very hard to answer and may force you to examine your beliefs. Here's an example. I was at a conference where an expert analyst was talking about trends in technology. Discussing the next generation of smart weapons, he explained how accurately a bomb can be dropped on a target, and the type of damage it can inflict. He also spoke enthusiastically about swerving bullets that tracked targets, as well as reviewing the latest drones and smart robot soldiers. A couple of people raised their hands and were passed a microphone to ask specific questions about the technology involved and the limitations or future enhancements. Then a woman at the back raised her hand. When the microphone was passed to her, she said:

"Thank you for the information on smart battlefields. When will we get smart diplomacy?"

The room fell silent, and the expert floundered. He stalled for a few moments, and then made some inane comments, before rapidly closing his session. Nobody in the room forgot the question. It was profound. It was definitely a killer question. Before you can ask a question with that power you need to:

- listen very carefully
- observe
- understand the subject
- view the subject matter from multiple perspectives
- understand how the question might have a big impact on you personally (good or bad)
- be aware that the question may have a strong effect on the receiver (good or bad)
- be prepared to handle the consequences

A killer question does not have to take a negative position. Many innovators have started down their path as an entrepreneur because a killer question occurred to them (or somebody else asked them one). Questions like:

- Why are computers made for big firms, and not for personal use?
- Why can't I carry all my favourite music around with me?
- How could we make healthier drinks with less sugar?

I've witnessed a handful of truly great questions over the years. They are a thing of beauty, almost a work of art like a painting, or a story. They don't usually spring out of nothing, but form around a core idea, a passion; and develop with knowledge and time. It's not a case of trying to ask a killer question; more that they emerge naturally, given the right environment. To cultivate a killer question, you must be patient, passionate about the subject, well-informed, and thoughtful—all at the same time! Then it will appear quite naturally, almost of its own accord. It's for you to decide whether to ask the question in a public or private setting, and always remember that the question will have an impact on the questioner, on the person answering, and on the audience.

Cautionary Tales #5

Would you like to come in for a coffee?

Some questions are only signals for what we really want to say because they have hidden meanings. Such questions can be useful if both sides share the subtext. This approach allows us to ask potentially awkward questions in a socially acceptable way and invite plenty of polite options to answer. On a personal level, I have asked and been asked the infamous question: 'Would you like to come in for a coffee?' answering yes, at least once, even though I don't drink coffee. Hopefully, you'll understand the reason I accepted the invitation without me being too specific. A rejection can be made in a simple way with a line such as 'I'd love to but I've got an early start for work tomorrow' that allows everyone to save face. These signal questions are very helpful, unless there is a cultural, language, or maturity issue that prevents one side from grasping the subtext. Signal questions should be treated like the 'trial close' examples we saw in the Advanced Techniques chapter.

Not all questions mean what they say. Be cautious in using such questions and wary of how you answer them.

What should I do now?

When Sally was taught French at school, she did well at first. She built a good vocabulary, some basic verbs and the grammar for common sentences. Over time, though, the grammar became increasingly complex as the teacher added more tenses and irregular verbs. Within a year, Sally reached a level where she couldn't say anything in French. Her brain would spend so long parsing sentences, breaking them into past/future/present or is it continuous present(?), wondering whether the object was masculine or feminine, if she was addressing a single person or a group in a familiar or formal way, that when she opened her mouth nothing would come out. We don't want to be in the same position with questions. This book isn't an instruction manual. Even so, it contains plenty of ideas that you could apply to your life or company. If you enjoyed the book as a piece of light entertainment and are ready to move on, then thanks for reading this far. If you'd like to improve your Q&A technique, then I have a couple of final thoughts and some checklists that summarise the main points we've discovered together. Let's face it, we love to have something to photocopy and store in a place we never look at, to be forgotten over time. Questions are so fundamental though that—now you've read this book and initiated your subconscious processes—I think you'll catch yourself thinking about them and about how others are using their questions.

I recently ran a short refresher course on questioning techniques for a group of executives. Although many of them were attending because it was required by their corporate organisation, everyone actively participated in the session, nonetheless. They particularly enjoyed the cartoons that accompanied the ten rules we proposed, often nodding their heads at the exaggerated scenarios the cartoons displayed. The general atmosphere was 'yes, very funny, but pretty basic—we're experienced people who already know all this stuff'. Then we surprised the team with a few role-plays. We threw everyone into a situation where they had to demonstrate the techniques, with teams of two or three holding a meeting with one of the other execs. In a series of 30-minute role-play sessions I made notes on every question asked. Here's what I found:

- Only *one* open question was asked in total, across all sessions.
- Some participants asked multiple concatenated questions, several times. 'Can you tell if xxx is deployed, and the cost for yyy?'
- There was no co-ordination within the teams, each person tried a different approach, sometimes interrupting another's questioning.

I was reminded of my badminton singles match, when my partner and I switched to playing left-handed and found it almost impossible to hit anything—we knew the theory but had never tested it with the opposing hand. For me, the lesson reinforced in these role-plays was that theory is easy to comprehend in principle, and we may think we understand it, but until we've tested it and practised it, then we don't truly know it. There's certainly some truth in the old saying that you don't really know any skill until you've taught it to somebody else.

My most important piece of advice then, for anyone who wants to get better at asking questions, is to **practice**. The old patient analogy still applies here, though. Don't operate on the heart, lungs, and kidneys all at the same time. The patient will die. Pick the most critical thing and fix it. Identify one questioning technique or approach from the checklists below, and use it for a specific meeting to see how it goes. Or try it for a whole day, or at a social event. Then keep practicing until you think it feels natural. Then try another.

The second critical point is to **stay curious**. I see that phrase everywhere, from National Geographic to a multitude of websites, schools, and business presentations. Questions flow from curiosity. When we question things, we learn, empathise, gain understanding and insight; plus we're engaged. That's a very different thing from being an interrogator. Don't ask question after question to prove your superiority or to expose a problem someone would rather hide.

Questioning can be an attitude, a stance, a way of life. You can make it positive and feel fascinated by the people and the world around you, or you can use questions like a stick to beat people down. Any tool has the potential to be used for good or bad purposes. A teaspoon can measure sugar or medicine, stir tea or dig a tunnel from a prison. You can hit somebody with a teaspoon, poke out their eye, break teeth, or feed someone who is not able to perform that basic task themselves. You can try to bend it with the power of your mind to demonstrate your psychic powers. All that with just a humble teaspoon. Questions are a far more powerful tool. We use them every day, in a million different contexts. They're the weapons of language, the sharp-end of our cognitive capabilities, and it's our responsibility to use them wisely. Questions can do many things, but at their core they're a tool for lifelong learning. Use them, get better at using them, and never stop. Ultimately, questions are what make us uniquely human.

Questions: knowledge summary

1. Humans probably asked questions by using gestures before we had language. Our language may have developed as questions expanded our cognitive capabilities, rather than the other way around.
2. Religion tackles important questions like: What happens when we die?
3. Science is developed through asking questions, coming up with a hypothesis, and then devising experiments to test the theory.
4. Modern science is built from layers of answered questions.
5. Animals do not ask questions (yet), although they can make demands and some animals can ask proto-questions.
6. Trained animals can be very good at answering questions.
7. Certain birds seem to have the most developed theory of mind and are showing signs of being the first species after humans to ask questions.
8. When the first human developed the ability to ask questions, other humans could answer them, as our trained primate relatives have shown.
9. Some computers can answer questions well enough to masquerade as humans and are interacting with you today on a regular basis.
10. Computers, like animals, cannot (yet) invent good, original questions.
11. When (not if) computers achieve super-intelligence, their capabilities will be significantly advanced compared to those of any human being.
12. Some of the most important questions facing humanity revolve around how we deal with this shift, as computers become smarter than humans.
13. Google is the world's most popular way to ask questions using technology.
14. There are multiple ways to categorise questions, and many professions have devised their own sets. Certain categories

are banned in specific scenarios; e.g. 'loaded' questions in a courtroom.

15. Patterns of questions are powerful, like a boxer's combination punches.
16. The sequence of questions is so important that some governments deliberately randomise the questions asked in their parliament. Order bias is just one type of issue, others such as anchor and acquiescence bias also affect our answers.
17. Questions can change our memories.
18. Self-education is not always the primary purpose of a question; it can be used for many other reasons—such as to buy time or to attack someone.
19. Sometimes it's best not to ask questions, e.g. when speed is critical.
20. Questionnaires are harder to write than they appear and are not as anonymous as they claim.
21. In group settings, people ask the appropriate questions for their role.
22. Much of the best artworks ask questions but leave the answer to the audience.
23. Every question generates a response, even if the response is silence.
24. The context of a question is key to understanding it.
25. Truth is slippery. A better filter for answers is to check their factual correctness and clarify the definitions on which the 'truth' is based.
26. Recognise the situations where accuracy and precision are critical—such as in a health test.
27. The answers to questions about the future are rarely accurate or precise. The value comes from thinking through the scenarios rather than making a prediction.
28. Big data lets us ask questions that were not possible before. It's not magic, but it can appear so.
29. Crowds can be good at answering certain types of questions. They're not so effective in framing the right question in the first place, though.
30. Swarms (interacting groups of software or biological entities)

are very efficient at answering complex questions, especially in fast-changing situations; but are still not so skilled at constructing questions.

31. The best questions to use for education are the ones that make people think, act, and engage.

32. Many countries have specific rules for their legal systems regarding the type, pattern, and time at which questions can be used.

33. A large proportion of politicians in western democracies have a legal education, where they're trained in formal question and answer techniques.

34. To become an expert on a subject, encourage others to bring their questions to you.

35. Most professions give training on specialist questioning techniques.

36. Children begin to ask questions towards the end of their second year. By the age of 4–5 they ask 70+ questions per day. After that, the number of questions they ask declines through adulthood and into old age.

37. One popular theory on why we ask less questions as we age, states that society rewards us for answers, not questions.

38. The key role of journalists in society is to ask questions in a public forum.

39. Philosophy is the study of key questions, such as 'What is a good life?' A PhD (doctorate in philosophy) is the pinnacle of achievement in western education.

40. The questions we ask and don't ask reveal as much about ourselves as they do about our subject, and often reveal more than our answers.

Questions: technique checklist

Philosophy
- Stay curious.
- Practise. Pick a single technique at a time, and use it.

Techniques
1. Ask one question at a time, then listen to the reply.
2. Practise active listening with three 'A's (Attention, Attitude, Adjustment).
3. Watch out for hooks—these are the subjects people want to discuss.
4. Remember we're all subject to bias:
   - Anchor: give an anchor value if you don't want the person you are questioning to find their own.
   - Order: your sequence of questions will affect the answers.
   - Acquiescence: if you want someone to say yes, get them answering yes to other questions first. The same applies if you want them to say no.
5. If you know the most likely questions you'll be asked in a scenario (like an interview), then prepare some good answers in advance.
6. Phrase a question differently when asking about a sensitive subject, e.g. by labelling: 'Do you mind if I ask...'
7. Groups asking questions should agree on roles and responsibilities, so everyone is clear who will ask the questions on each specific area.
8. If you're aiming to learn something, don't question someone who won't know the answer.
9. Repetition of a question can strip away layers. Use it with caution though.
10. To find the root cause of a problem, try using the Five Whys. Focus on the process, not the blame.
11. The purpose of a question can be at least as important as the

content.

12. If a question is hard to ask, try prefacing it with a sincere compliment (not flattery).
13. Don't forget that silence is a powerful tool. Learn to use it.
14. Recognise when there's not enough data for the answer and know how to rectify this.
15. Frame your next question in the context of the last answer you received.
16. Listen to the questions others ask you. Why did they ask *that* question?
17. You may not be the best person to ask a certain question. In that case, obtain the help of others, or use alternative means to identify the answer.
18. Use trial questions to test situations to avoid embarrassment for everyone involved, and increase your chance of success at the same time.
19. Never feel obliged to ask a question. If you must, then ask a good open question to buy yourself time to think.
20. The questions you don't ask are just as important as those you do. Journalists and lawyers (both questioning professions) are experts at 'errors of omission'.

Cautionary Tales

1. Our biggest regrets may be the questions we didn't ask. Don't keep your questions to yourself.
2. Don't ask a question if you're not prepared to hear the answer.
3. Some questions won't go away. Save time, money, and stress by answering them earlier.
4. Some questions are just as hard to answer as they are to ask. Spare a thought for the other side.
5. Not all questions mean what they say. Be wary of how you answer such questions, and be cautious in using them.

Acknowledgements

Let me state this plainly; the book you are holding would not have been possible, in any reasonable timeframe, without Wikipedia. They do a tremendous job and I would encourage everyone who uses the service to donate. Wikipedia was my primary research tool, and I would like to thank the editors and contributors who have inspired and informed many aspects of this book.

There are also far too many people to mention by name that have inspired me over the years, using questions effectively, or with their advice and guidance, or simply leading by example. People like Barry Hennessey, Paul Huntley, Liz Quelch, Eric Kraemer, Nicholas Brand, John Power, Anil Suren, Matt Wright, Carl Mayhew, Luis Vasquez, Caroline Hayward, Randy Lunn, Tamer Farag, Ralph Kemperdick, Dominique Grelet and many more – I'm just sorry I can't list everyone.

I should also thank the people that have invested time, money or both into SWARM Engineering, allowing us to pursue the art of questioning to help improve organizations – especially the entire S2G Ventures team, highlighting Sanjeev Krishnan and Michael Robinson for their belief and support.

I'd like to thank the people that spent time reviewing the book and gave me invaluable feedback from those early drafts – Linda Klug, Michael Levin, Grant Stapleton, and others. In particular, my sister Anne and my brother Alan, who each provided a unique perspective and were never afraid to tell me what worked and what didn't, in pure constructive criticism. This book wouldn't be the same without that honest advice.

Finally, there are people who appear inside this book,

either in disguise or plain view. I am still in frequent contact with many of them, while others we have lost touch over the years. That doesn't mean I don't think of them, and the friendship and lessons learnt – how could I ever forget those hours of playing badminton together Mr Bone? Thank you, one and all.

Nobody Will Ever Love You

A collection of award-winning short stories by A. M. Howcroft

Short stories are like miniature films, and this collection by Howcroft delivers a potent screening of art-house tales and Hollywood blockbusters. They are studded with a memorable cast of characters, such as a chicken-factory worker balanced high on a slippery roof, a woman carving saints out of driftwood, teenage boy-racers who've solved life's mysteries, through to a business-woman who dies nine times. Each story is set within a rich-cinematic backdrop to reveal people at critical turning points, with delicately balanced risks and rewards. Whether starting riots in Paris, breaking into a friend's house in California, or killing time before being busted by customs officers, the narrators are flawed, unpredictable, smart and stupid in equal measure. Funny, moving and often provoking, these compelling stories will entertain; giving you images that linger and dialogue you'll want to repeat in fake accents.

An exciting new talent who really knows how to write and keep the reader thoroughly engaged.

Katie Fforde, best-selling novelist

Intellectually stimulating, funny and poignant, his work is full of new ideas, invention and philosophical what-ifs.

David Gaffney, Author of Swan-off Tales, Aromabingo

A Splash of Ink

Edited by A. M. Howcroft

What does it feel like to stand on stage and play the opening three chords of a song that all the audience knows by heart? Or to suddenly see your mother, as you sit in a café with the two grandchildren she has never met? Flash fiction penetrates to the core of an issue, delivering powerful emotions of love, fear, hope and joy, in barely a page of writing.

This volume collects together the prize-winning stories from a decade of flash fiction contests at InkTears. Each story a ripe fruit, picked from thousands of entries, with a variety of tastes to suit every palate. And much better metaphors than that last one.

If you are a flash aficionado, this book will fill you with pleasure. If you are still to be convinced that flash is relevant and worthy, then I implore you to pick this book up and start reading.